"America's leading source of self-help legal information." ★★★★

—YAHOO!

P9-DEE-447

LEGAL INFORMATION ONLINE ANYTIME

24 hours a day

www.nolo.com

AT THE NOLO.COM SELF-HELP LAW CENTER, YOU'LL FIND

- **Nolo's comprehensive Legal Encyclopedia** filled with plain-English information on a variety of legal topics
- **Nolo's Law Dictionary**—legal terms <u>without</u> the legalese
- **Auntie Nolo**—if you've got questions, Auntie's got answers
- **The Law Store**—over 250 self-help legal products including: Downloadable Software, Books, Form Kits and eGuides
- **Legal and product updates**
- **Frequently Asked Questions**
- **NoloBriefs**, our free monthly email newsletter
- **Legal Research Center**, for access to state and federal statutes
- **Our ever-popular lawyer jokes**

Quality LAW BOOKS & SOFTWARE FOR EVERYONE

Nolo's user-friendly products are consistently first-rate. Here's why:

- A dozen in-house legal editors, working with highly skilled authors, ensure that our products are accurate, up-to-date and easy to use
- We continually update every book and software program to keep up with changes in the law
- Our commitment to a more democratic legal system informs all of our work
- We appreciate & listen to your feedback. Please fill out and return the card at the back of this book.

An Important Message to Our Readers

This product provides information and general advice about the law. But laws and procedures change frequently, and they can be interpreted differently by different people. For specific advice geared to your specific situation, consult an expert. No book, software or other published material is a substitute for personalized advice from a knowledgeable lawyer licensed to practice law in your state.

3rd edition

GET A LIFE

You don't need a million to retire well

by Ralph Warner

NOLO

Keeping Up to Date

To keep its books up-to-date, Nolo issues new printings and new editions periodically. New printings reflect minor legal changes and technical corrections. New editions contain major legal changes, major text additions or major reorganizations. To find out if a later printing or edition of any Nolo book is available, call Nolo at 510-549-1976 or check our website at www.nolo.com.

To stay current, follow the "Update" service at our website at www.nolo.com. In another effort to help you use Nolo's latest materials, we offer a 35% discount off the purchase of the new edition of your Nolo book when you turn in the cover of an earlier edition. (See the "Special Upgrade Offer" in the back of the book.) This book was last revised in August 2000.

THIRD EDITION	AUGUST 2000
Editors	MARY RANDOLPH, STEPHANIE HAROLDE & TERRI HEARSH
Illustrations	MARI STEIN
Cover Design	TONI IHARA
Book Design	TERRI HEARSH
Production	STEPHANIE HAROLDE
Index	SUSAN CORNELL
Proofreading	ROBERT WELLS
Printing	BERTELSMANN SERVICES INC.

Warner, Ralph E.
   Get a life : you don't need a million to retire well / by Ralph Warner. --3rd ed.
     p. cm.
   Includes index.
   ISBN 0-87337-583-1
   1. Retirement income--United States--Planning. 2. Old age pensions--United States. 3. Social security--United States 4. Finance, Personal--United States.   I. Title.

HD7125.W375 2000
332.024'01--dc21   00-021356

Permissions:

Material from *The Art of Friendship*, by Christine Leefeldt and Ernest Callenbach, which appears in Chapter 4, is used with the permission of the authors. Material from *Simple Living Investments*, by Michael Phillips and Catherine Campbell, which appears in Chapter 4, is used with the permission of the authors and Clear Glass Publishing of San Francisco, CA.

For information on bulk purchases or corporate premium sales, please contact the Special Sales Department. For academic sales or textbook adoptions, ask for Academic Sales. Call 800-955-4775 or write to Nolo at 950 Parker Street, Berkeley, CA 94710.

Acknowledgments

Many people have generously helped me deepen my understanding of what it really means to enjoy a successful retirement and how people in midlife can best prepare to enjoy life after 65. In both regards, I'm particularly indebted to Ernest Callenbach, Afton Crooks, Bernie and Bob Giusti, Arthur Levenson, Babette Marks, Henry and Althea Perry, Hazel Peterson, Yuri Shibata, Cecil Stewart and Peter Wolford, whose fascinating observations appear throughout this book. I'm sure you'll agree that this would be a far lesser work without their wisdom.

I have also received valuable suggestions and guidance from Leslie Armistead of the Career Action Center, Palo Alto, California; Gail Drulis, Director of the Albany, California, YMCA; Doris Sloan, a friend from the Board of Directors of the Save San Francisco Bay Association and Amy Ihara, my inimitable and inspirational mother-in-law.

Thanks, too, to Linda Hanger, Denis Clifford, Naomi Puro, Rod Duncan and Sarah Stromeyer, all of whom made helpful contributions to my research and fact-gathering efforts. Beth Lawrence has also been of huge assistance by contributing Internet savvy to this third edition.

Much inspired research for this book was done by Stanley Jacobsen, a twice-retired librarian who, at age 70+, cheerfully arrives at work at Nolo every morning at least an hour early. Stan's skill at mining online databases for golden nuggets about retirement and aging has been particularly helpful.

I'm also greatly indebted to Michael Phillips and Catherine Campbell, whose groundbreaking little book, *Simple Living Investments* (Clear Glass Publishing, San Francisco), I first read over 15 years ago. Still in print, this excellent work was one of the first to emphasize that when it comes to enjoying a successful retirement, who you are is far more important than how much you earn.

Finally, I owe mega-thanks to my good friends and editors Stephanie Harolde, Terri Hearsh, Mary Randolph and Susan (Lulu) Cornell. Each of them has cared about this book almost as much as I have. By dint of numerous suggestions and lots of hands-on editing, they have coaxed, cajoled and sometimes flat-out demanded that I work harder to make it better. Every author should have such wonderful colleagues.

Dedication

For my kids: André, Andromache, Eddie, Joe and Vilaylock.

It would be hard to find a nicer bunch.

Table of Contents

Introduction

"Life begets life. Energy creates energy. It is only by spending oneself that one becomes rich."

—Sarah Bernhardt

The premise of this book is simple: Popular advice that says you'll need to save a big pile of money to have a successful retirement is hugely exaggerated and sadly incomplete. Instead, we should focus on the things that will truly make our years more enjoyable and fulfilling: our health, spiritual life, relationships with family and friends and a full plate of interesting things to do.

I decided to write this book after reading hundreds of books and articles about retirement. Most have titles like "Don't Die Poor," "If You Think You're Saving Enough, You're Wrong" or "Baby Boomers in Denial About the Need to Save More." And it's not only the titles that are depressingly similar. The message is also pretty much the same: To avoid being destitute and dependent later in life, each of us needs to put aside an impossibly large amount of money during our working years, money we should have begun saving at least 15 years ago. Many of these publications implore readers to spend less (often far less) and place the resulting savings in mutual funds, annuities and other investments—an approach that usually assumes the reader either has a hefty income or is willing to live almost exclusively on beans and potatoes.

But in addition to reviewing retirement literature, I did something that was a lot more fun. I sought out and talked to lots of people who are enjoying their retirement years. I wanted to know what set these zestful people apart from the many other retirees who spend their last years bored, lonely and depressed. Among the questions I asked were:

- What is your typical day like?
- What things have been truly important to you during your retirement?
- Do you work for pay or do volunteer work?
- How do you explain the fact that some older people enjoy energized and interesting lives while so many others are depressed, angry and misanthropic?
- Do you exercise?
- Do you have many friends? If so, how old are they?
- As you age, do spiritual concerns become more important and if so, how do you express them?
- How much money do you spend in a year? Is it more or less than you anticipated when you were younger?
- If you could tell a middle-aged person just one thing about how to prepare for retirement, what would it be?

What I learned from these discussions, and from my own observations, is that there is a huge gap between the "save more money" message of the personal finance press and investment industry and what active, interesting retirees themselves say is important. The successful retired people I've talked with are, for the most part, not primarily interested in money—either in spending lots of it, piling up more or worrying about having enough.

True, a few of the retirees I queried had ample savings and no money worries; their focus on other retirement challenges is hardly a surprise. But many others, with more typical middle-class incomes, also don't give money much thought. Some have chosen to live fairly frugal lives; others are so busy thinking and doing interesting things they simply don't have the time or desire to focus a large amount of energy on their finances.

If you doubt this, be sure to read the comments of the energized, life-embracing seniors whose comments appear in the conversations interspersed between the chapters of this book. When each was asked, "What is the most important thing a middle-aged person can do to prepare for retirement?", all came up with pretty much the same list:

- "Learn new things"
- "Develop lots of interests"
- "Find useful ways to connect to the world"
- "Cultivate important family relationships and friendships"
- "Take steps to protect your health."

But what about all those articles and books that claim that, to enjoy a successful retirement, you must save hundreds of thousands—or even a million—dollars? Don't they make a valid point when they argue that it should be a high priority to put enough money aside to guarantee a fun-filled retirement and pay for all foreseeable emergencies that could occur if you lived until extreme old age? Don't be so sure. True, the successful retired people I've talked to almost uniformly say it makes sense to accumulate at least a modest retirement savings nest egg, but most caution that too strong an emphasis on earning and saving during one's middle years can actually be counterproductive to enjoying a successful retirement. If you don't take pre-retirement steps to help ensure you will enjoy a healthy, active, friend-filled and interesting retirement, no amount of money will buy those things later.

I'll go a step further and argue that there is often a direct connection between a midlife obsession with work and saving and an unhappy retirement. Imagine an overweight, poorly conditioned 50-year-old man returning tired and harried from a ten-hour day at the office. He tells his wife (who has just staggered in from her own full-time job) and children to please keep the noise down while he has a drink, eats a bag of chips and watches *Washington Week in Review*. Assuming this fellow lives long enough to reach the affluent retirement he is straining so hard to achieve, chances are he will confront a life of poor health, a family he hardly knows and, now that he no longer works, few true interests besides reading *Forbes* magazine. Against this unhappy background, the fact he and his wife own a large portfolio of blue-chip stocks is unlikely to do him much good.

But if accumulating lots of money in midlife does not guarantee successful retirement, why do so many people think it does? Here are my best answers:

- People saving for retirement have never experienced it, and have only the haziest idea of what their financial needs are likely to be. They don't know that they are likely to spend a great deal less—often about half—of what they spend now. (Chapter 8 shows you how to estimate how much retirement income you'll really need.)

- Because most people tend to socialize with people their own age, they typically know few retired people outside their own families who can serve as role models.

- The retirement industry's siren song—"work long hours and save, save, save or you'll end up poor, miserable and a burden to your family"—tends to fall on receptive ears. After all, most Americans have been brought up to believe it is wise to sacrifice present gratification for future benefits. (If you fool around instead of doing your homework, you'll never get into college or graduate school, or get a good job or make something of yourself.)

- Much of what people think they know about retirement comes from the media or retirement planning seminars. Although rarely disclosed, the "experts" who create these materials are almost always directly or indirectly paid by the securities or insurance industries. To keep earning cumulative annual profits in the tens of billions of dollars, these businesses must convince Americans to save huge sums for retirement.

- Fear sells newspapers. As a result, Americans are bombarded with false messages, such as:
  - "The Social Security system is sure to be bankrupt in a few years—anyone who counts on getting a penny from it is nuts."
  - "The cost of living is going up so fast that whatever you put aside now will purchase pathetically little when you retire, so you need to save much more."
  - "As people live longer, they face a high probability of spending many years in a nursing home or other institutional care facility. Unless you have lots of money put aside, you're likely to end your life in a snake pit. Good care is so expensive you can never save too much."

The fact that we are so often importuned to save for retirement isn't all bad. A little anxiety about the future can be a healthy thing if it motivates us to put aside a reasonable financial cushion. The real problem occurs when we become so preoccupied with saving for retirement that we fail to invest enough time and energy in areas more likely to help us enjoy a satisfying retirement. ■

Chapter 1

What Will You Do When You Retire?

"Old age ain't for sissies, honey."

—Bette Davis

Many Americans already in midlife will live from one-quarter to one-third of their lives after the traditional retirement age of 65. In short, even if after you officially retire you continue to work part-time, travel widely and participate in sports or other leisure activities, you will have plenty of time to do many other things. After talking to hundreds of older people, I'm convinced that the degree to which most people's retirement years are fulfilling has a great deal to do with how they spend this large chunk of discretionary time. People who are busily involved in a wide variety of activities—both mental and physical—are likely to do well. That may not surprise you. But what you may never have considered is that if you wait until retirement to start figuring out how to stay happily occupied, it may be too late.

Plan to Keep Busy

Many retirees report experiencing a paradoxical situation. On the one hand, they have the sense that time is short and their life is running out. On the other, they don't have anything interesting to do after lunch. Even the most avid fisherman, gardener, traveler or dog lover is likely to find plenty of time to both follow her passion and do many other things—including, if she isn't careful, becoming bored, depressed and prematurely dependent on others. As my friend Babette Marks, now in her 80s, puts it,

> *The ability to maintain an active involvement in life in a number of different ways is one key to leading a decent life when you're older. Face it, what else have you got? Your health probably isn't great, half your old friends are dead and you don't recognize yourself in the mirror. If you don't keep interested and involved with lots of activities and interests, you'll end up a depressed old vegetable.*

Marks is as right as she is blunt. In my observation, most people—especially those who have been busy earlier in life—make a successful transition to a reasonably fulfilling retirement if, and only if, they stay busy doing things that reinforce their sense of self-worth. Usually this means being involved with others in activities that are felt to be meaningful. I can't find anyone in their 60s and 70s who tells me it's fun to spend most of their time watching TV, sitting on a park bench, sleeping late, or even reading. And even many people who are more active—jogging, walking, bike riding or swimming—report that continually doing these things alone can quickly become joyless. To the contrary, people whose lives revolve almost exclusively around these types of passive activities seem to be sicker and more depressed and tend to die sooner than those who are more actively involved with life.

One example of how keeping busy seems to correlate with long life and intellectual vigor can be seen in the careers of the justices of the U.S. Supreme Court, one of the few jobs in America where people have never been required, or even officially encouraged, to retire until they are obviously no longer able to do the work. Out of the more than 100 justices who have served on the Court since it began to function in 1789, over 50% have served into at least their middle 70s, an astonishing age when you remember that over half died before the year 1900, when the average U.S. life expectancy was less than 50.

You may think I'm belaboring a fairly obvious point. Chances are you don't want to be an old couch potato anyway, and accept that staying involved in life's daily affairs probably does increase the odds of enjoying a fulfilling retirement. Great, but can you back up your conviction by answering this simple question: "How are you preparing now to be able to lead an interesting life after you retire?"

The Importance of Thinking Ahead

Some of us look forward to retirement with an almost childlike sense of anticipation: "This is what I've waited for all my life—a really long summer vacation!" Depending on our particular retirement fantasy—gardening, travel, woodworking, painting, golfing, spending time with grandchildren or simply having the freedom to take a daily nap—leisure-time activities are likely to figure large. Finally we will be free to enjoy every bit of personal gratification we have postponed since the day our parents first said, "If you don't stop playing and do your homework, you'll never amount to anything."

Lots of other people in midlife, however, simply refuse to think about retirement. The idea creates a strong sense of unease because they can't conjure up any clear vision of what their lives will be like as they age. This inability to confront the inevitability that work, family and even recreational patterns will change later in life is especially common among people whose lives center around their jobs. As one midlevel manager I talked to remarked, "Once they take away my employee ID number, I'm not sure what I'll do or how I'll define myself."

At 65, Lots of People Are Just Getting Started

The notion that older folks are supposed to sit on a park bench and feed pigeons while they wait for the Pearly Gates to open is increasingly seen as baloney by people of all ages. Many people do their best and most creative work after normal retirement age, a fact that is finally gaining wide recognition.

Ronald Reagan served two terms in the White House after age 65, and George Bush served most of one. Michelangelo designed St. Peter's cupola at 83. Ben Franklin helped draft the U.S. Constitution when he was over 80, and Oliver Wendell Holmes served on the Supreme Court into his 90s. Many painters and musicians, including Picasso, Matisse and Casals, continued to create inspirational work well into old age. When, at 93, Georgia O'Keeffe could no longer see well enough to paint, she took up sculpture. May Sarton finished her last book, *At Eighty-Two: A Journal*, just before she died at age 83. And as we all know, septuagenarian John Glenn retired from the U.S. Senate in order to have enough time to rejoin the space program.

Missing, of course, from both the rosy and the dismal views of what retirement is much sense of reality. If you're one of those anticipating an endless summer vacation, it's fair to ask whether you really will be able to fill every minute with favorite leisure activities. Even if you live in a climate warm enough to smack golf balls every day, and never suffer from mah-jongg wrist, will a heavy diet of sports and games prove fulfilling?

What about hanging out with your grandchildren? Assuming they aren't too busy with school, gymnastics, soccer and music camp to make time for you, how many hours a week do you really want to spend with them? And if you can't even picture your retirement, are you really doomed to sit down in a recliner, pull out your new gold-plated watch and count off the hours until you die? Or will your very fear of all those empty days goad you into figuring out something interesting to do with the rest of your life?

The truth is that unless you are one of the few adults who has taken an extended sabbatical from work and child-rearing pursuits during the middle portion of your life, you have no idea whether or not you'll be able to easily fill your retirement days with interesting activities. All of your hopes, fears, plans and expectations are fantasies, plain and simple. The only way you or I can learn in advance of our own retirement about what works and what doesn't is to draw on the experience of people who have already retired. That's why, in putting together this book, I've included in-depth conversations with numerous retired people about how they really fill their days and whether, in retrospect, there were things they could have done in midlife to better prepare themselves for a fulfilling retirement. If you don't read another word, I urge you to carefully look at what they have to say.

Why should you worry about planning your post-retirement activities many years before you retire? After all, depending on how old you are, your retirement may be a number of years, or even decades, from now. Unfortunately, however, waiting until after retirement to figure out what you will do seldom works well. People who count on developing new interests, activities and involvements after 65 often don't. Ruth Cohen, a Beaverton, Oregon, geriatric specialist, puts it like this: "For the first time in history, older people have a plethora of choices. But unless you have a plan, you're not likely to get what you want." (*Business Week,* July 21, 1997.) Or as Fred Astaire remarked, "Old age is like everything else. To make a success of it, you've got to start young."

You may assume that finding plenty of interesting things to do after your retirement will be absolutely no problem, or that if filling up your retirement hours proves to be more of a challenge than you now think, that you'll nevertheless deal with it when the time comes. Don't be so sure. In a recent Harris poll, the typical retired respondent reported spending half of her free time watching TV and a good chunk of the rest doing housework. If this combination doesn't sound fulfilling to you, you're not alone. The majority of the retired people responding to the poll complained of feeling less useful after retirement than before. And in a 1999 *Wall Street Journal*/NBC News survey, 30% of retirees reported feeling bored or alienated.

Early Retirees May Have It Easier

Some people dream of escaping the work-a-day treadmill years early. And increasingly larger numbers of Americans are pulling it off, retiring in their 50s or occasionally even earlier. Indeed, there are so many early retirees that, according to the University of Maryland's Survey Research Center, only two-thirds of men aged 55 to 64 are still on the job. In 1948, 90% of men of this age worked.

What types of pressures and problems do early retirees experience? Leaving aside those who quit work early to engage in an activity of consuming interest, most people who retire in their 50s face the same sort of "what will I do" and "how will I replace the buzz of the workplace" problems so often encountered by older retirees. But early retirees do have several big advantages. For one, because they are younger, they tend to be healthier, which means they are more likely to be able to engage in fairly strenuous activities, such as joining the Peace Corps or walking the length of Italy— things that may be harder to do ten or 20 years later. In addition, the very fact that they demonstrated enough personal grit to make a big change in their life means they are more likely to actively meet retirement problems, rather than passively accepting them. Finally, being younger, early retirees have more time to use a trial-and-error approach to discovering activities and interests that will prove satisfying over the long term.

On the other hand, many people who retire early report at least a couple of problems less common to people who retire in their 60s. The first is the feeling (sometimes reinforced by the attitudes of friends) that by quitting early they are slackers. Although objective facts may make it clear that this is nonsense, a decision to leave the workplace well before the traditional retirement age nevertheless runs counter to many deeply held American attitudes about the value of work.

A second problem is that at a time when corporate America has shed tens of thousands of unneeded older workers, you may be viewed—whether fairly or not—by friends, business colleagues and even family members as having been cast aside early because you didn't quite measure up.

(continued on next page)

Finally, there is the problem of friends—or I guess I should say lack of friends. After all, just because you retire at age 53 doesn't mean your friends will. (See Chapter 4.) In short, unless a number of your friends are older and already retired, or you adopt a successful strategy to make new friends, you'll likely find that while you now have plenty of time for interesting activities, you have no one to do them with.

Why is it difficult for so many people to find interesting things to do once they retire? My talks with older people suggest that it's often a combination of:

- a lack of practical knowledge about how to get involved in new activities
- shyness—often the result of a dip in self-esteem that can accompany no longer having a job; shy people too often become isolated people
- insecurity about one's self-worth ("Who would want me?")
- declining physical abilities—people who have relied on their participation in sports both to feel good about themselves and as a way to make friends are particularly vulnerable to becoming depressed and isolated, should physical limitations mean they can no longer play
- the inability to find a job that really makes use of their skills—most retired engineers don't want to take tickets at the local amusement park
- unexpected boredom with planned activities—many people report that by the time they finish their third cruise, they never want to see another margarita—and
- the sometimes unwelcome childcare expectations of your children—if you must care for your grandchildren many hours a day, you won't have much time to do anything else. This can be great if caring for kids is what you love to do, but tough to cope with if it isn't.

If you're a busy, outgoing person in your 40s or 50s, it's probably hard to believe that factors such as these will ever combine to severely limit your retirement horizons. But one only has to spend a short time with people in their 70s for the blinders to fall off. Over and over again, you encounter people who have become far less optimistic and resilient and far more reticent, sedentary and isolated than they were even ten years earlier.

Here's a real-life example that does a good job of illustrating how these factors can combine to threaten an otherwise sensible retirement plan. After a busy and fairly prosperous career as an electrician, Ted retired a little early, at age 60. He and his wife Beatrice had long since paid off the mortgage on their house and saved a comfortable sum. Ted planned to fill up his time volunteering with several local youth groups that sponsored kids' sports. For the 20 years since he had successfully coached his own kids' Little League teams, he had carried in his head a vivid picture of himself again standing on a baseball diamond explaining the fine points of playing shortstop to a group of happy, attentive kids. And during school and evening hours, when there would be no kids to teach, he saw himself working behind the scenes with like-minded adults dedicated to improving kids' sports opportunities.

A few days after replacing what he hoped was his last substandard wiring system, Ted stopped by a local community center to offer his help. His anticipation of an enthusiastic reception was quickly dashed when several parent volunteers, busy trying to cope with a disorganized equipment room, were barely polite. But Ted persevered, making several phone calls to people who coordinated Little League volunteers. Finally, he was assigned to help coach a ten-and-under baseball team.

Unfortunately, on the first day of practice, Ted was shocked and dismayed. The kids who he had eagerly looked forward to coaching for so long simply didn't respond to his heavily structured approach, flocking instead around the other coach—a 19-year-old college freshman who wore his clothing three sizes too large, kept his hat on backwards and shouted bits and pieces of popular rap songs as he hit the kids hot grounders.

Nor did anyone in the community center seem to be particularly interested in Ted's repeated offers to contribute his organizational skills to the nonprofit corporation that ran the youth softball and soccer programs. When, after several of his phone calls were not returned, Ted received an aggressive call from a fund-raiser asking him to make a "significant" contribution to help develop a new ball field, he became angry and disgusted. Before long, he even stopped coaching the baseball team, explaining to his family, "Kids just don't want to listen these days. I'm not going to be ignored or treated like an old fool."

Later that summer, Ted tried his hand helping with a math tutoring project and a summer recreational program for low-income kids. Again he felt unappreciated by the kids and undervalued by the program coordinator.

In less than six months, Ted's retirement dream had crashed. After painting the house, rebuilding the garage and organizing the basement, he had so little to do, he decided to start up his business again, if for no other reason than to get out of the house and stop driving Beatrice nuts.

At this point, Ted's adult son, Peter, who understood from his own experience that his dad knew lots about teaching sports and that organizers of kids' sports programs always need help, figured out that something was badly wrong. Guessing that his dad had simply lost touch with how to relate to kids in the almost two decades since his youngest had entered high school, Peter took a week off from work and accompanied ("dragged" might be a better word) Ted to a well-organized week-long coach's clinic.

Peter's intervention was inspired. Ted loved the clinic, which was based on the theory that from the first moment, teaching and learning the fundamentals of baseball should be a positive experience. And although he never quite admitted it, Ted quickly saw the flaws in his drill-sergeant-type approach, which focused too much on telling kids what they were doing wrong. Armed with his new skills and confidence, Ted again signed up as an assistant Little League coach. This time, the kids were much more responsive, and Ted began to look forward to every practice and game. His success with the kids and his willingness to take on lots of extra tasks, such as lining the field and coordinating equipment, quickly led to a position as head coach, and then to running the summer tennis and soccer programs. Eventually, he was asked to coordinate the entire county-wide under-ten soccer program.

Somewhere along the line, Ted bought a bright red hat, complete with prominent floppy ears. The kids, by whom he was now increasingly surrounded, started calling him "Teddy Ears." A year later, when commissioners of the local kids' basketball program voted him coach of the year, he was given a plaque that read, "To Coach Teddy Ears, the one man we couldn't do without."

Ted was lucky. Thanks to timely help from a wise son, he overcame his lack of preparation and eventually settled into a retirement role remarkably similar to the one he had dreamed of. Sadly, many retirees are not as lucky. For a variety of reasons, they are not able to recover from their pre-retirement failure to hone old skills, develop new ones or make and nurture necessary personal contacts. As a result, they fail in their first attempts to realize their retirement dream, whether it be finding a new job, becoming a successful volunteer or going to school. Of course, an initial failure or two probably won't faze self-confident people. But many others, particularly those coping with one or more of the common problems of aging—such as declining health, depression brought on by the death of a family member or shyness—simply settle into the recliner and turn on the TV.

Making an Action Plan

Okay, now it's time to focus on your own retirement. Exactly what will you do? Yes, I'm challenging you to come up with a detailed list. Take a few minutes to sit down with a pen and paper and write down the things you anticipate being actively involved in. Don't include solo activities such as reading, watching TV or jogging. While fine in themselves, these are not likely to keep you energized and interested for long. Be as specific as you can. For example, if you plan to participate in charitable activities aimed at helping immigrant children learn English, put down the details of who you will work with and what your helping activities will consist of. If you plan to learn a new skill, whether it be oil painting, how to develop an Internet site or Japanese calligraphy, where and when will you do it?

How long and detailed is your list? In my experience, too many people list a few general things such as travel and adult education courses and then get stuck. Sorry, but that's not good enough. Unless you can answer this all-important question with a list of things you are excited to learn or try, you are at risk of being one of the millions of older people whom my friend Stan Jacobsen describes as "spending lots of time in their favorite chairs contemplating their bodies falling apart." And Stan should know—he has already retired twice and each time found himself so bored he went back to work. (The last time, he landed as an editorial researcher at Nolo, where he helped me put this book together. See Stan's story in Chapter 9.)

If you're having trouble coming up with a fairly detailed plan, don't panic. After all, since you haven't retired yet, you have time to do some creative thinking and preparing. To help you get started, the rest of this chapter will focus on the main activities successful older people embrace to use their time well.

Working Part-Time

Many people who enjoy the bustle and creativity of the workplace find that continuing to work at least part-time after reaching retirement age offers the best opportunity to stay busily involved in life. And of course, planning to work a few extra years beyond retirement age (assuming you are pretty sure you can pull it off) can also go a long way toward helping solve any money problems you run into. The extra income will probably eliminate or greatly reduce your need to tap your investments until you cease working altogether. This, in turn, means that they will be busy earning additional interest or dividends.

How important are earnings after age 65? For Americans between 65 and 74, paychecks are the second largest source of income after Social Security, amounting to 25% of all income, according to the Department of Labor. Earned income is particularly important for single older women, a group particularly likely to have inadequate savings.

 For information on how earned income affects your right to receive Social Security, see Chapter 9, Where Will Your Money Come From After Age 65?

But money is far from the only motivation for working after normal retirement age. Lots of people enjoy the intellectual stimulation, social interactions and, most important for many older people, the sense of self-worth that accompanies having a job. (See the conversation with Ernest Callenbach that follows this chapter.) I don't believe it's a coincidence that my friends in their 40s and 50s who are in jobs with no mandatory retirement age seem far more relaxed about their prospective retirements than are other friends who face fixed retirement dates. Knowing that they can continue to work until they decide to give it up affords them a sense of security and control others lack.

How Anti-Age Discrimination Laws Protect Your Right to Continue Working

The federal Age Discrimination in Employment Act, or ADEA (29 U.S.C. §§ 621-634), prohibits age discrimination in hiring, discharges, layoffs, promotions, wages and other areas of employment. It is the single most important law protecting the rights of older workers. The key ADEA rule—which applies to workplaces with more than 20 employees—is that, subject to several big exceptions, no worker can be forced to retire. Unfortunately, the exceptions include:

- executives or policy makers if they would receive annual retirement benefits worth $44,000 or more
- certain police and fire personnel
- tenured university faculty
- federal employees in the fields of law enforcement and air traffic control
- any job where age is a bona fide occupational qualification. However, an employer that sets age limits on a particular job must be able to prove the limit is necessary because a worker's ability to adequately perform that job does in fact diminish after the age limit is reached. Fortunately, this is difficult for employers to do.

For a good summary of the ADEA, see *Your Rights in the Workplace*, by Barbara Kate Repa (Nolo). Also, the AARP publishes several good pamphlets on age discrimination. You can check out AARP's AgeLine Database at www.aarp.org. It contains a searchable electronic database that includes references to books, journal and magazine articles and videos. You can also write to: AARP, 601 E Street, NW, Washington, DC 20049, or call 800-424-3410.

According to a 1998 survey by the AAAP, 80% of workers in the baby boom generation anticipate engaging in at least part-time work after they retire. It's one thing to look forward to working for a few years or more after 65, and quite another to pull it off. Leaving aside Supreme Court justices, popular authors and others who feel little pressure to retire, and despite laws prohibiting age discrimination, the great majority of older Americans have no assurance that work they want to do will be available to them. Certainly this is true when it comes to keeping active in their long-term or "career" jobs. Even in this age of low unemployment, American employers have become increasingly adept at orchestrating employee buyouts, push-outs and restructurings in an effort to rid themselves of more expensive older workers. Faced with the threat that they will be laid off with no compensation, millions of Americans "voluntarily" agree to accept a lump sum payment to leave the workplace early. The result is that most people who will reach retirement age in the next two decades but want to continue working will have to find a new job. And face it, even when employers are supposedly beating the bushes for workers, after age 55 it isn't always easy to find a job that is both interesting and even moderately well-paying. Good evidence of how difficult it can be to find satisfying work can be found in an early 1990s survey by Harold Iams of the Social Security Administration, which found that just 10% of men (and 8% of women) who retired for at least a year ever returned to the workforce.

If you hope to establish a new career—or even find a part-time job more challenging than flipping burgers or punching tickets at a movie theater—it's a good idea to plan well in advance. While your retirement job needn't be in your current field, it obviously should make use of skills you already have or can fairly easily acquire. And so much the better if it's something you can do part-time and—should you want to relocate—isn't tied to a particular geographical area.

Assuming you come up with a new career idea that meets at least some of these criteria, or otherwise seems sensible, I strongly recommend that you take the time to test whether it's really likely to work. Just because you think you would enjoy teaching, working in a plant nursery, consulting or caring for small children doesn't mean anyone will hire you to do it, or if they do, that you will find it satisfying. Unless you have hands-on experience in your prospective new field and know there will be a job waiting for you, your post-retirement work plans are little more than a fantasy. And as we all know, fantasies come true a lot more often in Disney movies than they do in real life.

Here is an example of someone who clearly understood the barriers to transitioning to a new career and creatively worked to overcome them. Betty, an English teacher, planned to retire in her middle 50s after 30 years in the classroom. With her house paid for, a decent teacher's pension and modest savings, Betty felt she could scrape by without working, as long as she faced no major financial emergencies. But to afford a few amenities—especially to fulfill her dream of seeing much of the world—as well as to increase her savings cushion, Betty wanted to continue working, at least part-time, in a field that truly interested her. As a single mother who had worked hard to support and raise her children, and in the process necessarily limited her own social life, Betty was also conscious of the need to make new friends and develop fresh interests.

Betty's dream was to work in book publishing. From the time she was a small girl, she had been drawn to books and everything to do with writing, editing and producing them. She not only read books by the armload, but their authors' biographies and acknowledgments (and even the copyright information on the back of the title page). It was as if she wanted to inhale the publishing process.

Instead of waiting until after retirement to explore the publishing field, Betty started investigating local opportunities as soon as her youngest child was in college. Since she lived in a fairly populous area, it turned out there were a surprising number of small publishers within easy driving distance. Over a few months, Betty was able to arrange informational interviews with half a dozen. She then got to know a couple of her favorites better when they accepted her invitation to participate in career day activities at the junior high where she taught.

In the course of this practical research, Betty quickly saw that there was a continuing demand for people who were skilled at using a computer to do graphics and page layout. Since this seemed both challenging and fun, she signed up for an introductory desktop publishing course at the nearby community college. When

Betty found herself looking forward to every class, she knew she had made a good choice and invested in a relatively inexpensive Macintosh computer, page layout software and several how-to books so she could practice at home.

After six months of classroom and self study (and still two years before her retirement), Betty felt confident enough of her new skills to call the two publishers she liked the best to inquire about part-time freelance work over the summer. Since she cannily proposed charging what she knew was a modest fee, both quickly found projects "to try her out." One involved incorporating the revisions necessary to update a guidebook to local bed and breakfasts, the other laying out a "favorite recipes" book commissioned by a local children's shelter as part of a fund-raising campaign. Both publishers were more than pleased with Betty's work and told her she could have more whenever she wanted it. To celebrate, Betty took her two children (the older one had just finished college) to a local book- store, where the books she had helped produce were on display. She was proud to point to her name on the back of the title page under the small heading "Graphics and Production."

It's easy to see Betty's wisdom in investing time, energy and even a little money in developing the skills and contacts necessary to work in a field she had felt drawn to all her life. Planning like Betty's is particularly wise for anyone who intends to change fields. But even people who plan to work at an occupation closely related to what they did much of their adult life can usually benefit from careful preparation. For example, assume a successful small business owner plans to sell his business and become a home-based consultant, providing marketing advice to other small business owners in the same field. Although he may know virtually everything about how the underlying business works, chances are he'll nevertheless need to hone other skills. This might include developing or improving his writing (grown rusty after many years of delegating such work to subordinates), learning how to use a computer quickly and easily and coming up with cost-effective ways to market his services—something that every consultant needs to be able to do.

Learn How to Sell Yourself

Many people who work for large corporations, government entities or academic institutions haven't a clue when it comes to marketing their services to a wider world. If this describes you—and especially if you plan to work as a self-employed consultant or service provider—you'll need to develop this skill. One good approach is to arrange to work with someone who is already successfully running a small business you respect.

If you want to run your own shop, it's often best to start massaging your own network of business friends and colleagues well before you retire. With a few years of planning and thought, you should be able to develop your digital rolodex into a powerful tool to market your new business. One innovative technique that can often prove effective in helping you establish credentials as an expert is to contribute articles to professional journals and online sites respected by people in your field and, if you can find a publisher, to write a full-length book.

Similarly, anyone who wants to turn a hobby—for example, designing gardens—into a business will usually need to master a basketful of small business skills. Many years spent learning about plants and how to create lovely landscapes won't be preparation enough. Among the many additional things any landscape garden entrepreneur will need to know are how to market her services, purchase plants wholesale, hire help for heavy digging and lifting, charge and bill for services and collect on overdue accounts.

The Exciting New Career of Professor Grout

Alan, a smart guy from a poor family, ended up with a limited education. As a result, he spent most of his working life as a maintenance man and then maintenance supervisor for a local hospital. He didn't hate his work, but after 30 years, he didn't love it either. Alan's dream had always been to run his own small business.

At age 55, with his kids out of the house, Alan decided that if he was ever going to change his career, it was time to begin. But without a lot of money to invest in buying or starting a business, and no obviously bankable skills, he was at a loss as to what his new work should be. Alan's personal epiphany came one day as he was fixing some broken tiles in the kitchen of the teacher's lounge at John Quincy Adams Elementary School. It suddenly dawned on him that tile grout was always falling apart, and what the world truly needed was more people expert at replacing it.

After checking out the local tile scene, Alan found that while lots of general contractors did tile work and several local tile layers specialized in custom work, most preferred bigger jobs such as tiling new bathrooms and kitchens. Not many, it turned out, really wanted to patch a few broken tiles or replace degraded old grout. Alan got busy. He purchased every type of grout concoction on the market, scavenged a bunch of broken tiles from the dumpster behind a building supply warehouse and began to practice. Before long, he was a master at matching and patching old tile and ready to market his new service.

His first ad in a penny saver newspaper yielded five calls. Within a year, Alan, who now called himself Professor Grout, had retired from the school district (he was eligible for a decent pension) and was happily and profitably embarked on his new career.

Volunteering for a Good Cause

An active, maybe even passionate, involvement with an altruistic activity can be a hugely positive way for people to approach their later years. Among the benefits are staying busy, feeling needed and valued, making new friends, especially younger ones, and the personal satisfaction inherent in doing something you believe in. At a time when many surveys find that one-third of retired people feel bored or alienated doing valuable work in the nonprofit sector can be a powerful antidote.

It's almost a cliché that Americans will organize to support almost any good cause, and more than a few causes that are slightly wacky. As a result, about 11% of the nation's entire economic activity takes place in the nonprofit sector, much of it dependent—at least in part—on the unpaid work of volunteers. Oddly, it seems to be something of a secret that "senior power" is a powerful reason why so many nonprofit groups achieve so much. If you doubt this, take a look at any local educational, religious, environmental or health care group—even the volunteer fire department. You'll probably see that much of the behind-the-scenes leadership, as well as the bulk of volunteer help, is provided by retired people.

When you consider how stretched for time so many younger adults are as they simultaneously try to work and raise a family, it should be obvious that much of the good work our communities have come to rely on wouldn't get done without the energy and commitment of older people. But time and commitment aren't the only help that older adults offer. Commonly, their most important contribution is competence. For example, a retired bank manager or accountant can bring a level of financial savvy to a growing community crime prevention group that the organization could never hope to buy. And when a church or hospital needs a new building, it will almost always search the roster of volunteers in hopes of finding a retired contractor or other person familiar with the many pitfalls of construction to help guide them.

The fact that nonprofit work is usually unpaid doesn't alter the fact that, like any other work, success depends on competent people conscientiously and creatively applying themselves. As such, it's often a great fit for retired people who have no compelling need to earn more money, but who want to stay actively involved in community concerns.

Occasionally, people become involved in nonprofits because of the status they think they will gain as a result of membership on the board of directors or other responsible position. Participation primarily for this reason is almost always a mistake. Serious involvement in the nonprofit sector is hard work, with recognition—if it comes at all—usually being noteworthy only in the relatively small circle of people who truly care about the activity.

Older Americans Do Well by Doing Good

Here's what one researcher concluded about older volunteers with the U.S. Government's Foster Grandparents and Senior Companions programs:

"In addition to evidence that seniors can contribute in important ways through service, there are indications that the seniors greatly benefit themselves by serving. In fact, the engine driving senior service may well be less airy altruism than a strong and straightforward desire for structure, purpose, affiliation, growth and meaning....

"Research on benefits to Foster Grandparents ... found that participants' mental health and social resources improved over the three years, while those on the waiting list declined in these areas. Among the study's other findings: 71 percent of the Foster Grandparents reported they 'almost never' felt lonely, compared with 45 percent of the waiting list group. Also, 83 percent of participants reported being 'more satisfied' with their life, compared with 52 percent of those waiting to become Foster Grandparents."

("Seniors in National and Community Service," a report prepared for the Commonwealth Fund's Americans Over 55 at Work program by Mark Friedman.)

In thinking about my own not-so-far-off retirement, one question that interests me is whether volunteering for a good cause provides pretty much the same personal benefits as does working in the private sector—except, of course, no paycheck—or if volunteering is likely to be more fulfilling. After talking to many people who have done both, my tentative answer is this: When it comes to staying busy and providing structure or discipline to one's life, there is often little difference between "for profit" and "nonprofit" work. But especially for those retirees whose jobs haven't been particularly fulfilling, there are several reasons why working with nonprofits can prove more satisfying:

- *Doing interesting work:* Nonprofits often allow retired people to do work that they find more interesting and satisfying than would be possible working for a company busily trying to make money. After all, there aren't too many corporations whose main goals are to preserve a rain forest, record the oral histories of elderly Estonian immigrants or teach low-income children to read. By contrast, the nonprofit sector offers an array of fascinating activities that should be sufficient to inspire even the most jaded imagination.

- *Looking to the future:* Almost by definition, nonprofits aim to improve the quality of life. Working with an organization dedicated to making at least a little slice of the world better seems to help at least some participants cope with the inevitability of their own death. The fact that your good work will live on after you die can make your life seem more meaningful. Or as psychologist Erik Erikson put it, "I am what survives me."

Doris Helps Preserve a Marsh

While working on this chapter, I attended a board meeting of the Save San Francisco Bay Association, an environmental group I volunteer with. As part of a discussion of preserving wetlands, Doris Sloan, a retired University of California professor and long-time environmental activist, recounted how recently she had looked out the window of a jet as it descended toward San Francisco airport.

She explained that when a large green wetland on the north shore of San Pablo Bay came into view she remembered that, ten years before, it had been slated for a development containing up to 10,000 homes. Doris then reminded the Save the Bay board members that the group's work—along with that of other Bay Area environmentalists—had been essential to preserving this biologically rich and diverse stopping place for migrating birds. Doris movingly summed up her feelings by saying, "When I looked down at that big, beautiful spot of green, I felt good all over."

- *Paying one's karmic debts:* Working with nonprofits gives people the chance to indirectly repay those whose efforts have smoothed their own way. Whether it be a grandparent, teacher, older friend or helping organization, we all know and cherish the memories of people and groups who did something extra to enrich our own lives or help us achieve something that might otherwise have been out of our reach. Helping others lets us pass on the love and support once given us.

- *Meeting interesting people:* Work with nonprofits may lead to more rewarding friendships than are likely to occur in the private sector. I say this not because the job site isn't a good place to make new friends; to the contrary, it's one of the best. But because nonprofit groups, which by definition tend to attract the like-minded people, can be even better. Or as a friend who spends lots of free time supporting girls' sports recently said, "Where else can I find people interested in talking about the best way for a fast pitch softballer to throw a rise ball?"

Just as it is obvious that preparation is necessary to get a good job in the private sector, planning ahead can be key to succeeding as a volunteer with a nonprofit organization. At first you may think this is silly—after all, you're not asking to be paid, only to help out. Think again. As Ted, the retired electrician who wanted to help with kids' sports programs, found out the hard way, not all volunteers are welcomed. Increasingly, many nonprofits use the same sorts of management and training techniques as do for-profit enterprises. And an increasing number of nonprofits hire paid staff to accomplish most key tasks, with the result that only skilled and experienced volunteers are needed—and even they are too often relegated to tasks such as stuffing envelopes or staffing fundraising tables.

There's no question that even professionally staffed nonprofits still need help from at least a small cadre of skilled volunteers—some of whom will likely be retired—to sit on their board of directors and key advisory committees. But these people are usually drawn from those who have been active in the field for many years or who contribute cash to the cause. The unfortunate result is that retired volunteers who don't have a history of working in a particular field or deep pockets may have a difficult time finding satisfying work. This is especially likely to be true if, as is common with older people, the volunteer is a little shy or insecure or is physically limited.

NONPROFITS DON'T THROW OUT THEIR VETERANS

In too many parts of American life, the old are often needlessly and callously cast aside. For example, corporations and governmental entities usually force their senior executives into retirement at or before age 60 or 65, just when many are enjoying their most productive years. Happily, this "discard-the-old" mentality often doesn't extend to nonprofits. Especially when volunteers have been involved for many years, most nonprofits bend over backwards to find useful work for them to do well into old age. Unfortunately, because people wait until after they retire to volunteer, they have less time to find a useful role and this type of bonding may not occur.

You may think I'm exaggerating. After all, no matter what your age, isn't it possible to begin working with a helping organization by performing a simple task, such as answering the phone or doing office work? Don't be so sure. The group you want to work with may have paid clerical staff. And rapid technological change is squeezing out what used to be regarded as unskilled tasks in the nonprofit sector only slightly more slowly than in corporate America. In many nonprofits, people who can't skillfully operate a computer can't be of much help.

Even if you do find a nonprofit which needs you to stuff envelopes, there is no guarantee this will lead to more interesting work. A 1998 study by the UPS Foundation found that 41% of people who regularly volunteered stopped because the nonprofit organization did not make good use of their time and talents. Close to 60% reported they would volunteer more hours if their time were better used.

The lesson in all of this is much the same as it is for those interested in continuing to work for pay: to find a fulfilling role in the nonprofit sector, it's best to prepare in advance. Volunteering well before you retire gives you plenty of time to look for a group that will be able to make good use of your existing skills, and also affords you a chance to determine whether you are really suited for a particular type of work and to look elsewhere if you aren't. You may learn that you need additional education or training to do volunteer work that will be truly satisfying.

Finding a good nonprofit you can truly bond with is sometimes harder than you might guess. For example, one friend, Joan, who had planned for years to help out with a marine animal rescue project, retired early so she could begin this exciting work. She was hugely disappointed to discover that being around cold salt water caused her arthritis to flare up so badly that she couldn't continue. And for various reasons, her efforts to volunteer with several other wildlife organizations didn't work out. After consulting the staff at a local volunteer center, Joan finally found a good match—helping out in, and eventually running, the animal lab at a children's science museum. Looking back at her experiences, Joan feels she was lucky things worked out so well. "I can see I was naive about my future plans. Being active in animal rescue and teaching kids about animals on a daily basis not only involves a big time commitment, but also involves a level of planning, management and physical stamina that I was unprepared for. I realize now that I didn't understand how much I would have to grow to be able to handle it. I was lucky to get inspired help from our volunteer center—otherwise my lack of preparation might have doomed my whole plan."

Similarly, Rob, a law librarian friend, thought that after retirement he would like to help average people learn legal survival skills. But a few years before retirement, when he volunteered as a counselor at a legal aid office, he was disappointed to find that dealing with lots of anxious, impatient people caused him so much stress he couldn't sleep. After reluctantly facing up to the fact that he wasn't willing to live with this much personal anxiety, but still wanting to use his legal experience to help people, he looked for other places to volunteer. After floundering unsuccessfully for almost a year, he asked a group of volunteer lawyers who helped low-income people accomplish their own legal tasks if they needed research help. This time the fit was excellent. It turned out they badly needed someone to organize their library and help research legal issues—tasks Rob could do and still get his rest. But again, the lesson is clear—a little more planning would have made Rob's transition from the workplace to the nonprofit sector much smoother.

Pursuing Personal Interests

The last thing some recent retirees consider is continuing to work, in either the profit or nonprofit sector. For them, retirement offers a chance to finally have the time to do many of the interesting things they have put off all their lives. If this describes you, I have an important question to ask: Outside of your work and family, name the truly fascinating activities on which you currently spend a significant amount of time.

If, like many people in midlife, your answer is that you haven't had time to follow up on old interests or develop new ones, but plan to do both after you retire, please pay attention. You are at high risk of having a difficult—perhaps even an unhappy—retirement. The reason is simple: Few people who have not developed and cultivated authentic interests during their middle years are able to do so in their 60s, 70s or 80s. Many people in this category end up bored and disappointed in their retirement, whether they are scraping by on a yearly income of $20,000 or luxuriating in five times that amount.

I'm convinced that if middle-aged people allow too many years to pass without developing new interests or renewing old ones, they may never again be able to tap into their creativity. Much like the 12-year-old left to her own devices on a beautiful summer day, who plaintively calls to a parent, "I'm bored," retirees who have forgotten how to be interested in new things don't seem to know how to relearn this incredibly important skill. Sure, after retirement they finally have plenty of time to develop a new hobby or rediscover an old one, but all they seem to be able to do is turn on the TV.

Think back. Chances are good when you were in your teens and 20s, you were interested in all sorts of things. I can certainly remember periods in which I tried on new hobbies, artistic endeavors and sports at the rate of at least two a month. But as we age and our responsibilities increase, most of us become less interested in new things and gradually lose interest in some of our old pastimes. We may remember fondly when we wrote poetry, climbed rocks or took painting classes, but we are no longer so adventurous.

How long has it been since you've had a genuine new interest? And how much time has passed since you dabbled in an old one? If you can honestly answer yesterday, last week or even last month, chances are good you are still deeply curious about all sorts of things and make the time to do at least some of them. And it follows that there is a high likelihood you will revel in the extra time your retirement years provide. After all, now you really do have time to make that boat, hike to the top of Mt. McKinley, develop your watercolor skills or write your book. By contrast, warning flags should be flying if you are currently in your 40s or 50s and do not participate in at least several interesting activities. Or put another way, if besides working you do little more than consume passive types of entertainment while fantasizing that you'll become more active when you retire, your fantasies are likely to turn out to be just that.

Especially if at any time during your life you thought of yourself as a creative person (painter, musician, poet or whatever else), I urge you to make a real effort to rediscover or enlarge upon these impulses. The reason is simple: Older artists often do well, commonly experiencing a sustained burst of exciting creativity after 65. And because art is almost by definition of great interest to its creator, artists tend to remain vital and purposeful in their own eyes, which of course is one of the keys to continuing to be respected by others.

Continuing Your Education

We humans are an extremely curious lot. Hence the success of all sorts of large organizations dedicated to bringing us news. And it isn't only current events we are anxious to learn. In every human community the world over, we make it a high priority to establish schools to tell our children the most important events of the past, going all the way back to the Big Bang (or was it a whimper?).

In our own student years—whether we specialized in science, music, politics, art, language, agriculture or whatever else—many of us experienced moments of genuine excitement as we learned fascinating pieces of human history or, if we're really lucky, helped to extend human knowledge in a particular field. Looking back, we may still regard our high school and college years as among the most satisfying of our lives and possibly even wish we could have had a longer period in which to engage in systematic learning, free of midlife responsibilities.

Enter our retirement years, when finally we will have plenty of time to learn new things. Given the fast-growing number of affordable opportunities for older Americans to study, chances are good that without much inconvenience we will have the opportunity to learn a great deal about almost anything that interests us, whether it be how to sculpt, read Latin, teach autistic children, design a Japanese garden or any one of thousands of other endeavors.

Against this background, it is fair to ask why today's typical American retiree watches 26 hours of TV each week and takes advantage of few, if any, learning opportunities. Or to put the question more directly, why is it statistically unlikely that in retirement you will go to school part-time or engage in any other program of systematic learning?

Although neuroscientists and others who study aging can't conclusively tell us why older people seem so resistant to learning, evidence is accumulating that it has a great deal to do with how we use—or, in too many cases, under use—our most important muscle (our brain) throughout our lives. At the risk of oversimplifying, the old workout mantra, "Use it or lose it," seems to apply to exercising our brain just as it does to the rest of our body. A brain that is not challenged to learn new things for an extended period will actually become smaller and less capable of learning in the future.

What's the evidence for this claim? Two sources are most interesting. The first consists of over 30 years of studies on the brains of rats by a group of scientists led by Marian Cleeves Diamond and Mark Rosenzweig. After enriching the lives of one group of rats by putting lots of creative toys in their cages, while depriving other rats of stimulation, Diamond and Rosenzweig examined their brains. The rats in the enriched environment developed far more brain cells in their cerebral cortexes than did the others. And this phenomenon didn't apply just to young rats; older rats also grew more brain cells when they experienced a more exciting environment that gave them the chance to learn new things.

A second source of exciting information about how stimulated brains continue to function well comes from a study conducted by University of Kentucky professor David Snowden with the help of the School Sisters of Notre Dame, a community of nuns in Mankato, Minnesota. Snowden has found that nuns who remain intellectually active by teaching and learning well into old age not only live longer than their less educated sisters, but suffer significantly less from dementia, Alzheimer's and other diseases of the brain.

The physiological explanation for why hardworking brains are likely to do well is that their stimulated cells (neurons) branch frequently, with the result that millions of new connections (synapses) are created and your brain actually becomes larger. Unfortunately, the reverse also seems to be true—an unchallenged brain, like an unchallenged biceps, soon loses size and tone. But assuming you are determined to keep your brain active, there is good news—evidence is accumulating that your larger brain can help cope with the effects of brain diseases, such as Alzheimer's and stroke. Here the hypothesis is that a brain that is made up of more active tissue has a greater number of ways to work around diseased or damaged areas.

To understand how intellectual stimulation can strengthen the brain, it's helpful to know that in the normal course of living our brains are constantly reorganizing themselves, and that this process (called neuroplasticity) speeds up with the amount and complexity of new information the brain receives. Or in the words of Paula Tallal, a Rutgers University neuroscientist quoted in the January 1, 2000, issue of *Newsweek*, "You create your brain from the input you get." Against this background it is easy to see why continuing to be an active learner throughout your life may contribute to a larger, healthier brain, which in turn may help you be more inquisitive and less bored during retirement.

It follows that, just as during midlife you need to adopt a plan to get enough physical exercise, it also makes sense to think about how you can challenge your brain to stay active. To make the necessary time, why not turn off your TV at least three days a week and substitute more brain-stimulating activities? Arnold Scheibel, head of UCLA's Brain Research Institute, believes that the brain's axons and dendrites (threadlike appendages to neurons), which send and receive messages, grow fastest when dealing with new material. In a fascinating article, "Building a Better Brain" (Golden and Tsiaras, *Life* (1994)), he says, "The important thing is to be actively involved in areas unfamiliar to you. Anything that is intellectually challenging can probably serve as a kind of stimulus for dendritic growth, which means it adds to the computational reserves in your brain."

It follows that it not only makes sense to continue your education, but it's best to challenge yourself to learn a new subject. For example, if you are already fluent in three languages, rather than master two more, you will stimulate more brain cell growth if you learn to paint, play a musical instrument or strive to understand basic physics. And those who don't enjoy formal schooling will be happy to know that it's not only traditional academic subjects that stimulate the brain. Anything that's both new to you and challenging will do it. Thus a Latin professor might do better to learn how to prune fruit trees, line her car's brakes or even solve difficult jigsaw puzzles than to write a scholarly essay parsing Cicero's rhetoric.

More Information About How Human Brains Age

If you want to stimulate your brain by learning about how brains work, here are several good places to start:

- *Enriching Heredity: The Impact of the Environment on the Anatomy of the Brain*, Marion Cleeves Diamond (Free Press 1988). A fascinating book detailing Dr. Diamond's early work on the effects of learning on the brains of rats.
- "The Brains Behind the Brain," Marcia D'Arlangelo (*Educational Leadership*, November 1998). Interviews with five prominent brain researchers provide an excellent review of current knowledge.
- "Rewiring Your Gray Matter," Sharon Begley (*Newsweek*, January 1, 2000). A breezy, but nevertheless fascinating review of current research.
- *Keep Your Brain Alive*, Lawrence C. Katz and Manning Rubin (Workman Publishing 1999). A fun little book that offers 83 practical brain exercises to help prevent memory loss and increase mental fitness.

Finding the Time to Learn

Many of us spend hours each week on public transit or behind the wheel of a car. And others conscientiously invest hours exercising our bodies using equipment such as a treadmill, stairstepper or stationary bike or by simply going for a jog or long walk. With a little planning, time we spend commuting and exercising offers a great opportunity to learn new things. For example, why not use a Walkman to listen to a language tape while you jog, or do the reading for a continuing education course while you sit on the subway? Not only will you experience the fun and pride that comes with learning something new, you will be developing habits that should serve you well after retirement and may even increase the learning capability of your brain.

Denis Prepares to Retire

Probably like many of you, I know lots of people who not only work a 40-hour week but often put in extra hours besides. Most of them believe they need every penny they make both to finance their current lifestyle and, if anything is left over, to save for the future. But I have at least one friend who approaches life differently. Instead of maximizing his income as a well-known Nolo author, Denis Clifford (*Nolo's Will Book*, *Plan Your Estate*, *Make Your Own Living Trust*) works two-thirds time, so that he will have time for other activities. In addition to affording him time for daily exercise, this relaxed work schedule allows Denis to maintain an art studio, where he paints and displays his work, as well as to study French. And each summer, Denis stops working entirely for two months to venture out and explore the world.

Now and then, Denis questions himself a little, wondering if he is making a mistake by not working full-time and, as a result, being able to save more for retirement. But in his heart, he understands that if you can stay truly interested in your life in middle age, your retirement will take care of itself.

Can You Buy an Action-Packed Retirement?

Single parents and others who must work incredibly hard to support their families will probably want to skip this section. For better or worse, they are in no danger of having to worry about whether it's possible to purchase a fulfilling retirement.

As noted often in this book, some people in midlife become so obsessed with working long hard hours to save money for retirement that they are too busy to develop new skills or interests. Commonly, business executives and professionals who experience their peak earning years in their 50s or even 60s fit this profile.

When asked about what they will do when they retire, these affluent people often say they plan to travel the world or move to a resort-like retirement area, with easy access to a plethora of leisure activities. In short, they seem to believe that after retirement they will be able to use their big financial nest egg to purchase a fun-filled life. Can they? Is it a viable retirement strategy to concentrate on earning piles of money, even though it may well leave you little time to become involved with a good cause, bond with your family or make new friends outside of work?

My answers are "possibly," and "no," in that order. Let me explain why I appear to be so confused.

My first answer is "possibly" because, to my surprise, a good number of affluent retirees achieve at least a measure of retirement success for at least a few years after retirement by substituting spending lots of money for taking the sensible pre-retirement steps I discuss in this book. If they are in decent health—something that really can't be bought—affluent older people obviously have retirement options others don't enjoy. They can spend their winters skiing at Aspen, golfing in Palm Springs and sailing in the Bahamas while the rest of us are home shoveling snow or doing laps around the mall. And because each of these glamorous activities comes with lots of opportunity for socializing, affluent retirees may even be able to make new friends while they spend their money.

Of course, upmarket vacations aren't the only thing the affluent can buy. They can also buy or build new homes, start hobby businesses or otherwise spend money in ways that interest them. Take my friend Mike, an independently wealthy 75-year-old who in his middle years did none of the things that I advocate to ensure a fulfilling retirement. Mike largely ignored his children when they were young, with the result that he now has little contact with them. He cultivated no new friendships, with the result that he is often lonely. And he developed no new interests, with the result that he now has very few. Despite all his mistakes, Mike has found a way to use his wealth so that he isn't a miserable guy.

Mike, who owns a number of commercial buildings, constantly renovates or adds on to them. And he doesn't just plan the additions, he dons a hard hat and cheerfully works alongside the people he hires. If it seems wacky to other members of the crew to see a millionaire in his 70s coming to work at 6:30 in the morning to pound nails, they have the good sense to keep their mouths shut. And now and then, when Mike feels bored with pouring concrete, he does what he has always done when he's at loose ends—he jets to Sun Valley for a little skiing or to Paris to check out the ever-changing gallery scene.

Now let's look at why my second answer to the question of whether a successful retirement can be bought is "no."

Although Mike and some other affluent older people have found a way to use their money to enrich their retirement, it remains true that good family relationships, good friends, good health and your own spiritual development can't be bought. If in your struggle to become wealthy, you do nothing to nurture the interests and people who will afford you a sense of purpose and fulfillment in your retirement years, there is an excellent chance you'll end up being a rich, miserable old fart. And all the fancy toys money can buy and all the exotic places it can take you probably won't fill your empty life. Or put another way, while your first cruise to paradise may be great fun, your third is likely to be a bore.

I don't mean to suggest that retiring with a seven-figure net worth is a bad thing. Certainly, having a comfortable portfolio of investments can make you and your family feel more secure and independent, as well as providing you with the wherewithal to pay for decent long-term care should you need it. And, of course, a fat bank account will also afford you the pleasure of being able to provide economic help to family members (a down payment for a child's new house or tuition for a grandchild's education). No, the problem with being wealthy at retirement is not with the money (although being rich can make some people obnoxious no matter what their age), but with the sacrifices it often takes to attain it. For example, many of the midcareer lawyers, doctors and other professionals I know routinely work a 60-hour week. With this type of schedule, helping to raise the children, spending time with friends and developing new interests outside of work are simply not a realistic part of their picture.

Recently I had occasion to briefly talk to Jamal, a successful but overbusy physician in his late 40s, about his life. Almost the first words out of his mouth were, "I know I work too obsessively, and may even be putting my health at risk." Jamal believes his inability to slow down is the product of several factors: the nature of his job (his employer expects long hours); his desire to be a leader in his medical specialty; and his desire to lead a fairly affluent lifestyle while at the same time saving lots of money for the future. When I remarked that he and his wife (also a physician) must together earn well in excess of $350,000 per year and that it's my guess they have already saved well over $1 million, his very serious response was "You're right, but we will feel much more comfortable when we have saved twice as much."

I next asked what he did with his leisure time. Jamal answered with a shrug. "I get up at 5:45 a.m. and am out the door by 6:40 most mornings. I don't get home until close to 8:00, sometimes even after my children are in bed. By the time I eat, I'm usually so tired that I fall asleep in front of the TV set before 10. On Saturdays, I catch up on reading medical journals and correspondence, and maybe run a few errands. But I do try to save part of Sunday afternoon to spend with my family."

What do you think? Even if Jamal saves another million dollars and trades his BMW for the biggest Jaguar, will he be well-prepared to enjoy a successful retirement? Leaving aside the possibility that Jamal will die of exhaustion first, my guess is that, without his work, he will have a tough time figuring out who he is and finding things to do that truly interest him. Given all the money he and his wife have already saved, both of them might do far better to cut back their work hours and begin to learn how to live a sensible life.

ARRANGE TO WORK A FEW HOURS LESS

Figure out a way to trade some of your income for increased free time—that is, to work a little less in order to have some time to volunteer, explore a different line of work or develop a new interest. This may involve some jawboning with your boss—especially difficult if you work for yourself—but in this era of flex time, it's often possible. What about the money you'll lose? Unless you are living close to the poverty line, don't fret. Your successful search for activities that truly interest you will pay bigger dividends throughout the rest of your life than a mutual fund ever can.

A Tale of Two Railroadmen

In my research for this book, I often met older people with very modest incomes who were nevertheless doing things they loved. Instead of taking the all-too-typical American approach of buying their pleasures, these creative people used common sense to achieve their goals at low cost. Here's an example based loosely on two older men who have in common a love of trains. One of them, John, is a retired businessman whose investment portfolio runs into the double-digit millions. The other, Cedric, is a retired supermarket checker who lives on his Social Security and a small military pension, supplemented by his wife's part-time babysitting business and a few thousand dollars a year he earns from his small business sharpening garden and household tools.

John expresses his passion for railroads by building—and constantly rebuilding—the largest and most elaborate hobby railway set-up I've ever seen, which occupies the entire basement of his multi-million-dollar retirement home. John does most of the designing and construction of his little empire by himself, occasionally inviting some neighborhood kids or other train enthusiasts to come and share his creation.

Cedric expresses his similar love of trains by volunteering a couple of days a week at a steam railway in a local park. There, a group of railroad buffs—most of them retired—operate a two-mile, small-gauge train. For a modest fare, kids and their families can ride in small open cars pulled by one of several steam locomotives. Several days a week, low-income and school groups enjoy free admission. None of the volunteers, including Cedric, are paid, since all income—supplemented by a yearly fund-raising event—goes to maintain and expand the railroad. In the course of a year, tens of thousands of people ride the steam train. Because Cedric is actively involved with others in making this happen, he has made a load of "railroad friends" and enjoys an active social life.

Although John seems to be doing fine working on his trains in what can best be described as splendid isolation, I am impressed by how much more interesting Cedric's life is. Not only is he doing something that fascinates him, but he is helping others and making friends—many of them children.

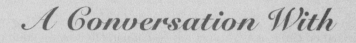

A Conversation With

ERNEST CALLENBACH

Born in 1929, Callenbach grew up in the tiny town of Boalsburg, Pennsylvania. Growing up in the country gave him basic training in gardening, carpentry and other skills, which he has practiced all his life. He attended the University of Chicago and has lived most of his adult years in Berkeley, California, where he worked at the University of California Press as editor of the respected film magazine *Film Quarterly,* the Press's Natural History Guide series and the country's leading line of film books. He has also written a number of books including *Ecotopia,* a best-selling novel portraying a society that embraces biological survival over economic profit to reach what ecologists call "sustainability."

RW: You retired early, at 62, from a job you apparently loved—editing books and the magazine, *Film Quarterly*.

EC: Yes, my job really was great fun.

RW: So why did you leave early?

EC: I had a pretty decent retirement plan and was also covered by Social Security. Once I hit 62 and qualified for Social Security payments, I would have gotten very little more by continuing to work. In addition, my wife works, which also adds to our family income.

RW: But still, you loved your job.

EC: Yes, it was a great job, but I had done it for a long time and was ready for something different. Add to that the fact that I already had another occupation as a writer and lecturer. Since the publication of *Ecotopia,* years ago, I have been invited to lecture on environmental issues all over the world. So in a way, my retirement from U.C. Press just let me devote more time to my second career.

RW: Had you planned to do this consciously? In other words, did you say to yourself 20 years ago, I better get busy with something besides my job so I'll have interesting work when I retire?

EC: No, I really didn't think about retirement back then. But I did consciously plan to be independent all along—to protect some time for myself. For example, for many years I only worked at U.C. Press four days per week so I could do my own projects—though, of course, this meant only getting an 80% paycheck. As it turned out, doing this served me well when I retired.

RW: You've been retired for over three years. How busy have you been?

EC: I feel just as busy with my writing, lecturing and other projects as when I was working at U.C. In fact, I'm always trying to cut back. I have a pleasant fantasy of becoming more like a primitive person, working only when work really needed to be done—to get food, for example—with no need to accomplish a list of 27 things every day. You know, it really is a great pleasure to sit in the sun, listen to music or take a nap.

RW: Sounds great. Is that what you get to do?

EC: Not much. I just spent two years writing a book called *Bring Back the Buffalo! A Sustainable Future for the Great Plains,* which involved lots of research and a fair amount of travel. In addition, I do other writing—shorter pieces mostly—and still give lectures, sometimes overseas. For example, I've been lucky to have been invited to speak in Spain, Germany, Quebec, and in Japan several times. I've been active in the Elmwood Institute, a small think tank concerned with planning a sustainable future.

RW: And you have a family?

EC: In addition to my dear wife, Christine, with whom I enjoy doing all sorts of things, my daughter, son-in-law and granddaughter, Anya, who is shown with me in the picture at the beginning of this interview, live nearby. My son and daughter-in-law live in New York City.

RW: Imagine you were asked to give a lecture entitled "What I've Learned About Retirement" to a group whose average age was 40 or 45. What would you tell them?

EC: First, I would ask them to focus on the question of what they will do with their time. The truth is, even if you love fishing or golf, you are likely to become quickly bored if those are the only activities on your plate. The key is to find useful ways to connect to the world—otherwise, you'll drive your

spouse or anyone else you are close to nuts. Men, especially, often suffer a big dip in their feelings of self-worth once they are no longer working and don't get all those strokes from colleagues or subordinates. This is something that must be confronted and turned around to have a successful retirement. Often this means having to start from scratch to reconstruct one's self-esteem. Fortunately, there are a number of ways to do it—for example, turning an occasional hobby into a small business. Providing service through a nonprofit organization is another good approach. Getting involved in local politics to try and improve the way your community works is a third. The larger point is to recognize that we humans are a sociable species and we need to connect to others in a positive way.

RW: Great. What would be next on your list?

EC: Perhaps it will surprise you, but I would put "space" next. At a workplace, you have your space, even if it's just a corner of the shop floor or a desk in the shipping department. When you retire, assuming you're married or live with someone else, you must share space in a way you never have before. And I mean all types of space, including even using the telephone. Especially for men, who have typically seen the home as being more a woman's environment, this can be a huge problem. Whether it's in the basement, attic, spare room or out of the house altogether, everyone needs their own defensible space. And I would add that once a domestic partner retires, a spouse who mostly managed the home also feels his or her space has been invaded, so by creating a space for the recently retired person, the spouse also minimizes conflicts created by the change.

Third on my list I would put health and fitness, including diet. Start right this minute to improve all of these things and you'll be grateful when you retire. If you don't, you may not even live that long. Not only will paying attention to your physical well-being likely result in your living longer and feeling better, it will also save you a pile of money in expensive medical care. Incidentally, I recommend a publication called *Nutrition Action*, published by the Center for Science in the Public Interest (1875 Connecticut Avenue, NW, Suite 300, Washington, DC 20009-5728), to help you clean up your diet. (They're the outfit that describes fettucini Alfredo as "a heart attack on a plate.")

But in addition to eating better—less salt, fats and sugar—you need to be active, to exercise every day. Whether you join a gym, ride a bike regularly or just walk briskly doesn't make a big difference as long as you really do it. Also, look at your life and find ways to accomplish your daily rounds more actively. For example, instead of getting in the car to drive to the neighborhood market or a friend's house, walk or bicycle.

RW: You and your wife Christine Leefeldt wrote a book called *The Art of Friendship,* which I quote from in Chapter 4, so I suspect friends must be on your list someplace.

EC: Next, in fact. As we become older, it's critical to have a network of real friendships—people with whom we enjoy close emotional contact. Again, this is an area that can be tougher for men, since by the time they retire, many have few real relationships beyond the workplace and their immediate family. When they retire and lose most of their work friends, they can be profoundly lonely. They can also begin to lose their sense of attractiveness—or maybe I should say sexuality. Friendships with younger people—and I don't mean sleeping with them—can do a lot to make older people feel more attractive and less vulnerable to isolation. Of course, by paying attention to one's health and physical fitness, it's a lot easier to maintain a healthy self-image.

But it's also important to remember that a big component of self-esteem comes from playing a part in shared work—or play. Actively pursuing shared interests is the single best way to make sure you remain a worthwhile person in your own eyes, so people should practice it all along, to be ready for retirement.

A few self-starters will have no trouble getting involved in loads of activities and making new friends, but many, if not most, retirees won't know how to do it. You may not believe this now, but lots of older people tend to withdraw from the world and gradually lose interest in things they used to be involved in, which in turn means they don't have much chance to make new friends or maintain old friendships. Incidentally, this is an area where people who have younger spouses or partners often benefit, since the younger person helps the older one stay tuned in to the world as it is now, and not as it was 20 years ago.

RW: All this is fascinating. How about one more category middle-aged people ought to think about?

EC: Money. Sure you'll need some, but if you are willing to change your attitudes about consumption, probably less than you think. Most Americans way overdo it with buying luxuries they don't need. You really can learn to live better at the same time that you spend less. And if you do, you won't have to work so hard and save so much.

RW: Let me interrupt. Are you proposing that Americans go cold turkey on the shopping mall?

EC: That would probably be impossible. And anyway, they may find some bargains there. No, I'm suggesting that if we change our attitudes about what we consume, and particularly about the bad trade-offs we make in spending too much of our precious lifetime to get money, we free ourselves from worrying so much about money. For lots of middle-class Americans who aren't ever going to be as prosperous as their parents were in the late 1950s bubble economy, this is important. Once you really accept that spending money doesn't equal happiness, you have the battle half won. I know it's hard for most Americans to believe, but there are tens of millions of poor people in this world—desperately poor by our usual standards—who are in better spirits than we are. Hundreds of millions!

RW: Think back 10 or 13 years. Did you worry about saving for retirement?

EC: My wife and I have always lived within a pretty sensible budget, so we did accumulate modest savings. More important, we learned how and where we could save further if we needed to. You know, there are all sorts of rea-sons—taxes being just one—that a dollar saved is far more valuable than a dollar earned.

RW: Are you continuing to save money now that you are retired?

EC: Despite traveling quite a bit this last year or two, the answer is yes, a little. Remember, lots of costs decrease when you retire. You don't go out to lunch as much, or buy business suits, and you have lots more time to save money by doing your own household projects. For example, I need to replace some old sewer pipe a tree root has gotten into. If I call a sewer guy, it will cost nearly $1,500. But with a few days digging and my hiring a neighbor's kid to help, I can not only do it for about $100, but I can feel good about getting the exercise. And of course, I have lots more time to shop sales and buy things at a reasonable price. You know, in many ways, we now live in a deflationary age—prices for many things are actually going down, especially if you have the time to shop discount stores. (Health care and coastal real estate are two things that keep going up, of course.)

RW: Despite being frugal, you have a nice house, decent cars, go out to dinner fairly often and travel a lot.

EC: Christine and I are careful connoisseurs of cheap restaurants. We also really like to get out and see the world. Middle America, in particular, is an incredibly cheap place to travel. Some of our travel gets paid through my lecture fees and expenses, but even without that, between senior discounts and common sense, you can see loads of interesting things for very little. For example, United Airlines allows people over 65 to buy four tickets, each good for travel anywhere in the continental U.S., for $600. Not bad.

RW: What about Social Security?

EC: It's a much-maligned program that's actually pretty decent. Twenty years ago, everyone predicted it would be bankrupt by now. Instead, adjusted for the real cost of living, benefits have gone up. It's one of the few real success stories of American government. And I'm sure with a few modest adjustments it will still be doing fine 20 or 30 years from now. ■

Chapter 2

Health and Fitness

"Every man desires to live long, but no man would be old."

—Jonathan Swift

We all know people in their 70s and older who are in excellent physical condition. Many still jog, swim, ski, dance, hike or golf with much the same verve and stamina they displayed 20 years ago. We know other retired people—unfortunately, far too many—who are so sedentary they become tired going to the grocery store.

I find it odd that although most people currently in midlife say that after retirement they hope to count themselves among the active, energized group, a great many follow a lifestyle that almost guarantees they will be in such poor physical condition they will spend most of their retirement on a couch. Even odder is the fact that many sedentary middle-aged people whose health and stamina are already in obvious decline nevertheless quickly and cheerfully agree that staying physically active is a key factor to enjoying retirement.

To be sure, not everyone believes that maintaining good health is important. Some fatalists contend that because there is no guarantee that healthy habits will benefit us later in life—or that unhealthy ones will ruin our retirement years—there's no point in making sacrifices such as quitting smoking, exercising regularly or cutting back on fatty foods. After all, as many are eager to point out, apparently super fit athletes sometimes die in their 50s, while some people who smoke two packs a day and drink anything that comes out of a bottle cheerfully bustle about until they are 102.

Despite the fact that one of my favorite t-shirts says "Eat Right, Exercise, Die Anyway," I find this reasoning silly. Although there is no guarantee that taking good care of one's health means living a long, healthy, active life, there is clearly a strong correlation between the two. The better our health and physical fitness after age 65, the more fulfilling our retirement years are likely to be. You don't have to take my word for it. Dr. John Rowe, a gerontologist and president of Mt. Sinai Medical Center, puts it like this: "Only about 30 percent of the characteristics of aging are genetically based; the rest—70 percent—are not.... People are largely responsible for their own old age."

If you, like many middle-aged people, are less healthy and fit than you should be, it makes sense to put more energy into maintaining or improving your health than into growing your investment portfolio. If you retire rich but in poor physical condition, you have achieved little, except to provide a comfy nest egg for your inheritors. I'm often asked how much can good health and exercise habits influence how an older person feels and acts. After reading more studies than I could list in the next three pages, my guess is that a person committed to staying in excellent physical condition can roll back the clock about 15 years. That is, at 85 he or she can live the life of a healthy 70-year-old.

And while affluence won't make up for poor health later in life, maintaining good health will be even more important if you have saved little. Because of a poor education, low pay, bad luck or heavy family responsibilities, many people—especially single women—need every penny they earn during their middle years just to live from day to day. When they retire, people in this group will have little more than their Social Security income to live on. (Despite what you may have read to the contrary, this doesn't doom them to a miserable retirement; about 25% of current retirees receive over 90% of their income from Social Security, and many of them are living interesting and fulfilling lives. See Chapter 9.) But for low-income retirees, good health is particularly important. Not only does it reduce out-of-pocket costs for health care and drugs not covered by Medicare, but even more important, it makes it far easier to produce needed extra income by continuing to work past age 65.

Some Immediate Ways to Improve Your Health

To help us stay healthy as we age, there's certainly no shortage of advice. Magazines and books constantly tout the newest drug, herb or wonder food: Fish oil! Tryptophan! Echinacea! Oat pasta! Soy milk! St. John's Wort! Melatonin!

The truth is, we don't need quick fixes; we already know the key ways to improve our health and, for the most part, they don't require odd chemicals, esoteric vitamins or homeopathic supplements. Individually, some of these things may be helpful, but putting your faith in them—or any wonder cure—will probably be counterproductive, especially if it serves as an excuse not to do more sensible, but boring, things such as eating lots of fruits and vegetables, cutting back on fats and sugars and getting plenty of exercise.

This isn't a health textbook, and I'm not a doctor. But I can still say with absolute confidence that adopting a healthy lifestyle as early in life as possible really does greatly improve your odds of both living to retirement age and enjoying it once you get there. So let me remind you of some simple and medically sound strategies you probably already know. But before I do, here is a brief disclaimer, courtesy of the inimitable Mark Twain: "Always be careful when reading books about health. Otherwise you might die of a misprint."

Stop Smoking

As you already well know, smoking often brings with it a long list of potentially life-shortening and life-degrading health problems, including a number of kinds of cancers, emphysema and heart disease. The risk of encountering one or more of these problems is so serious that if you smoke, kicking the habit will very likely have a greater positive influence on your retirement years than any other single act.

Clean Up Your Diet

Most of us already understand that we should be eating far healthier meals. Consuming lots of fruits, vegetables and whole grains, and cutting way back on fatty, salty and calorie-laden foods, is an obvious way to begin. Take a close look at your dinner plate; it should contain no more than a few ounces of lean meat, but plenty of vegetables. If, instead, it is heaped with six or eight ounces of meat (and especially if you think a butter-laden potato qualifies as a vegetable), you're getting at least double a healthy level of fat and calories.

For lots of people, the key to quickly improving their diets is to cut out most fast foods and poor quality restaurant meals. At many traditional Chinese, Mexican and Italian restaurants—and virtually every hamburger, chicken, pizza and hot dog establishments—foods are typically prepared with huge quantities of blood-vessel-clogging saturated fats. Food quality isn't the only issue; it's a lot easier to pay attention to the size of our servings at home than when eating out.

⚠ DON'T BELIEVE STORIES THAT SAY FAT IS GOOD FOR YOU

Recently, the media has widely hyped several studies which seem to say that a little fat in your diet may reduce the risk of heart attacks. Sorry, but the truth is far less fun. Very few Americans eat a diet containing so little fat that a bit more might be beneficial, and even for these folks, only those with low HDL—"good" cholesterol—are likely to benefit from more fat. Most of us could cut our fat intake in half and still be in no danger of consuming too little.

Maintain a Healthy Weight

One-third of American adults are significantly overweight. As a result of the sedentary lifestyle and poor diet that typically accompany obesity, many are at a comparatively higher risk for a number of diseases, including heart attack, cancer and diabetes. And although you may not want to hear it, considerable evidence indicates that being moderately overweight (pleasantly plump, if you will) is a major negative health factor. Specifically, two studies—one involving 115,000 female nurses and the other 19,000 male graduates of Harvard—indicate that gaining even 15 or 20 pounds after age 18 significantly increases one's chances of early death. By contrast, people who are lean and strong—for example, a 5'5" woman weighing 120 or less—are significantly more likely to retire in good health.

What's strong got to do with it, you may be asking? Simple. As you age, you lose muscle mass. Even if you maintain your weight, the percentage made up by muscle significantly decreases over time. In turn, this means your weight will probably go up even if you eat sensibly, since muscles burn calories and you now have less. This is where strength training can make a big difference. If you exercise with light weights or use a strength-training machine, you will build muscle mass as you burn fat and keep your weight under control.

⚠ IF YOU WEIGH OVER SEVEN PERCENT MORE THAN YOU DID AT 22, YOU PROBABLY WEIGH TOO MUCH

Despite all the evidence to the contrary, many Americans deny that we are too heavy and as a result are unwilling to change our bad habits. Partial evidence for this assertion comes from the fact that three quarters of the letters and emails I've received from readers claim I'm far too critical of middle-age weight gain, which most writers claim is inevitable and not something to worry about as long as cholesterol and blood pressure are under control. Nonsense. Even moderate obesity slows you down in numerous ways and contributes significantly to the early onset of all sorts of nasty health problems, diabetes being just one. Perhaps it will help stop denying the truth that being overweight really is harmful to health and longevity if you think about many of the smokers you know who similarly refuse to fully accept the fact that their habit is likely to measurably shorten their lives (and contribute to a long list of miserable illnesses).

Here's a fast and practical weight gain reality check that works for most people who were reasonably trim as young adults: Think about what you weighed when you were in your early 20s. If your current weight is more than seven percent higher, you probably weigh too much—something that is almost surely true if your weight has increased 10% or more from what it was in your early 20s. If you conclude that your belt really is too tight, take a serious look at making the changes necessary to take off—and keep off—a few of those extra pounds. And don't try to justify a higher weight by claiming you are now more muscular; unless you work out often and strenuously with free weights or resistance-based exercise machines, the reverse is almost surely true.

Do You Weigh Too Much?

To find out the U.S. Government recommends a body mass index of 25 or less, with anything higher signaling that you are too fat. Here is how to figure yours.

Step 1:   Multiply your weight in pounds by .45 to get kilograms.

Step 2:   Convert your height to inches. Multiply this number by .0254 to get meters. Multiply that number by itself.

Step 3:   Divide this into your weight in kilograms.

Your answer will probably be a number in the 20s or low 30s. It is your BMI.

Control Your Blood Pressure

After stopping smoking, the single most important thing Americans can do to improve their long-term health is avoid high blood pressure. According to the Center for Science in the Public Interest, by age 60, 60% of Americans have blood pressure so high that it should be medically treated. Millions more, although not prescribed medication, nevertheless have blood pressure levels sufficiently elevated that they are at substantially increased risk of heart attack and stroke. Put another way, by the time they retire, only one in three people has a healthy blood pressure.

Is moderately high blood pressure really so bad? The answer may shock you. Because high blood pressure so greatly increases your risk of heart disease and stroke—two of the three biggest premature killers of Americans—even a slightly elevated level is a truly significant threat to your heath, and by extension, to your ability to enjoy your retirement years.

High blood pressure may even increase your chances of being diagnosed as senile. While there is no evidence that diseases such as Alzheimer's (senile dementia) are affected by blood pressure, people who suffer a series of tiny localized strokes in the brain are often misdiagnosed as having dementia. It follows that because people with healthy blood pressure suffer far fewer strokes, your chances of becoming senile and maybe even being incorrectly diagnosed as having Alzheimer's can be significantly reduced by improving your diet.

Senility May Not Be Inevitable

The Baltimore Longitudinal Study of Aging, the long-term federal effort to understand the aging process, which has tracked 2,438 participants over four decades, provides a fascinating conclusion. For most Americans, senility is not inevitable. That's because only about 10% of older people will develop true dementia. For others, loss of cognitive function will occur because of avoidable or treatable medical conditions such as diabetes, hypertension and depression. True, many older people will experience a slight decline in short-term memory and physical reaction time, but neither of these impairs one's intellectual capacity.

Fortunately, there is some good news. You can take effective steps to lower your blood pressure. How do you do it? The short answer, according to the U.S. government's National High Blood Pressure Education Program (NHBPEP), is to take these steps:

1. Reduce your salt intake. An average adult American consumes two teaspoons of salt a day, much of it in processed foods or restaurant meals. Hypertension expert Rose Stamler says that if starting at age 25 we reduced this amount of salt by half, it could mean a 16% drop in coronary heart disease deaths and 23% fewer stroke deaths at age 55. (*Nutrition Action*, July/August 1995.)

2. Lose weight if you need to (and most adult Americans darn well do).

3. Exercise. The U.S. government now recommends 30 minutes per day. More is definitely better.

4. Use alcohol moderately. Here the medical evidence diverges, depending on your sex. Drinking up to two or three ounces of alcohol per day—preferably wine—reduces everyone's risk of having a heart attack or stroke. But other studies indicate that regular use of alcohol may increase the risk of breast cancer in women. ("Breast Cancer," by Bonnie Liebman, *Nutrition Action*, January 1996.) Balancing the benefits and risks, the consensus view of medical experts is that drinking one small glass of wine each day makes sense for women.

5. Eat lots of potassium-rich foods, such as fruits (particularly oranges and bananas) and vegetables. Most experts recommend about seven servings of fruits and vegetables per day.

But don't just assume your blood pressure level is okay because you have taken a number of steps to improve your health. High blood pressure is called the silent killer because you can have it and still feel fine. So have regular physicals, attend a blood pressure screening or get a home test kit and find out what your level is. If it's elevated (or even at the high end of the normal range), it's important to promptly take steps to lower it. Damage occurs long before you suffer a stroke or heart attack. The good news—confirmed by a 2000 study led by Dr. Frank Sacks of the Harvard Medical School called "Dietary Approaches to Stop Hypertension" —is that adopting a low-salt diet with plenty of fruits and vegetables can quickly lower your risk. The bad news is that damage done to your blood vessels while your blood pressure is too high can't be completely reversed later.

⚠ DON'T FALL FOR MEDIA HYPE THAT SALT ISN'T A PROBLEM

News stories sometimes quote studies—some funded by food companies that manufacture salty food—claiming that eating lots of salt isn't a problem for people with normal blood pressure. What often isn't mentioned is that blood pressure almost always increases with age (and that most older Americans have elevated levels), suggesting that consuming lots of salt now is highly likely to cause blood pressure problems later.

Control Your Cholesterol Level

Excess "bad" cholesterol, or low-density lipoprotein (LDL), results in fatty gunk building up in your blood vessels. For people in midlife with a high LDL cholesterol level, a drop of one percent reduces the risk of heart disease by two or three percent. In short, it is important to have your cholesterol checked regularly and to act quickly to reduce elevated bad cholesterol levels. Beginning a determined program to reduce LDL as early in life as possible will significantly reduce the chances you will be killed or debilitated by a heart attack.

You may also want to increase "good" cholesterol (high density lipoprotein, or HDL), which actually picks up bad cholesterol from body tissues and transfers it to your liver, which gets rid of it. Again, for most people, the best way to do this is to lose weight, reduce their intake of most fatty foods and engage in fairly strenuous daily exercise. People already on a low-fat diet may wish to slightly increase their consumption of unsaturated fats, such as olive or canola oil.

When it comes to cholesterol, the enemy comes in three forms. The first consists of cholesterol- and fat-rich products like butter, cheese, beef and pork. Second, saturated fats such as coconut and palm oil, which don't themselves contain cholesterol, are nevertheless loaded with fatty acids, which also raise blood cholesterol levels. Third, and recent evidence indicates even more artery-clogging, are partially hydrogenated oils (called trans-fatty acids or trans-unsaturated fat) found in most margarines and in many foods such as french fries, doughnuts and commercial baked goods. Again, while these don't contain cholesterol, they increase bad cholesterol (and may reduce good cholesterol) in your blood.

If your cholesterol levels are too high, your first steps should be to eliminate as many trans-fats from your diet as possible while also cutting down on saturated fats (substitute unsaturated fats found in nuts, fish and olive and canola oil). It's

also important to get lots of regular exercise, since extra pounds and extra cholesterol tend to be shed together. If this doesn't work fast enough, your doctor will
probably prescribe cholesterol-lowering medicines.

💡 YOUNGER WOMEN NEED TO WATCH THEIR CHOLESTEROL, TOO

Because pre-menopausal women don't suffer many heart attacks (probably
because their bodies produce estrogen), some are not greatly concerned about
maintaining healthy cholesterol levels. This is a big mistake. After menopause,
when estrogen is no longer produced, women's heart attack rates take a huge
jump—so big that as many as one-third of all women will eventually die of heart
disease. In short, a woman's poor eating habits in her early adult years, which
result in clogged blood vessels, are likely to come back and haunt her in later life.
True, post-menopausal women can cut the risks of both heart disease and
osteoporosis by taking estrogen, but since this also increases the risk of cancer, it's
hardly the ideal solution. (Raloxifene, a synthetic estrogen medication, may
produce many of estrogen's benefits without its worst side effects, but it is too
early in the testing process to be sure.)

Good Resources on Personal Health

It is both liberating and life-affirming to make an honest commitment to clean up your diet, reduce your weight and get more exercise. Unfortunately, as too many of us well know, good intentions have a way of fading quickly when we are faced with a tasty plate of fettuccini Alfredo, a nice fatty steak or a butter-filled slice of chocolate cake. One good way to periodically recharge your healthy resolve is to subscribe to one or more monthly magazines or newsletters on the subject. Here are some I like:

Nutrition Action. This well-written, hard-hitting newsletter should really get you to sit up and pay attention to the many ways you can improve your health. (It's especially hard on fast food outlets and manufacturers of unhealthy foods.) Center for Science in the Public Interest, Suite 300, 1875 Connecticut Avenue, NW, Washington, DC 20009-5728, phone 202-332-9110, fax 202-265-4954. Also check their website at www.cspinet.org.

Health magazine. It's intelligent, interesting and geared toward women. Subscription information: phone 800-274-2522 or see their website at www.healthmag.com.

University of California at Berkeley Wellness Letter. A straightforward newsletter that contains the latest research on diet and exercise, as well as information on the effectiveness of traditional and herbal medicines and general "wellness" tips. It also regularly looks at other health and safety risks, such as highway safety and household toxins. *Wellness Letter* Subscription Department, P.O. Box 420148, Palm Coast, FL 32142.

For a reference book on health issues, I recommend *The PDR Family Guide to Nutrition and Health (Medical Economics).* It does a good job of distinguishing health facts from health fads.

Finally, on the Internet check out Cyberkitchen (www.shapeup.org/kitchen). One of its interesting features allows you to enter your weight and the amount of exercise you get, at which point Cyberkitchen provides you with an estimate of how much you should eat each day.

Prevent Brittle Bones

Many of us fear that diseases of the brain like Alzheimer's will sentence us to spend our last years in a nursing home. Actually, it is far more likely that we will be institutionalized because of broken bones, most commonly hip fractures. Most of these injuries are the result of bone loss, or osteoporosis, a disease that is as preventable as it is horrible. Twenty-five million Americans, 80% of them women, suffer from this debilitating disease which results in 1.25 million annual skeletal fractures, of which 300,000 are hip fractures. (*Nutrition Action*, October 1997.) When you see a frail and bent older person hobbling down the street, you can be almost sure that one of her or his most serious problems is osteoporosis.

The good news is that osteoporosis—and the height loss, pain and high risk of bone fracture it causes—can largely be prevented. The keys are to get enough vitamin D and calcium and to engage in regular weight-bearing exercise. The most natural way to get adequate vitamin D is to expose your skin to sunlight for a few minutes several times per week without first covering it with sunscreen. Exactly how long depends on where you live and the time of year. Yes, this may slightly increase your risk of wrinkled skin or possibly even skin cancer, but as long as you carefully limit the time you spend in the sun without sunscreen these dangers are small as compared to those posed by osteoporosis. Other common sources of vitamin D include milk and vitamin pills, but according to the National Academy of Sciences, you need 400 IU a day at age 51-70 and 600 IU over age 71. Since a whole quart of milk contains only 400-600 IU, few people get enough via this route.

In addition to vitamin D you need plenty of calcium. This can be found in non-fat milk products, green leafy vegetables and a variety of supplements.

PEOPLE OVER 50, ESPECIALLY WOMEN, SHOULD CHECK BONE DENSITY Measuring bone density isn't difficult. Talk to your doctor about the desirability of doing this and what to do if you are suffering bone loss.

Manage Stress

Many people believe that reducing stress can decrease the likelihood of heart attack; for one, Dr. Dean Ornish, director of the Preventive Medicine Research Center in Sausalito, California, puts people with coronary artery disease on a strict low-fat vegetarian diet and prescribes stress-management techniques such as yoga and meditation for an hour per day. And some believe that one reason why older people who attend religious services regularly appear to be healthier than those who don't is that their stress levels are lower.

But a number of studies have failed to produce clear evidence that for healthier people stress is linked to heart and other diseases. Some people actually seem to thrive on stress. My own gut feeling is that if you keep your weight down, eat well and exercise every day, a moderate amount of stress, with an occasional period of more intense tension, shouldn't be a problem. Because the causes of stress, and the ways we handle it, vary so much from one individual to the next, you are probably the best judge of whether you are experiencing too much, too often, and therefore need to make some significant changes in your life. If you are drinking too much, sleeping poorly or are chronically tired and depressed, warning flags should be flying. If you are experiencing none of these problems, don't worry about it.

Get Needed Medical Tests

Forty or fifty years ago, an annual physical examination wasn't likely to do you much good, because tests available then couldn't spot more than a few serious health problems early enough to do much about them. That's no longer true. Today, many invisible but life-threatening problems can be discovered early, with the high likelihood of being eliminated or contained. To take one example, periodic examinations of the colon after age 50, using procedures called "sigmoidoscopy" and "colonoscopy," can discover polyps and other suspicious growths, which can then be quickly removed years before they turn cancerous. Checks of cholesterol levels are another life-saving must. Middle-aged women should have regular mammograms (to find breast cancer), pap smears (to detect cervical cancer) and bone density scans (to identify osteoporosis). And men should have regular prostate exams.

My point here is not to list all the tests you need and when you need them, but to suggest that today there really is a powerful reason to get an annual physical checkup. Certainly, if problems are spotted and corrected early, your chances of enjoying a healthy retirement will be greatly enhanced.

Exercise Often

When she was 88, the great actress Helen Hayes remarked, "If you rest, you rust." This pithy advice doesn't just apply to the aged. Regular exercise, especially activity that provides both an aerobic workout and builds muscles, bestows a wide range of truly significant benefits on people of all ages. These include weight control, improved cardiovascular health and stress reduction. Exercise also wards off mild depression and greatly improves strength; people who exercise into old age are far less likely to become frail than are couch potatoes. But perhaps just as important to the quality of our lives, both now and after we retire, regular exercise makes us feel better and look better and can even enhance our sexuality.

FIND A TYPE OF EXERCISE YOU REALLY ENJOY

It's easy to exercise every day for a few weeks, but far harder to keep at it. Your best hope of sustaining an exercise program is to find an activity that meets two criteria: you enjoy it, and it's relatively easy for you to do it. Swimming, jogging, jazzercise, step classes, fast walking, bicycling, kickboxing and aerobic calisthenics, to mention a few popular ways to work out, are all terrific as long as you have an easy way to do them on a regular basis.

When I began the first edition of this book, I was pretty sure that exercising frequently as part of a determined effort to maintain physical fitness was important to a healthy retirement. The hundreds of conversations I've had since then with current retirees have only strengthened this conviction. Almost without exception, the most energized, vital seniors I have talked to exercised regularly and fairly strenuously. And as you'll see when you read the conversations with retirees whose lives seemed interesting and fulfilling, the importance of physical fitness was really brought home to me. Although my interviewees were a very diverse group, one factor was evident: Whether wealthy or poor; traveler or homebody; single or married; male or female; African-American, Japanese-American, or Caucasian; age 67 or age 81; virtually every one of them exercised regularly. I was particularly surprised at how many people walked or ran as many as four or five miles a day, sometimes supplemented by fairly strenuous calisthenics to strengthen the upper body. Although I don't think most of my interviewees would ever define themselves as "older athletes," in my view most fit this description.

Exercise, especially exercise that maintains and builds muscle tone, is also a significant factor in maintaining good mental health as you age, for several reasons:

1. How you look will influence how you feel about yourself just as much at age 75 as it did at 25. In fact, maintaining an attractive physical appearance may be more important after you stop working and lose one of your main sources of personal validation.

2. Older people who don't exercise enough to maintain their strength often become frail, which can result in their becoming afraid of physical attack, so fearful in some cases that they are reluctant to venture out of their own houses.

3. Seniors who can't do things for themselves (carry groceries to the car, twist off a bottle cap or move a piece of furniture) become overly dependent on others, which is never a good way to live.

4. Exercise wards off the mild depression that troubles so many older people. (See "Exercise to Avoid Depression," below.)

How much exercise is enough? Many studies have concluded that even moderate exercise, such as taking a walk a couple of times per week, can significantly reduce the risk of heart attack and therefore increase the length of your life. Pulling this research together, Peter Jaret, writing in the September 1994 *Health* magazine, concludes that every hour of activity like fast walking will add an hour and a half to your life.

But while a few brisk walks per week will reduce your chances of a heart attack or stroke, my conclusion is that it really won't improve the quality of your life much in other ways. To elevate your mood, improve your strength and lower your blood pressure and cholesterol levels, I agree with the U.S. government's recommendation that you do at least 30 minutes of daily aerobic exercise—that is, enough exercise to work up a light sweat. But to really get all the mental and physical benefits exercise can produce, you need to work out more vigorously— up to 60 minutes of daily swimming, dancing, jogging or other aerobic activity such as fast walking, coupled with calisthenics or light work-outs with weights to shape up your otherwise atrophying muscles. If you are currently a couch potato, even the idea of doing this much exercise may seem impossible. I can think of nothing to say more convincing than the old cliché, "no guts, no glory." Or put another way, if you have read this far, you obviously want to make some changes in your life. Go do it now.

Exercise to Avoid Depression

So many Americans are chronically depressed that the names of anti-depressant drugs such as Prozac, Zoloft and Paxil have become household words. Unfortunately, the chances are good that many of us will face increasing bouts of depression as we age, a condition that is both miserable in itself as well as a significant risk factor in the development of heart disease. Estimates vary, but many experts suggest that as many as 20% of people over 65 suffer from depression. Some of these people will become so depressed they'll end up in a long-term care facility.

For years, many health professionals observed that people who exercise regularly are less likely to be depressed. Athletes also found that regular vigorous exercise could produce much the same mood-lifting results as a drug like Prozac. Then scientists discovered what is likely to be at least part of the biological explanation for this phenomenon. Both anti-depressant drugs and exercise, it turns out, increase a brain chemical called serotonin. ("Serotonin's Motor Activity and Depression," by Barry Jacobs and Casimir Fornal, *American Scientist*, October 1994.)

For people who are deeply depressed, this information isn't likely to be of much help. If you have ever lived with a deeply depressed person—especially an older person—you already know how difficult it is to motivate that person even to get out of a chair or bed, much less exercise vigorously. But it can be a big boon to the rest of us. Once we accept the fact that, as we age, we are at higher risk of experiencing at least mild depression, we can begin a regular and fairly vigorous exercise program that will help combat it and lift our daily sense of well-being. And if exercise alone doesn't solve the problem, it probably will when combined with an antidepressant medication.

Finding Time to Exercise

Finding time to engage in strenuous exercise four or more times a week can be difficult. For example, if you have a full-time job plus a long commute, or you must care for and support a disadvantaged child or senile parent, or you are a single parent, just finding enough time to go jogging or take a brisk walk will obviously be a challenge. And even if your life isn't quite so over-full, there will always be plenty of reasons to put off exercising until mañana. This section offers suggestions on finding the time and making the commitment to regularly work up a sweat.

Make the Commitment

If you are about to conclude that, given all your responsibilities and burdens, making enough time to exercise is just plain impossible, I have a simple favor to ask: After reading the next three paragraphs, get out of your chair and take a brisk 30-minute walk. Yes, I mean it—just put down this book and slip into some comfortable shoes and start perambulating.

As you stride briskly along, think about what kind of life you envision after you retire. And as you do, ask yourself whether you are really likely to be sufficiently healthy and physically fit to live this life. Particularly if your retirement is many years in the future, you may not know how to give a good answer. Fair enough—no one can predict with anything close to 100% accuracy what their physical condition will be like 20 years from now. Nevertheless, you can gain much useful information by looking at the trend of your general health and fitness over the last few years. That's because unless you make a determined effort to change it, this trend will very likely continue and may even accelerate. For example, if you are significantly heavier and less aerobically fit than you were a decade ago, you'll probably be in even worse shape by the time you retire unless you modify your eating and exercise habits.

Also, as you walk along give some hard thought to how you can find the time to begin a daily exercise program. And don't just plan to put an exercise bike in front of the TV. Although I know a few people who make this strategy work, your chances of doing yourself much good with this low level of commitment are pretty slim. More than likely, your bike will be abandoned in three weeks and in the back of the garage in three months. Far better to begin a regular program of movement classes at the local community center or "Y," join a gym or simply continue to take fast walks. Again, at least 30 minutes of aerobic exercise per day, supplemented by working with light weights or a strength-building exercise machine three or four days a week, will quickly improve your physical condition and health and probably also your mental outlook.

Thanks for listening and enjoy your walk.

Mall Walking: It May Be Weird, But It Works

Every day, at about the time the rest of us go to work, groups of retirees gather at many of America's enclosed shopping malls. They are not typical shoppers. Instead of their credit cards, these folks bring their running shoes. And they put them to good use, as they form pairs or small groups to walk three, five or even ten miles, up and down and around the relatively safe, weather-protected mall corridors. For example, at the huge Mall of America in Bloomington, Minnesota, over 3,000 mostly elderly "Mall Stars" regularly stride the halls. Although personally I can imagine more fulfilling activities, mall walking has lots going for it—simultaneously allowing retired people to visit old friends and make new ones while enjoying several hours of fairly strenuous exercise. And when the walking is done, many stick around to socialize over tea or coffee.

Work Less

As part of writing this book, I made a list of ten people I know well who regularly work more than 50 hours per week. (It wasn't hard, given the fact that Americans, on average, work more hours than do people in any other industrialized country—yes, even more than the hard-working Japanese.) I next asked myself how many of these people I thought legitimately needed to put in extra-long hours to support themselves or their families. My educated guess was that, at most, only two could convincingly argue they really needed to keep the pedal so close to the metal. By any reasonable assessment, the other eight could fairly easily afford to cut back on their work, freeing up five to ten hours per week. But in talking to these people about this possibility, a huge psychological obstacle immediately appeared: They were hooked on their jobs and just didn't know how to cut back. A few weren't even able to take regular vacations.

If you work more than 45, or certainly 50, hours a week, why not ask your friends, co-workers and family how they see your "work habit"? My guess is that most of them will respond that they see your "overtime" work as far less essential than you do. And if you're willing to listen, they may make valuable suggestions about how you can cut back enough so that you have the time you need to exercise, spend time with your family and pursue non-work-related interests.

Yes, this may mean that you are able to save less money for retirement, but if you use your extra time to exercise more or develop authentic interests and friendships, you'll have made a good choice. To understand why this is true, carefully read my conversations with energized, successful retirees included in this book. To a man (and woman), they say that, after retirement, enjoying decent health is key to feeling good about life—far more important than an affluent lifestyle. Arthur Levenson, whose comments appear just after this chapter, puts it like this:

> Exercise is a great tranquilizer, and one of the best ways to relieve stress. By contrast, a sedentary lifestyle is a risk factor [to enjoying one's retirement], perhaps as dangerous as smoking.

Of course, you may face practical barriers to cutting back your hours—perhaps your boss expects you to put in a 50-hour week or you have convinced yourself that your small business can't operate without your constant presence. But the point remains that if you currently enjoy even a modest financial surplus (or could if you changed your consumption habits), you have a golden opportunity to confront and overcome whatever barriers make it difficult for you to work less. Put more directly, you really can trade a percentage of your income for the extra time you need to exercise and otherwise improve your health.

Tom and Adrienne: Making Time for Mental Health

Tom was a busy lawyer with a law firm that represents companies producing multimedia products. Adrienne, his wife, was a university librarian with a specialty in music. Both liked their jobs, which together brought in more than $175,000 per year.

Tom and Adrienne had two children, a house in a nice neighborhood and comfortable savings for the kids' college education and for their own retirement. In short, they thought they were living the American dream. Then the dream threatened to turn into a nightmare. Tom started to drink a little too much and put on weight. Not only was he too busy to exercise, but his work schedule was so hectic that he began to substitute fast food for healthy meals. Adrienne began to worry about how she could possibly meet all her daily responsibilities to her children, husband and job, with the result that her sleep began to suffer and she became chronically irritable. At about the same time, Jack, the couple's younger child, whose life was jam-packed with after-school activities calculated to keep him busy until his parents got home from work, began to complain of being tired.

One morning at 6:00, while preparing the kids' lunches, Adrienne started to cry. Tom, who was halfway out the door for another 11-hour day, immediately understood how she felt. That evening they had a long talk and decided that the whole family was experiencing too much stress. They decided they would each cut back their work week to four days, at least until the kids were older.

Tom's boss promptly agreed to the new schedule. But Adrienne's supervisor, a workaholic himself, denied her request. But the day before Adrienne planned to resign, her boss had a mild stroke. His deputy promptly approved Adrienne's request for a four-day week.

The new schedule allowed Tom and Adrienne to do three important things: spend more time with their children, begin personal fitness programs and plan a healthier diet. At first they expected their savings program (both for retirement and the kids' college educations) to take a huge hit, but by tighter budgeting and eliminating some luxuries (Tom always felt pretentious in that Lexus anyway), they were able to keep saving, albeit at a slower rate.

Cut Down Commute Time

As a parent, business owner, author, Little League coach and active participant in several civic organizations, to mention a few of my roles, I probably have almost as many excuses not to exercise as you do. So how do I practice what I preach—that is, find the time for daily exercise? I can tell you in three words: I don't commute. By working less than ten minutes from where I live, most days I have enough time to comfortably fit in 40–60 minutes of exercise, either before or after work. And when that's not possible, I stop by a nearby gym or go for a jog at lunch time. I don't mean to suggest that, on some days at least, making enough time to exercise doesn't take both willpower and planning (or that I don't occasionally skip a day). My point is that by not spending time commuting, I really can and do make time to exercise.

And in case you think I'm just lucky not to spend an hour or more getting to and from work, I should add that my decision not to commute has been a determined tenet of my adult life, one I arrived at as a young boy when I watched—and occasionally accompanied—my grandfather and father to work. Both traveled a little over an hour each way to get to and from work in New York City, meaning that they left home before 8 a.m. and returned after 6:30 p.m. Refusing to commute has meant that several times I've turned down attractive job opportunities; it was even a major factor in my decision to start my own business.

And guess what? Although I can look back at my life and see that I've made my share of bad choices, just saying no to commuting has been one of my best. The extra two hours per day has allowed me to do all sorts of things my father and grandfather never had a chance to enjoy. Top on the list has been the ability to spend more time with my wife and children. A close second has been the ability to exercise enough to stay in decent physical shape. Not only does this make me feel better, but it contributes to a positive self-image—one I know I wouldn't have were I frail or substantially overweight.

Squeezing Out a Few Hours to Work Out

Still think you can't find enough time to begin a meaningful exercise program? Sorry, but I simply don't believe you. Here are a few more ways you can find the time to work up a sweat:

- Turn off the television. If, like the average American, you spend about 40% of your free hours a week in front of the TV (as reported in *Time for Life, the Surprising Ways Americans Use Their Time*, Robinson and Godbey (Penn. State Press)), you obviously have all the time you need to exercise.

- Join an exercise facility near work and go during your lunch hour.
- Share child care with other parents, so you each have a free hour or two several times a week.
- Spend less to work less. For many people, the most powerful strategy to find extra time is to lock up their credit cards, so they need less monthly income. To have the guts to do this, most of us—and our families—will need to truly distinguish what's important in life (good heath, a functional family, true friends) from what isn't (a bigger house, a newer car, buying more things at the mall). No question—living frugally can be tough in America's consumer-driven society, where lots of people really seem to believe "you are what you buy." But if you can learn to live happily on less, you really can make the time to improve your life in major ways, including taking better care of your body.

■

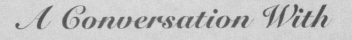

A Conversation With

ARTHUR LEVENSON

Arthur Levenson, shown above running a 20K (12.5 mile) race, was born in New York City and attended Brooklyn College and Columbia University. As a young mathematician, he was working for the National Bureau of Standards when the Second World War broke out. During the war, he was stationed in England as part of the U.S. Army's top secret team that worked with the British organization (GCHA) to break Germany's most sophisticated codes, including the Enigma machine—a breakthrough that shortened the war significantly. Retired in 1974 after a long and successful career in the U.S. defense security services, Arthur, who was born in 1914, lives with his wife, Marjorie, in Bethesda, Maryland.

RW: Arthur, when I called you this morning, you were out running five miles. Do you do that every day?

AL: When I turned 80, I cut back to six days a week.

RW: Do you work out in other ways?

AL: I do various stretching exercises after I run and 100 push-ups per day to keep my upper body in shape.

RW: Is exercising something you began doing when you retired?

AL: No, I started running about age 50, when I read a book by the Yale swimming coach advocating exercise. It was easy for me to do because I quickly found that running was enjoyable. Running just makes you feel good all over.

RW: You obviously enjoy life. Do you attribute that to getting lots of exercise?

AL: Well, to stay healthy, you should follow the advice of the medical profession —don't smoke, moderate drinking, watch your weight and eat sensibly, avoiding too much fat. But beyond that, yes, I'm a great believer in exercise. It has enormous benefits, both psychological and physical.

RW: You mean it has benefits besides keeping your body fit?

AL: Certainly. Among others, it's a great tranquilizer, and one of the best ways to relieve stress. By contrast, a sedentary lifestyle is a risk factor perhaps as dangerous as smoking. Incidentally, I once participated in a study at Johns Hopkins that compared older athletes with younger athletes and older sedentary people. It turned out that, by most measures, older athletes were much closer to younger athletes than they were to older sedentaries.

RW: Do you believe people in their 40s and 50s ought to be jogging, swimming, biking or doing something else to work up an aerobic sweat so they will be in decent shape later on?

AL: Yes, but it's hard for many people to find the time when they are working. It takes some determination and commitment. I used to get up at 5 a.m. to run, and it was worth it. If you wait until 65, it's not easy to reverse a poor physical condition, but it's not impossible.

RW: Let's shift gears. Suppose you read an article entitled "The Seven Things You Really Need to Know About Retirement," which was devoted exclusively to saving and investing money. Assume also that you decided to write a letter to the magazine editor pointing out that other things were also involved when it came to planning for a fulfilling retirement. Besides finances, what would you talk about?

AL: Well, first, as far as money is concerned, it is important. Being old and poor is a bad combination. But while some personal financial security is necessary, there is no need to be rich. I think Aristotle had it right when he said, "Virtue is in the mean, not the extreme," and that this applies to wealth. In other words, it is better to be comfortably well-off than very rich.

RW: Do you mean having lots of money might even be bad for a retired person?

AL: Being rich is problematic because it often leads to overindulgence. Most of us aren't wise enough to live well if we can easily give in to all of our whims. It's better to have limits on our foolishness. Also, it makes no sense to save every possible penny earlier in life just so you can be wealthy when you retire—you need to give yourself and your family some pleasure during all phases of your life.

RW: Great. But now, for your second paragraph, what else would you write about in your letter to the editor?

AL: Interests. Outside of your work, you need to devote some time to activities you enjoy. As Oscar Wilde put it, "Work is the last refuge of people who have nothing better to do." Having many interests is very important when you stop working. If your entire life centers around your work, then your life stops when your work stops.

RW: Do you have a prescription for how to develop lots of interests?

AL: No, except to do it early—if you wait, you might not do it at all. Sean O'Casey said, "If you've never read a book in your life, you won't start at age 60."

RW: Is reading a big part of your life?

AL: Yes, it's a wonderful habit. I especially feel that people should read widely outside of their own immediate field. And music does wonders. I try and listen to a Bach fugue every day. Jazz, too, has produced some marvelous music. Duke Ellington was a truly great composer.

RW: What about a good friendship network? Would this be something you would write to the editor about?

AL: I'm kind of a loner. I enjoy solitude. As the French philosopher and mathematician Blaise Pascal said, "The sole cause of man's unhappiness is that he doesn't know how to sit quietly in his own room."

RW: So you haven't really needed an extensive friendship network?

AL: No—I'm very comfortable with my own company. But just the same, I have good friends who are very important to me. For example, I'm sitting here in California talking to you because my wife and I have just taken the train across America to visit friends. I particularly believe it's important for older people to have younger friends. Younger people bring you a new energy and outlook.

RW: Let me ask you a little more about solitude. Do you think learning to be alone has contributed to your enjoying your retirement years?

AL: Definitely. It's essential that a person learn how to be comfortable with himself or herself. As you get older, you'll almost surely spend more time alone, so learning to enjoy your own company is very valuable.

RW: Anything else you would you put in your letter?

AL: Family. Having good family relationships has been important to me. My wife, Marjorie, who I've now been in love with for 51 years, is a lovely person and a huge asset to me. There is no question that being with Marjorie makes my life better. And I have three fine children who I enjoy very much and am pleased to be on good terms with. One of our (Marjorie and I) great joys is visiting with, and being visited by, our children. They are all married and we are very fond of our two sons-in-law and our daughter-in-law. In addition, we get pleasure from spending time with our wonderful grand-children.

RW: When you were working, did you think about things you could do to help ensure your family relationships would be strong late in life?

AL: Not directly or consciously, but I definitely did look forward to retirement as another phase of life to enjoy. I tried to raise my children to be independent people, but at the same time, I hoped they would be part of my life. And while I never want to be a burden to them, I know that if Marjorie or I need help, we can count on them.

RW: It sounds as if you and Marjorie have enjoyed a good relationship these many years. Any secrets about that you can share?

AL: It will probably sound rather ordinary, but in a word—commitment. A good marriage demands a high level of commitment. I don't mean that with the stress of work and raising kids you and your spouse won't occasionally have what today would be called "a bad hair day." No, I'm talking about the basic determination to hang in there for a lifetime. Incidentally, having a sense of humility about yourself really helps. Remember, you're no bargain.

RW: You believe in marriage through thick and thin?

AL: Not necessarily. Some people should divorce. But I do think a sense of commitment can pay big dividends later on. At my age, it's just great to live with and do and share things, like travel, with someone I love. ■

Chapter 3

Family

"Mary and I have been married 47 years and not once have we had an argument serious enough to mention the word divorce—murder, yes, but divorce, never."

—Jack Benny

Nurturing good family relationships and repairing broken ones in midlife is extremely important to your chances of enjoying your retirement years. The reason is simple: As you age, your psychological and practical need to be part of a loving, supportive family will grow, just as your ability to create or solidify these relationships is likely to decline. Sadly, if you reach retirement age with poor or nonexistent family ties, you will be significantly impoverished, whether or not you are materially wealthy.

Today, people are likely to live a quarter, or even a third, of their lives after retirement, and the four-generation family has become commonplace. Given this long span of years, it's easy to see why the many positive influences of a loving family—or the negative influences of a dysfunctional one—can have an enormous effect on whether or not you enjoy your retirement. For those without a loving family, 25 or 30 years is a long time to be lonely.

The Value of Close Family Ties

Since the dawn of history, the family has been humankind's most efficient economic unit. Although its primacy has been challenged in centuries past by feudal overlords and the church, and in recent times by corporations and governments, for most of us, it still is. If you doubt this, remember that despite what is sometimes called government's social safety net, it's families who pay the many costs of feeding and clothing their children, help fund much of the cost of their higher education and often give them a helping hand as young adults. But our families are not only our true economic safety net when we are young—for many millions of Americans, they also provide love, many types of practical help and, if needed, considerable financial assistance, in our retirement years.

Of course, families are much more than economic units. For most of us, parents, grandparents and older siblings serve as our most important early role models and teachers. And throughout our lives, our relationships with parents, spouses, children and grandchildren have very likely been our most reliable vehicle for giving and receiving love. In a universe that is big and empty beyond our ability to comprehend, watching an inquisitive grandchild crawl across the living room floor, a seven-year-old grandniece get her first hit in a softball game or an eager grandson graduate from high school can help us understand ourselves in ways we will never put in words.

Lest you fear I'm about to evaporate into a romantic haze, let me quickly add that, like all other human institutions, most families are far from perfect. Many of us are members of families that simultaneously manage to do some things very well and others poorly or not at all. And a few of us must cope with families that get far too many things wrong far too often. But although the ideal family doesn't exist, and more than a few have disintegrated (or are on life support), many millions of American families nevertheless manage to provide their members—especially the very young and the very old—with a great deal of material and emotional sustenance. Sadly, it is also true that when a family fails to function well—no matter what the reason—all of its members suffer. Among the biggest losers are its older members, who, just when they need it the most, are deprived of affection, social interaction and help with everyday concerns.

It follows that people in midlife who are thinking about their retirement years should focus on the major role a functional family can play in enhancing their lives. The key word here is "functional." A family can love and, if necessary, care for its older members only if it is relatively strong and unified. And that strength won't be there unless you and other key family members invest a good deal of time and attention to be sure that your family ties really do bind. Happily, if you do a good job of fulfilling your family obligations to care for the young and nurture the old during your middle years, your chances of being similarly helped later in life will be excellent. By contrast, if you let business, personal recreation, civic or other activities so dominate your life that you pay little attention to your family, these crucial relationships are very likely to atrophy, with the result that you may receive little or no support in your retirement years.

The Barber Family in Action

John and Emily Barber, in their early 80s, are at the center of a family consisting of their own three children—Katherine, Brian and Sabina—as well as June, a high school friend of Sabina's whom the Barbers adopted (emotionally, not legally) as a teenager almost 35 years ago. In addition, the Barbers have two sons-in-law, a daughter-in-law and eight grandchildren, two of whom are from one son-in-law's previous marriage. Most of the members of this 19-person family live in the San Francisco Bay Area, which allows for frequent group get-togethers, including about eight large yearly holiday or birthday gatherings and many smaller ones. Obviously, the geographical proximity of many of its members makes it easier for the Barbers to function as a meaningful group. But it is interesting to note that this didn't happen accidentally; John and Emily, realizing that distance is no friend to the maintenance of close family ties, relocated from Los Angeles at their own retirement 20 years ago.

While the Barbers have fun together, they are seen at their best when one or another family member quietly helps another cope with day-to-day concerns. Here are just a few of many ways John and Emily have helped their children:

- When grandchildren—and now the first two great-grandchildren— were born, they were always there with loads of TLC and, on the few emergency occasions when it was necessary, an open checkbook.
- They followed up with much-needed babysitting and after-school child care.
- They loaned money to all their children to help them purchase their first homes.
- They handed down their old cars to the children who needed them most and quietly paid for the occasional plane ticket when one of the kids couldn't quite afford a family reunion.

But it's not just the senior Barbers who help other family members. A few years ago, when John broke his hip, it was the turn of the younger family members to help him out (fetching, carrying and lifting and visiting were

(continued on next page)

just part of it) and give Emily emotional support. As it turned out, June, the adopted daughter, who hadn't married and wasn't raising a family of her own, was able to help the most during John's lengthy convalescence.

Among other Barber family helping activities are:

- a part-time job for Emily and summer jobs for teenage grandchildren in a business owned by Sabina and her husband
- providing a home away from home for teenage grandchildren who occasionally need a short break from their parents
- tutoring for several teenagers with bad math genes and
- shared vacations to interesting places, organized by more adventurous family members.

How Healthy Is Your Family?

Take a minute to assess the health of your own family. Are its key relationships likely to be in good working order after you retire? When you become older and possibly mentally or physically frail, are you confident that members of your family will be there to provide emotional support, include you in family activities and, if necessary, provide practical day-to-day help?

As part of thinking about this, ask yourself a few key questions:

- If you are married, do you get along well with your spouse in a relationship built to last?
- If you are a parent, how emotionally close are you to your children, and if they are married or living in long-term committed relationships, with their spouses?
- If you have grandchildren, have you made yourself an important part of their lives, or are you simply someone they peck on the cheek occasionally at family get-togethers and send a pro forma thank-you note to after birthdays and holidays?
- Are you meaningfully connected to your brothers, sisters, nephews, nieces, cousins and their families?
- If you live far from key family members and see each other rarely, what are you doing to make sure close bonds are nurtured and fraying ones repaired?

- If your own family is very small or absolutely incapable of giving you support, have you been able to join a new one?

If you conclude that most members of your family are already reasonably close and communicating fairly well, taking steps to make yourself a catalyst for further positive interactions—and, if necessary, trying to reach out to the temporarily disaffected—should be relatively easy. But for too many people in midlife, the answer to these questions will reveal at least some family relationships in serious disrepair and others in a kind of limbo—neither dead nor really functioning well. Of course, there are a variety of reasons why the glue of shared genes and history that holds most families together can lose its stick. Perhaps the two most common are divorce—something that one out of two married couples will experience—and the fact that Americans are prone to relocate to distant parts of the country. It's hardly a secret that family members who see each other infrequently and lack a shared determination to maintain close emotional bonds are likely to drift apart.

But distance and divorce aren't the only enemies of family togetherness. Differences in temperament, economic status and even political or sexual orientation can also strain family relationships, with the all-too-common result that at least some family members become, at best, lukewarm about even relating to others. For example, an autocratic, distant or abusive father or a whining, selfish mother can result in children growing up with the conviction that the best way to deal with their family is to put it in the rear view mirror as quickly as possible.

If distance, busyness, lack of commitment or garden-variety personal spats threaten the cohesion of your family, restoring close relationships is clearly your first job. Fortunately, this isn't usually impossible. If one, or better yet several, respected family members will step forward to lead the way, it can prove relatively easy to convince others that it's worth the effort to work together to deal with problems and restore family cohesiveness.

Unfortunately, as a result of many types of stresses, such as the divorce, mental illness or uncaring behavior of one or more key members, some families are in such bad shape that people have already begun running for the exits. And obviously, when serious alcoholism, drug abuse, criminality or abusive behavior towards other family members is present, the family is likely to become so seriously dysfunctional that putting it back together is a Herculean task.

Ways to Improve Family Functioning

Especially if your family is more or less typical—less than perfect but with at least some members shouldering their responsibilities and others at least hoping to do better—here are some suggestions you may find helpful. Just in case you think some of these sound like too much trouble, let me add that I know of no other ways to invest your time that are as likely to provide you with as much post-retirement payback.

Spend More Time With Your Children

Sadly, lots of overbusy parents spend far too little time with their children. In many middle-class families, both parents work ten to 12 hours per day (or even a 40-hour week plus a long commute). It is easy to point to entire suburbs where houses are big, cars expensive and retirement plans fully funded, but children are too often left to fend for themselves. Less affluent families (and especially those headed by a single parent) face the same types of pulls and tugs between work and home. But because they live closer to the ragged financial edge, they are even less able to cut back work hours to spend more time with their children.

To try to convince themselves that they are nevertheless doing a decent job of parenting, some parents call the few hours they do spend with their children "quality time." Humbug. No human being—and especially no child—can be trained to accept scheduled nurturing. Raising healthy, happy kids requires lots of hands-on parenting. The more you try to measure out your love by the teaspoon, the more you will fail.

No matter what your reason for spending too little time with children, your first step towards being a better parent is to honestly face up to the fact that absentee parenting doesn't work. Sooner or later, undernurtured children—and spouses, for that matter—will suffer and, if your conduct continues, may never completely re-cover. What's all this got to do with retirement, you may ask? Simple. When chil-dren are poorly nurtured, they are likely to repay their parents several times over later in life, when it's their turn to decide how much time they want to spend with their now-older parents. In short, working too much and parenting too little may mean you retire to a fancy condo next to a perpetually warm beach, but that your children will have permanently lost your phone number.

Of course, there are plenty of important reasons to spend more time with your children beyond trying to ensure that you won't be lonely after retirement. Never-theless, it remains true that creating a loving, attention-filled environment for your kids, especially through their early teen years, is likely to pay dividends all your life—more satisfying ones than you'll get by putting that time and energy into enlarging your investment portfolio.

Work for a Family-Friendly Employer

Most employers don't concern themselves much with their employees' family lives. In their view, a good employee works hard and never bothers supervisors with family problems. Some employers are even less sensitive, sending a clear message that despite what it may say in the employee handbook or, for that matter, the law, employees are expected to show up early, stay late and never take off time to nurture a sick child.

Fortunately, some employers are beginning to do better, realizing that in the long run workers will be more productive if they have a reasonable chance to cope with family needs. For example, Nolo, the publisher of this book, employs many parents who prefer to work three- or four-day weeks. At least partially as a result, it enjoys very low staff turnover and is besieged by highly qualified applicants whenever a new position opens. And, of course, Nolo isn't alone—an increasing number of employers have begun to adopt more family-friendly policies, including flex time, onsite child care, generous family leave policies, and for some types of jobs, the opportunity to telecommute from home. For example, the accounting firm of Ernst & Young, worried that it wasn't retaining enough high-level women, recently established a women-retention effort designed to look at every aspect of corporate operations, from cutting back on 50-plus-hour weeks to reducing travel expectations and even restricting weekend email.

If you plan to look for a new job, ask questions designed to discover whether a potential employer has family-friendly policies. For example, will your employer permit you to come in a little early twice a week so you can leave in time to help with your son's drama group or your daughter's softball team, or to get your mother to her doctor? If you are told in response, "Don't worry, we have a whole book full of flexible policies," be a little skeptical. Too many companies adopt rules that sound great on paper, but then in practice subvert them by subtly—or sometimes not so subtly—letting employees know that if they take advantage of flex time, elect to work a four-day week or simply take a day off to cope with a family emergency, they will be labeled underachievers and their fast-track career sidetracked.

The best way to find out whether or not a particular employer walks its pro-family talk is to speak to parents who hold jobs similar to the one you are investigating. Another way is to get information about large companies from one of several surveys published by magazines. One of the best is authored by business writer Milton Moskowitz and appears annually in *Working Mother* magazine. *Fortune* and *Business Week* also publish very useful annual ratings of the family-friendly—and too often unfriendly—policies of major corporations.

WORKING AT HOME OR A SHORT WORK WEEK CAN MAKE A BIG DIFFERENCE

Millions of Americans have decided to work at home—sometimes at the sacrifice of some income—to nurture small children. Having done this myself, I know it can be a good way to supply a warm hello and a cookie when school is out and still get a fair amount of work done. Other parents choose to work a three- or four-day week or not to work at all when children are small. True, if you follow either of these plans, it may mean your finances will be tight for a few years, but in my experience an anorexic bank account is far more easily remedied than is a dysfunctional child.

Keep Your Family Unit As Extended As Possible

As important as it is to stay emotionally close to your children, doing so is only part of the challenge of creating a rich family experience. Especially in the era of the two-child family, it is essential to maintain and strengthen relationships with your parents, siblings, nieces and nephews, grandchildren and cousins. Not only will doing this enrich the lives of everyone in your family (a sense of belonging to a good-sized clan can be particularly important to your children), but it is almost guaranteed to pay you huge dividends as you age. Unlike so many American seniors who are close to only one or two family members, your phone and door-bell will ring regularly.

THINK TWICE BEFORE MOVING FAR FROM FAMILY MEMBERS
In modern America, where it's not uncommon for people to move 3,000 miles on little more than a whim, it is close to heresy to suggest that your life will be easier, and probably more fun, if you live fairly close to family members. There are plenty of good reasons for family members to scatter—a better job, a good school, a change in lifestyle, the needs of a spouse or lover—but I'm convinced that the benefits of families sticking together far outweigh any sacrifices necessary to make it happen. A person lucky enough to be part of a family where members of four generations live in close proximity, I experience how enriching this can be on a daily basis.

For many people, even figuring out who is really part of their family isn't easy. Divorce, death, remarriage and non-traditional relationships, including gay and lesbian unions, all play a part in redefining what the very term "family" means. For example:

- Is your son's former wife still part of your family? Does it make a difference if there are grandchildren?
- If you remarry or live with someone late in life, does your new partner join your existing family? If so, for what purposes?
- If your adult daughter has been living with a man, is he a member of your family? Does it make a difference if her living-together partner is a woman? Does it make a difference if your daughter and her friend have or adopt a child?

Obviously, there is no one correct answer to any of these or many similarly perplexing questions. Nevertheless, my own life experience has taught me that a family almost always becomes stronger when its members are willing to be inclusive, and weaker when members erect barriers to admission. There are at least two good reasons for this:

- People who are generous in defining who is in their family during the early and middle parts of their lives will obviously enjoy more—and probably richer—family relationships after retirement than will a person who hands out family memberships as if they were the Nobel Prize.

- The experience we gain in welcoming outsiders into our own family may prove invaluable later in life should unforeseen circumstances, such as the premature death of a spouse or other close family member, mean that we suddenly find ourselves alone and hoping to bond with someone else's family. Just recently, for example, I attended a very romantic wedding of two 75-year-olds. Alice has seven children and six grandchildren; Walt has no close relatives. It's not hard to predict that a significant portion of both Walt and Alice's future happiness will depend on how and whether Walt and members of Alice's family will be able to create close and loving bonds. Unfortunately, I'm also familiar with another family where bonding didn't happen. Instead of embracing their mother's second husband, her two adult sons barely tolerated him. The unhappy result was that a decade later, when mental and physical illness made it impossible for the couple to live on their own, a very nasty situation developed. Mom's boys were anxious to care for her, but not her spouse. Mom, on the other hand, wasn't willing to be separated from her husband and felt betrayed by her children, whom she saw as primarily interested in guarding their inheritance.

Don't Take Family Leadership for Granted

Many extended families are headed and defined for many years by a charismatic person or couple. Other families stay in reasonably close touch in large part because a small group works together (two sisters, for example) to make sure it happens. Often, being a family leader amounts to little more than having good human skills, including the ability to notice when a family member needs an extra measure of nurture, support or coaching, and to see that appropriate help is quickly forthcoming. Especially when a crisis looms—as might be the case when there is a divorce—sensitivity, sagacity and plenty of patience will be required.

People who are lucky enough to be in families headed (or coordinated) by a good leader often have the luxury of coasting. As long as they show up at a reasonable number of family activities and don't make too many waves, they can receive many of the benefits of active family life without doing much work. But few people get to coast downhill indefinitely. When long-time family leaders become very old or ill, die or, for some other reason, no longer play their familiar role, one or preferably several of the people who have been getting a free ride must start to pedal. Ideally, it's best to consider the inevitability that new leadership will be needed well in advance, so that younger people have time to gradually assume leadership roles. But this doesn't always happen; if a vacuum suddenly develops, one or more new leaders will need to quickly step forward.

The Carroll Family: New Leadership Emerges

For years, Frank Carroll's parents, Tim and May—mostly lovingly, and sometimes autocratically—headed their brood of nine children and 15 grandchildren. Even though the Carroll children settled all over the U.S., close relationships between them, their spouses and the grandchildren were developed and nurtured through a number of activities and get-togethers—most importantly, the family's yearly summer gathering at their vacation cottage in the Adirondack Mountains in Northern New York, and Christmas at Tim and Mary's home in New Jersey. While not every child attended both events every year, it was an unwritten—but nevertheless unbroken—family rule that no one ever missed more than two in a row. The entire Carroll family came to see the get-togethers as essential to keeping the Carroll family a functioning unit.

Then Tim died one October. With May now in her mid-80s and feeling her age, no plans for the next summer were being made. Frank, the middle child, now in his 40s, became increasingly bothered by the family leadership vacuum. His first solution was to do what he had always done as a child: He called his older sisters, Maureen and Kathy, to talk them into playing their traditional roles as junior parents and organizing the August reunion. When Mo pleaded job problems and Kathy said she and her husband were having a tough year emotionally and wanted to go to Europe by themselves, Frank got angry. His first thought was that neither of his sisters—and for that matter, none of his younger siblings—cared enough about the future of the family to do even a little work.

Then, a few days later, when he was out jogging, it occurred to Frank that at least one person did care about family solidarity and was in a position to do something about it. So he took a week off work and organized the reunion himself. For the first time in years, everyone came—even Kathy and her husband, who had apparently been able to patch up their relationship at home in Omaha—and Mo, who decided her overly demanding boss could stuff her job if he objected. Best of all, Frank's commitment and his demonstration of the crucial need for new leadership prompted a family meeting at which his siblings volunteered to form groups of two and take turns organizing future get-togethers. Plans were even made to have several teenagers coordinate an online family bulletin board.

Try to Develop a Sense of Humor About Lifestyle Differences

Few things make me sadder than seeing a family pulled apart by a political or religious disagreement, or conflict over sexual orientation or choice of lifestyle. One family I used to know fairly well (let's call them the Martins) comes to mind as a most unhappy example of this sort of stupidity. When John, the oldest of three children, announced he was gay, his mother dissolved into nearly perpetual tears and his father disowned him. June, the second child, sided with John and voluntarily removed herself from the family. Tim, the youngest child by eight years and still in high school, was so traumatized by the family rift that he lost much of his self-confidence and with it his good grades and active social life. Eventually, he dropped out of high school and did poorly at a series of dead-end jobs. It wasn't until his mid-20s, after a stint in the army and marrying a loving woman, that Tim enrolled in college and began to put his life back together.

How is the Martin family doing today? It barely exists. John died a lonely death of AIDS in San Francisco a few years ago, still estranged from both of his parents. June and Tim, both fortunate in their marriages, have been welcomed into the families of their respective spouses and are planning to get together soon. The senior Martins have retired and live in Florida. They haven't seen or talked to either of their surviving children in years. Each year June sends them a Christmas card with a picture of her children. Tim doesn't.

The moral of this story should be obvious. When lifestyle differences threaten to strain family relationships, you have a choice: Open your arms and heart wider—perhaps wider than you thought possible—or risk losing the people and family you care most about. My own experience is that the best way to do this is with as much humor as you can muster. After all, if your daughter marries a member of an ethnic or racial group you have never liked and your son settles down with his long-time boyfriend, a hearty laugh may be the only way you'll ever get those tight arms of yours open wide enough to wrap around your interesting new family.

HELP FOR FAMILY MEMBERS DEALING WITH NON-TRADITIONAL RELATIONSHIPS

Anyone worried about how best to deal with the gay or lesbian relationship of a close family member or friend needs to know about an organization called Parents and Friends of Lesbians and Gays (PFLAG). As the name suggests, this group provides support and counseling to help family members and friends become comfortable with a loved one's sexual orientation. For a chapter near you, contact PFLAG at 202-638-4200.

Don't Give Up on Black Sheep

One of the big things that distinguishes your family from your job, hobbies or even many of your friendships is that for better or worse, it's yours for life. Even if you turn your back on a brother, father, mother or child for what seems to you an excellent reason, it's impossible to erase your ties of blood and shared history. And especially if estrangement makes your entire family disintegrate, it will make little difference who was at fault. Even if you are entirely in the right, you'll carry the emotional pain of your family's breakdown until you draw your last breath.

It follows that it's almost always worthwhile to work hard to salvage damaged family relationships before they dissolve entirely, and even to try to recover those that seem irretrievably lost. No question, taking the first steps to reach out to a family member from whom you are seriously disaffected can seem daunting. But procrastination, while understandable, is a mistake. The longer you wait to repair bad family relationships, the more you reinforce them, and the harder it becomes to break the pattern of non-communication. Certainly, if you wait until retirement to try to heal serious family breaches with your children, grandchildren or other key family members, it's likely to be too late.

When it comes to keeping your family together in times of trouble, here are some ideas you may find helpful:

- **Try to prevent family drop-outs.** Family members who are socially awkward or who judge themselves as unsuccessful in some important aspect of life, particularly work or marriage, often begin to avoid family get-togethers and ceremonies, pleading illness or some other excuse. If you see a person starting down this lonely path, it's important to quickly find ways to prevent her from exiting the family entirely. If a family member has already become isolated, take immediate steps to do everything possible (and then some) to recover him. Not only is providing support for a troubled member one of the most loving roles you and other family members can play, but your act of reaching out may actually end up benefiting you. After all, by keeping the disaffected person part of your family, you increase the chances that someone will be there should you need help.

- **Don't give up on substance abusers.** One common reason for excluding a family member (or for that person excluding himself) is a serious drinking or drug problem. Here, the best rule is to never give up on the troubled person, at the same time you don't condone or support the destructive habit. Of course, this tough love approach is easier to say than do. Fortunately, however, many organizations and publications can show family members how to intervene constructively. One good source of information is *The Recovery Book*, by Mooney, Eisenberg and Eisenberg (Workman).

- **Get quick, effective help if someone in your family becomes physically abusive or seriously neglectful.** A child who has been neglected or abused (or honestly believes this has occurred) will carry emotional scars for life, and may even withdraw from the family. And a person found to be guilty of serious neglect or abuse is often immediately ostracized. Either way, family cohesiveness is likely to suffer, and the family may even fall apart.

There are obviously no easy solutions to the gut-wrenching situations caused by seriously abusive behavior. Start by accepting the fact that without outside help neither the perpetrator nor the victim of the abuse— or, for that matter, the rest of family—is likely to return to anything approaching healthy functionality. Almost always, a wise and determined family member (or a small group) will need to insist on, and arrange for, long-term counseling or therapy for both the abused and abuser before the healing process can even begin. People who are lucky enough to share strong religious bonds can often get inspired help through their church, temple or mosque. But sometimes even with lots of outside help, a particular person may seem beyond saving. Even when redemption seems impossible, I recommend at least staying in touch with the blackest of black sheep. If you are never able to bring him back into the family fold, you'll at least be well-positioned to extend the welcome mat to his children and grandchildren.

- **Don't let divorce be a family wrecker.** Without doubt, divorce raises a gaggle of tough problems for other family members, especially if the separating couple are parents of small children. At least in the short term, neither of the divorcing spouses is likely to show up at family gatherings where the other may be present. Even more threatening to the health of the family, each member of the divorcing duo may try to influence others to take his or her side, with the danger that a once fairly harmonious family may degenerate into warring camps. And of course, additional practical problems arise if one or both ex-spouses remarry. Fortunately, members of many families have the wisdom to stay on good terms with both divorcing spouses, resisting being sucked into their emotional tantrums. Sometimes it can actually be easier to do this when the divorcing couple has children to act as a kind of family glue.

EXAMPLE: When their son and daughter-in-law divorced, the Lees were at first shocked, and then angry, fearing that their grandchildren would be emotionally scarred and that they might lose their close relationship with them. They blamed their son, who had precipitated the break-up by becoming sexually involved with another woman, and even considered barring him from upcoming family Christmas activities. But on the advice of good friends, the Lees decided to keep their judgments to themselves and try to steer a neutral course, even though this involved staging two Christmas parties, so their son and his ex wouldn't have to meet. Three years later, with both their son and former daughter-in-law now married to nice people—and even willing to attend the same Christmas party—the wisdom of this approach is apparent to all.

Of course, it isn't just your children who may divorce. Statistically, chances are good that if you are in midlife, you have already experienced at least one divorce. If so—and especially if you were already a parent—you know, as I certainly do, just how tough post-divorce family relationships can be. My best advice is, no matter how unpalatable, define your family as your children do. If this means occasionally spending time with your ex at family social events—and making it a golden rule never ever to criticize him or her—you owe it to your kids to make the effort.

For Couples: Improving Your Relationship

It's easy for middle-aged people to begin to take their mates for granted. After all, many are simultaneously trying to cope with the pressures of work, the needs of children and friends and sometimes even the huge responsibility of helping a frail parent. It's nevertheless too bad, since keeping the candle of your romance burning is surely one of the most important things you can do to increase the chances that yours will be a successful retirement. Certainly, the alternative isn't likely to be any fun. Even if, like many romantically estranged couples over 40, you decide not to divorce, but instead to soldier through your retirement years with little more in common than the same address and an affection for your grandchildren, you won't have gained much.

Bernie and Bob Giusti

The quiet joy that comes with sharing one's later life with a soulmate was brought home to me when talking to Bernie and Bob Giusti, a couple who first met over 60 years ago when Bob was age 11 and Bernie 9. When I asked for the secret of their success, Bob replied, "Friendship and an honest commitment to each other form the basis of our relationship." "That and a determination to be a real part of each other's life," Bernie added.

"Sounds good," I said, "but give me some specifics. What would you two say to a 40ish couple who asked what they could do to nurture their relationship?"

Bob replied, "Maintaining a lifetime romance involves lots of things. Shared values, interests and friendships are a few. Also important to us has been an appreciation of each other's sense of humor. Life isn't always easy, and there are plenty of times when romance boils down to whether you can laugh together and gain perspective on a situation."

"What about practical things?" I asked.

"For us, putting our family and each other first has been important," Bernie answered. "For example, 45 years ago, Bob's career as an up-and-coming business executive almost guaranteed that we would be asked to transfer to a new area every few years. But we jointly decided that we would rather live near family and good friends. So Bob just said no to leaving the San Francisco Bay Area. As it turned out, even better opportunities for Bob became available where we wanted to live. But more important, not moving allowed us to nurture a lifetime's good relationships with our family and friends."

"Another thing that has been important to us has been community involvement," Bob added. "Whether through our church or working with young people or people in need, we both believe that caring for others enhances our relationship. While we don't always know exactly how, reaching out to others strengthens our family life and our commitment to each other. And many other small things make a difference, like dinner by candlelight and banishing the TV from our living room."

"We always eat dinner together, light a candle and say a prayer," Bernie explained. "You know, it's often the little pleasures you share in life—not big, complicated, expensive events—that truly bring pleasure. Instead of exhausting your energy, as can happen with a huge event, smaller activities allow you to grow in intimacy and sharing."

"Sounds good, but where does banishing the TV fit?"

"Like most people, we used to have one in the living room. But years ago, when our living room TV broke, we didn't replace it," Bob replied. "We still have one upstairs if we want to watch something special, but now we spend more time talking, reading and listening to music together. If you let it, TV can be a relationship and time killer."

Bernie added, "It's far better to enjoy a good laugh, some beautiful music or just a peaceful walk together. Romance really builds on so many very simple shared things."

Getting Close Again

If you and your spouse are still on decent terms, here are several steps you can take to increase your chances of spending your retirement years with a kindred spirit:

1. **Talk about your relationship.** How long has it been since you sat down and asked your mate how he or she really feels about you and your relationship? If you are reluctant to ask so direct a question, maybe it's because you fear you won't like the answer. This makes it all the more urgent to start communicating. But don't just blurt out, "I wonder if we even love each other any more." Even though your mate may not be any happier than you are, suddenly making negative comments about the health of your relationship is likely to be scary and counterproductive. Far better to introduce the subject in a setting where you both feel comfortable and in a way that encourages both of you to make suggestions for improvement.

2. **Do things together.** People's interests and passions often diverge as the years pass, especially after their children are grown. This has its positive side; we all need room to grow and change, and it's a truism that each of us must take charge of our own happiness. But to stay reasonably close, it's a big help if mates share at least some day-to-day enthusiasms. So whether it's bridge, bird-watching, cooking, or doing volunteer work, look for and build on common interests. Although this is easy to say, it is often a lot tougher to do. For many couples, finding things to happily do together requires a spirit of far more openness than either spouse has exhibited for many years. For example, a man who bewails his mate's failure to learn to play golf or tennis, but categorically refuses her invitations to go square dancing or work in the garden, misses the point of what it takes to build a sharing relationship. He needs to understand that buying a pair of dancing shoes may be the missing key that will open his wife's heart.

3. **Keep yourselves in good physical condition.** Your health will be an important factor in determining whether or not you enjoy your retirement. One reason is that how you and your spouse take care of your bodies—or let them go to seed—is likely to have a significant effect on the quality of your sexual relationship later in life, and that this in turn will contribute significantly to whether or not you will be close emotionally.

I can almost hear some readers saying, wait a minute, the process of aging itself is inconsistent with physical beauty, at least as defined by America's youth-obsessed culture—sooner or later we'll all end up looking like prunes and forget about sex. Nonsense. Many studies conclude that healthy active people enjoy mind-blowing sex well into old age. By taking decent care of our bodies and our health, there is lots each of us can do to maintain or improve our physical and mental vitality, and by doing so, our sexual attractiveness.

If you doubt whether it's worth the effort it will take to stay in good physical shape, compare the two or three most active, vital 75-year-olds you know with several others who view themselves as just plain old. At a guess, people in the first group probably have their weight reasonably under control, exercise regularly and have learned to cope fairly well with the inevitable health problems associated with aging. By contrast, I'm willing to bet that the other folks are heavier and more sedentary, have poor muscle tone and see themselves as victimized by a long list of illnesses, both real and imagined.

Now ask both yourself and your spouse a simple question: Which type of person would I (you) prefer to live with and make love to later in life? If you both conclude that being in good physical condition simply isn't important, fine—flip on the TV and put some more chocolate sauce on your ice cream. But if you agree with me that there is a huge difference between the vitality and attractiveness of healthy, fit older people as compared to those who are neither, you and your spouse may be motivated to make some changes in the way you eat, exercise and otherwise live your lives. (Chapter 2, Health and Fitness, discusses how to maintain good health as you age.)

DON'T SWEAT THE SMALL STUFF

"Throw away the score card," "take charge of your own happiness," "learn to accept apologies" and "don't bemoan your partner's failures for doing things you can do yourself" are just some of the good suggestions for marital harmony in the excellent book, *Don't Sweat the Small Stuff in Love*, by Richard Carlson and Kristine Carlson (Hyperion 1999).

LEAD BY EXAMPLE, NOT BY LECTURING

If you decide it's worth the time and energy necessary to get into better condition, your best bet is to change your own behavior—not to lecture your mate. If after a few months of exercise and diet you really are looking and feeling better, there's a good chance she or he will see the difference and start shaping up too. One good way to get your life partner into the fitness spirit is to suggest a walk. If he or she has trouble keeping up after a mile or two, your message will have been delivered.

4. **Celebrate the romance in your heart.** As young adults, many of us had an inner vision of ourselves as exciting, poetic or romantic souls, eager to embrace the opportunities life offered for fun and adventure. Meeting and courting our mates was likely to have been one of the most exciting and meaningful times of our lives. Too bad, then, that as the years rush past and life's many responsibilities pile up, our vision of ourselves as lovers and poets, and our shared vision of our relationship as being special, often dims.

   Although it's probably unrealistic to expect the original intense glow you experienced when you bonded with your mate to last a lifetime, there is no need for your relationship to grow dull. And who knows; if you are lucky you may even agree with the historian Will Durant, who wrote at age 90, "The love we have in our youth is superficial compared to the love that an old man feels for his old wife."

   Recognizing the potential problems that a loss of "romance" threatens, and sharing with your mate your desire to rediscover the excitement in your relationship, is almost always a good way to begin strengthening your romantic bonds. Obviously, there is no one-size-fits-all approach to doing this, but making a commitment to spend more fun time with your mate, even if it means cutting back work hours and saving a little less money, is almost sure to be a good start.

5. **Plan ahead if one spouse will retire years before the other.** Several generations ago, when a man retired, his typically non-working mate often considered herself to be retired as well (despite the fact that she was still almost surely responsible for cooking the meals, cleaning the house and doing the rest of her traditional tasks). Even in the last few decades,

when it has become routine for women to work outside the home, it has nevertheless been common for women to regard their jobs as of secondary importance. Again, the result was often that when the man collected his gold-plated watch, his wife was also ready for retirement. Although these male-centric family and employment patterns were not without problems, one big advantage was that both spouses were ready to retire at the same time.

Today, for a variety of reasons, there is far less certainty that spouses will want to retire simultaneously. Combine the facts that many women are quite a bit younger than their husbands, and that they are more likely to have interrupted their careers to care for children, and the result is often that women in their early or middle 50s are just hitting their career peak as their husbands either choose to retire or are pushed out of the workplace. This means that many couples now in midlife may soon find that their day-to-day lives are out of synch.

If you'll likely be part of a half-working, half-retired couple, you and your mate may both face some tough practical and psychological issues. To mention just a few, the retired spouse may want to travel, relocate or just share leisure time, while the other—now with the increased status of sole breadwinner—may have no desire to leave the workplace. The still-working woman may well be fed up with maintaining her traditional role as primary homemaker and expect her retired mate to do the shopping and chores before putting a good dinner on the table.

Of course, no two couples face the same situation. For some, the income of the still-working spouse will be essential, while for others it won't really be needed. And some working women will love their jobs and may even be eager to take on more responsibility, while others will be content to work just a few more years to qualify for a better pension. And, of course, just because one spouse is retired doesn't mean he will pine for something to do. To the contrary, many retirees will be so busy with interesting activities they won't feel threatened or inconvenienced by their spouse's continuing working.

But one thing is certain. Both spouses will have to come to terms with a very different lifestyle than they have been used to. And I'm convinced that the chances both will make a good adjustment to their new reality go way up if this major life change is faced and planned for well in advance. In fact, some marriages may be at significant risk of failure if this isn't done.

Just to get you thinking, here are a few ways couples I've talked to have coped with this situation:

- The retired spouse went back to work part-time (I've seen this work well for a number of couples, especially when that person found interesting work).
- The non-working spouse got deeply involved in nonprofit activities (again, as long as the work is really interesting, this approach seems to work well).
- The first spouse to retire enrolled in school full- or part-time (a great plan when a retiree has a genuine thirst for knowledge, since both spouses are likely to benefit when one becomes energized by a big new challenge).
- The retired spouse traveled widely (I know two couples who have pulled this off, but the long separations involved in one spouse taking long solo adventures definitely aren't for everyone).
- The retired spouse became a house-husband, with an occasional day on the golf course (no one I know has happily made this work for long, but surely some people must).
- Both spouses move to a new part of the country the retired spouse is yearning to explore (this takes lots of advance career planning by the still-working spouse, but it's a compromise that I've seen succeed).

For Men Only: Look Beyond Your Paycheck

Many men work hard—sometimes incredibly hard—to fulfill their roles as providers, but do a poor job of being family members. Even in an era where the majority of women also work outside the home, traditional male attitudes die hard. And lots of men make the terrible mistake of thinking that bringing home a large chunk of the family bacon absolves them of other family responsibilities. Too often, they fail to see that all children need gobs of time; wives or mates need help with day-to-day chores, as well as companionship and romance; and parents, siblings and other family members need their active involvement.

What's this got to do with retirement? Unfortunately, for many men, a great deal. A man who follows the fairly common male lifestyle of working long hours and then spending much of his free time watching sports on TV, bonding with his male buddies or participating in some other activity that excludes his family, is highly likely to fare poorly after age 65. If you doubt this, take a look at the older couples you know. Count how many more retired men as compared to retired women seem lonely and isolated.

Why do so many more men than women seem to have a tough time dealing with retirement? Easy. When work stops and physical limitations often make it more difficult to participate in sports, many men do not have good family relationships to fall back on. For example, I know a number of men whose careers were highly successful and whose bank balances run to the high six, or even seven, figures who are nevertheless desperately lonely and isolated, in significant part because children to whom they paid little attention earlier in life are now returning the favor.

Indeed, I believe that one of the reasons why women, on average, live substantially longer than men is the fact that so many men—in addition to being members of the more violent and accident-prone sex—are social misfits after they retire. By contrast, women, who have typically developed better social and family skills earlier in life, adjust far better to being old. Just as many aged Supreme Court justices (mostly men, of course) seem too busy to die, many older women seem too engaged in life to be ready to quit it early.

One of the best ways for men to increase their chances of enjoying a fulfilling retirement is to spend more time becoming close to their families during midlife. Of course, as mentioned earlier in this chapter, this advice applies to women as well, but men are much more likely to be inept in this regard.

If there is one key to a man's ability to really be part of his family, it's simply to spend more time together—that is, to be significantly involved in lots of day-to-day family activities. Yes, this includes changing diapers and getting up with a sick child in the middle of the night, but it also means being sure you have a close personal relationship with each child at each stage of his or her life. Many men never seem to understand that intimacy doesn't just somehow happen as a result of sharing genes, but must be earned by reading bedtime stories, helping with homework, driving carpools, volunteering in the classroom, coaching Little

League (for your daughter's team as well as your son's) and even helping your seven-year-old make a new dress for her favorite doll.

Unfortunately, too many men find most of these mundane tasks off-putting and too often use work as an excuse to avoid them. Sorry, but pleading busyness—whether real or feigned—is a prescription for failure. To experience the joy of being in close touch with your kids later in life, you'll need to become involved in the activities they care about now. I direct doubters to my conversation with Henry and Althea Perry, which follows this chapter. Few men will follow Henry's example and teach themselves to sew well enough to make a daughter's wedding dress. But Henry's spirit of family involvement and caring can nevertheless inspire all of us to surprise ourselves and our loved ones by learning to participate in their lives in new and meaningful ways.

INSIST ON BONDING WITH CHILDREN FROM BIRTH

Many women are so enthusiastic about caring for their newborns and toddlers that they unconsciously distance their mate during the early days—and sometimes even years—of child-raising. Some men willingly accept this, believing that, at bottom, nurturing babies is women's work. Nonsense. You need to be involved in your children's lives from the first day. Politely insist on doing your share of baby-related work, if necessary, by gently but firmly reminding your spouse to make room for you in the family bonding process.

Children, of course, aren't the only family members who need your caring involvement. Taking the time to be truly a part of the lives of parents, siblings, nieces and nephews and cousins will benefit all of you now and, especially, after you retire. And this doesn't mean just putting in a token appearance at a family event organized by your spouse. Making the telephone calls, planning the menu and, yes, even listening to why Aunt Agnes doesn't want to sit next to Cousin Fred is where real family glue is mixed. C'mon, let some stick to your fingers. ■

A Conversation With

HENRY AND ALTHEA PERRY

Henry Perry was born in Alameda, California, in 1915. His family had moved west from Louisiana, where they had been sharecroppers, about 1900. After graduating from high school in the middle of the Depression, Henry worked in construction, often on steel structures as many as 20 stories high. In World War II, Henry served on one of the Navy's first two mostly black fighting ships, USS 1264. He later joined the U.S. Postal Service, where he worked as a letter carrier for over 25 years. Henry and his wife, Althea, now live in Oakland, California.

(Author's note: When I arrived for my appointment to interview Henry Perry, I was delighted to also meet his lovely wife, Althea. It seemed the most natural thing in the world for the three of us to sit down together and for me to include Althea's occasional comments.)

RW: Henry, your maternal grandparents moved to California from Louisiana well before the First World War. Wasn't it somewhat unusual for a black family to move west in those days?

HP: They had to get away from Collinston, Louisiana, in a hurry, after my grandfather's boss came to him one day and said he wanted my mother.

RW: Wanted her?

HP: Yes, in the most basic way. My mother was only 12 at the time. So my grandparents had to quickly and quietly sell all their belongings and sneak away. They went first to Arkansas and then to California.

RW: Tell me a little bit about your early life.

HP: When the Depression hit in 1929, I was 14. It wasn't an easy time for anyone, especially black people. I finished high school and then had to scrape for work. At that time, black people couldn't get work except as cooks or waiters on the railroad or working in the Southern Pacific yards. I got on with the WPA for a few months and then got into the construction laborer's union, Local 304—one of the few unions open to blacks—and was able to hustle work at places like the Alameda Naval Air Station and the Oakland Army Base.

RW: Were you still doing that when the war started?

HP: Yes. The war gave me a chance to grow—since, at the time, I was really in a rut. I enlisted in the Navy, which, of course, in those days was completely segregated. Blacks worked in the kitchen or cleaning up, and that was it. But I guess you could say the very first hints of change were in the air—there was beginning to be political pressure to allow at least a few blacks to go beyond being servants. As a result, I was one of a very few black men chosen for training to serve on a combat ship—in my case, a Subchaser (USS 1264). Eventually, we went to sea with a crew of 52 blacks and five white officers and were assigned to convoy duty to protect merchant ships from the German submarine wolf packs. Later, a book, *Black Company: The Story of Subchaser 1264,* was written about us.

RW: You met Althea during the war?

HP: Yes, Althea is from Boston. We met on a blind date, set up by a friend.

AP: Yes, that was when Henry's ship was commissioned in New York. We got along so well, I moved to New York, where Henry was based, and got a job in a restaurant. When the war ended, Henry went back to California and got a formal divorce from his first wife. Then I took a bus out and we were married.

RW: Did the racial situation in the Bay Area improve any after the war?

HP: Thanks in large part to Harry Truman in the White House, it did improve a little. For example, I was able to get pretty decent construction jobs. But then, Althea stopped by with my lunch one day and saw me walking a beam five stories up.

AP: That was it. I didn't want him falling, and made him quit. After a short stint at the Oakland Army Base processing equipment and supplies, he passed the post office test in 1949 and worked there until he retired in 1975.

RW: Henry, as you know, the book I'm writing is about retirement. Let me ask if you consciously prepared for what has obviously been a very successful retirement.

HP: Yes, I did. For one thing, once my kids were grown, I went to college. It was something I wanted to do all my life. Because I was still working, and had to go nights, it took me five years to graduate from California State University at Hayward. In fact, I didn't get my diploma until I was 61—a year after I retired. But that wasn't all—I also took a course at the University of California's extension program on all aspects of the aging process. I wanted to be well-prepared for retirement.

RW: You were looking forward to retiring?

HP: Absolutely. I was never afraid of it. Lots of people are worried that they won't know what to do. That wasn't me. I stopped doing what I had to do to support my family and started doing what I wanted to do.

RW: You didn't miss your job?

HP: I never loved being a letter carrier. I did a good job and was happy from one day to the next, but I always knew that if I hadn't been born black, I would have been doing something more interesting.

RW: If a younger friend asked you for advice about how to retire successfully, what would you emphasize?

HP: Live for yourself, but do it by helping others. Take a look around you and make yourself useful.

RW: What's helping others got to do with enjoying your own retirement?

HP: Think of it like this: All your life, you're writing the speech someone will give at your funeral. If you have been concerned about helping others and making the world a little bit better, that speech will be about how your deeds will live on in the hearts of others.

RW: You mean, there is a sense of immortality in working for the good?

HP: Sure, but your work has to be genuine. It has to start with what's inside you. For example, as we are talking, it's only a few days before Christmas. I feel deeply sad that so many poor children don't have anything and won't be able to have anything. If I can do a little something about that, I'll do it.

RW: You're 80 years old and active in many community activities. You can't be doing all that without being in pretty decent health.

HP: I feel good about my life and what I'm doing to help others. Not only do I stay active, but I feel good inside. I'm not angry, I'm not envious, I'm not full of acid. I feel a sense of inner contentment. I believe all these things are important to good health.

RW: What about exercise?

HP: That's important, too. I still have my bike, and even when I drive someplace—say to the store—I park a little ways away and walk the last part good and fast.

RW: You're a bike rider?

HP: Let me tell you about that, because you'll see a little of how I work in the community. I was 52 when I got my first bike. Black kids just didn't have bikes when I was young. At any rate, when I rode my bike, I saw all the neighborhood kids watching me enviously. I had been thinking about how to approach them about such things as why it's important to do well in school, but until that moment, I hadn't figured out how to get their attention.

RW: It's useless to just go up to a kid and give him good advice, isn't it?

HP: That's it. I needed a gimmick, a way to break the ice, and I saw right away that the bike was it. But to make my idea work, I needed more bikes. So I talked to a family on my mail route who had an old bike they weren't using, and they let me have it. Later, I bought a few old banged-up bikes from a guy at a bike store. Soon after, I was able to get a truckload of broken bikes someone was taking to the dump for free. I bought some bike books and taught myself how to fix them.

RW: So you became a sort of pied piper of bikes?

HP: Yes, kids came from everywhere. Sometimes they would be here, knocking at my door, at 6 a.m. Saturday morning. I taught them safety, formed drill teams and did all sorts of other things. Many of the kids were from the housing projects and were just hungry to get on those bikes. It gave me a chance to really communicate the important things I wanted to talk to them about.

RW: Were all the bikes in your backyard?

HP: Yes, at the start, but not for long. The media heard about what I was doing and I was interviewed for some newspaper and radio stories. The result was that bikes came in from everywhere. The City Recreation Department and the Oakland Police Department began to help me and provided an old warehouse. By then we had 435 bikes.

RW: What a great story. I can see what you mean about looking around and making yourself useful. But let me bring things back to retirement and ask you about money. Is having a good bit of money put aside before you retired something you worried much about?

HP: Because I worked for the government, Althea and I knew we would have a decent pension and could get along all right. But to answer your question directly, money just isn't something I think about much. It's just not that important, especially if you use your common sense. For example, a few years before I retired, we paid off our mortgage early by sending in extra payments.

RW: So many Americans obsess about money. What makes you different?

AP: It's easy if you do just one thing—learn to live on what you have rather than on what you don't have. For example, when lots of people we know began to get a few dollars ahead, they sold their small working class houses in this area and moved to much larger houses in the Oakland Hills, which, of course, meant they started over with another mortgage. But we stayed right here in a house that's bought and paid for and we haven't had to worry for ten seconds. And you know what? When we want to go someplace, we do. There's a bus on the corner that goes to the Bay Area Rapid Transit system, and from there you can go around the world.

RW: Have you traveled much?

AP: I like to travel more than Henry. I've been to Jamaica and Hawaii three or four times with friends.

RW: Henry, what do you do for fun away from the neighborhood?

HP: My son and I went in together and bought a 28-foot boat. We go out on the Bay together and fish. Family bonds are very important at any age, but especially as you get older. If you asked my son, he would say I'm his best friend. I consider that the biggest compliment a person can receive. Althea and I are also very close to our daughters and grandkids. It's something you do all your life. In a good family, people always support one another. It's something that lasts a lifetime.

RW: What about religion? Is that important in your life?

HP: I'm involved with the church. I enjoy church, especially to the extent that it's involved in the community. Just the same, I'm not a particularly religious person. I've read the Bible, the Koran, the Book of Mormon and many of the other holy books, and as far as I'm concerned, they're all good. But when it comes right down to it, I believe in the Golden Rule and not some of the rest of it.

RW: Is anything else important to why you feel good about your life?

AP: Talk about the sewing. It's a good example of how you work in the community.

HP: Let's see. Going back a number of years, I became worried about so many poor children not having decent clothes, things they could be proud of. So I asked Althea if she would make the girls some beautiful dresses.

AP: "No way," I said. I can darn and mend, but I don't enjoy sewing beyond that.

HP: Well, since I firmly believe that, except for the arts, a person can learn to do anything, I called my sister and asked her to teach me to make a dress. That week after work, I went to her house every evening. (My kids knew where I was, but Althea didn't.) My sister taught me about patterns and how to use the sewing machine. By late Saturday night, I had a dress for Althea finished. I brought it home and hung it up where she could see it Sunday morning.

AP: I put it on and it fit beautifully.

RW: Somehow I just bet we haven't reached the end of this story.

HP: You're right—I got hooked on sewing. To improve, I first took a class in Berkeley and then started teaching teenaged girls here in the community. Some War on Poverty money was available, and soon the sewing project started to grow. Eventually, we had to hire more teachers, and it got pretty huge.

AP: Henry even made our daughters' wedding dresses.

HP: Yes, but then for a few years, I didn't sew much. Recently, I've picked it up again. I didn't want to lose it.

RW: Henry, since we've been talking, three people have knocked on the door. Your life is obviously extremely busy. Do you ever get frustrated about not having enough hours or even years to do all that you want to accomplish?

HP: No, when things get busy, I just pick out the activities where I'm most needed and concentrate on those. And I often remind myself of the serenity prayer.

RW: How does that go?

HP: "God grant me the serenity to accept the things I cannot change, the courage to change the things I can and the wisdom to know the difference."

■

Chapter 4

Friends

"Making and keeping friends may be among the most important things you can do for yourself; and relating sensitively and meaningfully to friends is an art you can learn."

—Ernest Callenbach and Christine Leefeldt

The message of this chapter can be summed up in one sentence: Whether you retire rich, poor or somewhere in the middle, you will almost surely be poor in spirit later in life unless you have both good friends and the skill to make more.

Having observed, with sadness, how lonely and increasingly isolated my father was in the years before he died at age 80, I understand firsthand how impoverished retirement can be without friends. My father's loneliness was palpable; for days at a time he had no one except my mother to do things with or even talk to. Undoubtedly he would have been happier—and probably would have lived longer—if he had even a few confidants.

Dad hadn't always been lonely. For many years, as a partner in a small law firm, he worked with lots of interesting people and made a few real friends. On the weekends, he relished the time he spent with a half-dozen or more golf and tennis buddies. Add to this the busyness of raising two sons, staying on friendly terms with the neighbors, belonging to several clubs, chairing the town recreation commission and playing semi-serious bridge, and it is fair to say that, although Dad was at bottom a fairly shy man, he was actively engaged with all sorts of people.

So why was my father so alone in the years before his death? I think he would have explained it something like this:

- My law partners and most of my old law business friends retired, so even though I tried to keep working, a lot of the fun went out of it.
- Many of my friends moved to Florida or other warmer places while I stayed in New York.
- My physical strength declined, to the point that my golf and tennis became so embarrassingly bad I couldn't play with anyone except an increasingly few old friends.
- In my mid-60s, my older friends began to die or become senile. In my 70s, the same thing began to happen to friends my own age. Before long, my address book consisted of little more than columns of crossed-out names.

- My two sons—my only close family—chose to live thousands of miles away, and I saw them only a few times a year. As a result, I never really became close to my grandchildren.

Although this accurately describes what happened during my father's later years, I don't think it reaches to the heart of his problem. I say this because once, earlier in his life, a series of tragic family circumstances resulted in his losing contact with a number of close family members and friends—a loss so severe that, at one point in his late 30s, he was close to despair. But instead of sitting down in a comfortable chair and giving up, as he did when he was older, Dad created a new family and made new friends. It's this difference in behavior that reveals the real reason Dad was so lonely when he died: In his last ten years, and probably closer to 20 or 25, Dad lost his ability to make new friends.

I mention my father's loneliness late in his life because I know that many other retired people also experience it, and for much the same reason: When old friends die, move away or become mentally or physically incapacitated, it becomes increasingly difficult—and often seemingly impossible—to replace them. The result is that for far too many people, old age is an intensely lonely time.

It's worth noting that the loneliness of older people is a fairly recent social phenomenon. It is at least partially attributable to the fact that today's retirees are, on average, far more affluent than was true even 50 years ago and, as a result, far more likely to maintain their own separate living spaces well into old age. While being able to live independently undoubtedly has many advantages, it's also true that, in a typical American suburb, it's easy for a person without a job to go for days without any significant human contact. Contrast this to the way people lived even a century ago, when multi-generation families typically lived close together, either in crowded urban areas or on the farm, and it's easy to see why today, older people have a greater potential to be lonely—and a greater need for close friends outside their family—than at any time in American history.

Few Friends = Illness and an Early Death

A large and growing number of studies conclude that people who enjoy close relationships with others live longer and healthier lives than those who don't. For example, a 1998 University of Michigan, Ann Arbor study of 100 recent retirees by Alicia Tarnowski and Toni Antoriucci, reported that the most powerful predictor of life satisfaction after retirement was the size of a person's social network. Those who expressed satisfaction with life averaged social networks made up of 16 people while those who were less satisfied had social networks of less than ten people. And these studies show the reverse is also true—people who are isolated and lonely are more likely to become ill and die prematurely. Interestingly, the negative effects of social isolation manifest themselves in people of all ages and physical conditions—healthy adults of working age, older adults, people who have suffered a recent heart attack and even women who suffer from advanced breast cancer. For fascinating details on the key studies which support this point, see *Overcoming Loneliness in Everyday Life*, by Jacqueline Olds, Richard Schwartz and Harriet Welster (Carol).

The Art of Friendship

Over two decades ago, my good friends Ernest Callenbach and Christine Leefeldt wrote an inspiring little book called *The Art of Friendship* (Pantheon Books, 1979). It's a shame more people haven't read it since it's by far the best book on this overlooked subject. In it, they do attempt to come to terms with what friendship means in modern America. Here are a few of their observations:

"When family ties falter, when love affairs or marriages end, friends relieve our loneliness, fulfill our need for affection, and bolster our morale. Making and keeping friends may be among the most important things you can do for yourself; and relating sensitively and meaningfully to friends is an art you can learn.

"Each friendship exists in a complex social network that creates both opportunities for friendship to thrive and obstacles to its development. We were endlessly fascinated by the strategies people adopt to maintain friend-ships, despite the stress of family responsibilities, marriage, love affairs, and power relationships.

"Old friends are comfortable, known qualities; you can count on them. You have a common history, which provides a sense of stability and continuity.... Old friends are your yardstick for measuring your changes: they 'knew you when....'"

"But with old friends, however precious, the entire weight of the past is always present. As a result, it is important for you to remain open to estab-lishing new friendships, which allow you to start with a clean slate. New friendships also give you the opportunity to concentrate on the process of 'creating yourself.' It's up to you to bring whatever you consider relevant from your past into new relationships. What's more, you're free to present yourself as you are becoming, not as you have been.

"The benefits we reap from our friendships are neither the cause of nor the basis for friendship so much as the consequences of it. Indeed, we tend to love people we help more readily than we love people who help us. The friendship bond thrives upon a sense of generosity and mutuality, not sharp

(continued on next page)

> dealing and rational calculation of gains and losses. Such sharing behavior, we suspect, goes back very far in our biological evolution and is probably far more 'human' than the cost-benefit analysis we so often allow to displace or outweigh emotional ties.
>
> "Americans too seldom praise each other for being good at friendship, although we give ample recognition to ambition, power and physical attractiveness. Perhaps this is a result of our apparent difficulty in pinpointing the qualities that make our friendships successful—though we often place a very high value on the happiness friendship brings."

Unfortunately, the ability to understand why our great-grandparents—assuming they lived beyond age 60—were less likely to have been lonely in their later years than we may be doesn't help us avoid the risk that we will be increasingly isolated after we retire. Even if we desired it, there is probably little chance of getting our parents, children and other relatives to buddy up with us in a large, rambling farmhouse or, for that matter, even a suburban condo complex. Instead, our task is to recognize that if we are to avoid loneliness after retirement, we will need to maintain a healthy friendship network—one we need to start building or at least strengthening as soon as possible. Here are a few suggestions that should help:

- Make at least some younger friends.
- Seriously commit yourself to continuing to make new friends in midlife and, if necessary, relearn the art of doing it.
- If you are married or living with someone, make at least some friends who are yours alone.
- Plan and carry out practical strategies to be around enough compatible people later in your life that you'll have a good chance to form new friend-ships.

Because each of these approaches to increasing your chances of having friends later in life is a subject unto itself, let's take a moment to reflect on each.

Make Some Younger Friends

If most of your friends are about your age or older, and you live into your 80s, many, if not most, will die or become mentally incapacitated before you do. Not only will this deprive you of their companionship and increase the likelihood that you will spend many hours and days alone, but a friend's death is almost always a painful event. This is true even though you still have other friends or the ability to make new ones. Here is how my friends Michael Phillips and Catherine Campbell, authors of *Simple Living Investments* (Clear Glass Publishing)—a small book I highly recommend—put it:

> *The death of friends, including lovers and family, will be a powerful and debilitating force. As we age, the names listed in our personal phone books will slowly be crossed out. To sense the extent of the problem, we can imagine a party to which a large number of long-time friends are invited. Now picture the same guest list when we are 65: One out of four, 25% of our male friends, will have died, and 15% of the females will be dead. By the time we are 85, only one out of five men who were our friends at age 35 will still be alive, and only two out of five women.*
>
> *When we travel to a city where we once had many friends, it will be painful to try to reconnect with them. Too often the person on the other end of the phone will say, "He died in March, didn't you hear?"*
>
> *To clearly understand how death will rob us of our friends as we age, consider that a person who had 200 friends, close associates and relatives in his/her life-circle at age 35 will—at age 75—be losing to death one male friend every two months and one female friend every four months. Ten years later, when that person is 85, the rate of loss will have doubled, with a male friend dying every month and a female friend dying every other month. The death rate difference between males and females means that those of us still alive at age 85 will have twice as many women friends as men, assuming we started with an equal number of each in our earlier days.*

Phillips and Campbell go on to point out that, "These actuarial figures don't apply to all ethnic and racial groups. For example, half of all black males will not even live to collect Social Security at age 65." But there is a simple way to plan ahead to cope with this unhappy eventuality: Consciously make and keep younger friends throughout your life—people who, statistically at least, are unlikely to die before you do. At first, this may sound calculating, or even selfish—after all, since authentic friendship comes from the heart, not the head, deliberately deciding to cultivate younger friends would seem to contradict friendship's most basic premise. I don't buy this argument, for two reasons:

- First, in the larger context of the inevitability of human aging and death, each of us must find a way to live out our final years with dignity and, hopefully, a little joy. Cross-generational friendships are simply one commonsensical and traditional way to do this.

- Second, and probably more important, making good friends with anyone— young or old—is never a one-way street. You can't force someone to become or stay your friend. Bridges of affection are built and maintained between people only to the degree that there is both a mutual attraction and sharing, which usually means that each person has something to offer the other. Younger people, for example, are often attracted to the knowledge and experience of a person who has resided on this planet a little longer. And older people are commonly drawn to the energy, fresh ideas and vivacity of people who are many years younger.

MAKE AN OLDER FRIEND; YOU JUST MIGHT LEARN SOMETHING

Just in case you are still concerned that deliberately setting out to make younger friends is a mite selfish, it's easy to even the score by making an effort to befriend several people who are older than you are. My experience of doing the interviews for this book has again forcefully reminded me that people who have lived a few years more than I have often have the experience and wisdom to teach me a great deal about how to live a more fulfilling life. I suspect if you take the time to talk about aging with the older people in your life, you will have a similar experience.

Forming New Friendships

If your experience of life is anything like mine, you found it easier to make friends in the first three decades of your life than you have after age 30, or certainly 40. There are undoubtedly lots of good reasons for this common phenomenon. Certainly, a big one is that the great majority of adults who both work and become parents have very little free time—so little that even keeping up with old friends can prove difficult or sometimes even impossible. If you are a typical American adult, you are probably having such a hard time meeting daily obligations (should I fix the water heater before or after I take the dog to the vet and go shopping for my daughter's prom outfit?) that you have begun to avoid at least some social obligations.

Withdrawing into one's immediate family circle in midlife isn't the only explanation for why we make fewer new friends as we grow older. Many people who remain or become single—as well as those who form long-term committed relationships but do not have children—also report that they make friends more slowly as they age.

How can we reinvigorate our social relationships in mid- and later life, so that our retirement years will be enriched by new human contacts? We must start by clearly understanding (as my father never did) that the ability to make new friends after age 40 is a skill each of us needs to nurture—or in some instances relearn—and that the failure to do so is likely to lead to loneliness and unhappiness later in life. Let me emphasize the huge importance of grasping this basic truth, since most middle-aged people who currently enjoy at least some close friendships don't even notice that they have begun to make fewer new friends as the years pass. As a result of this myopia they also fail to grasp how big a risk they are running of being lonely in their 70s and 80s.

If you are ready to take steps to rebuild a good friendship network now, here is a quick reminder about at least some of the ways good new friendships are typically made:

- *Common interests:* Friendships formed around real interests, whether it be surfing at Malibu or surfing the Internet, are more likely to last than those that grow out of more casual contacts. Witness the fact that people who meet and may even become inseparable at vacation resorts or on cruise ships often don't continue their relationships for long, while people who share a passion for chess, dance, fossils or women's ice hockey often do.
- *Sharing:* Honest friendship is achieved by listening, giving support, being open to talking about your real interests and worries. While friends often socialize together, real friendships are rarely formed at social events.
- *Commitment:* For a variety of reasons, as we become older, the chances become greater that we will fail to convert friendly acquaintances into real friends. But once we recognize this pattern, we are well-positioned to adopt strategies to reverse it.

- *Recovering old friends:* Close friends from our childhood and young adult years know us in ways that no one else ever will. Although it may not seem so in our middle years, having these people be part of our lives later in life is almost sure to prove meaningful. It follows that we should invest some time and energy getting in touch and staying in touch with old friends— something that ever-cheaper travel and communications technologies really do facilitate. So next time you get an invitation to a class, workplace, sport or other reunion, overcome your shyness (and, if necessary, your cynicism) and do whatever you need to do to get there. Better yet, why not be a little more ambitious and track down a few of your long-forgotten buddies and organize your own mini-reunion? It may just turn out that you have more friends than you think.

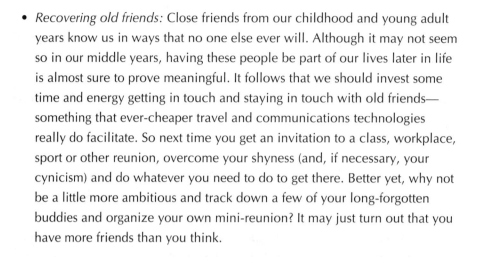

Gail Worries About Making New Friends

On a backpacking trip high in the Colorado Rockies, I asked a good friend who is in her mid-40s and has two school-age children how she makes new friends. Her response helped me understand why I have made fewer new friends over the years.

"I meet lots of people through work and parenting activities, but as the years have gone by, I have turned very few of these acquaintances into real friends. I've told myself the biggest reason is that by the time I complete the weekly rat race, I'm just too tired. Most evenings, all I want to do is climb into bed and read a book for a few minutes before sleep. But lately, I've begun to wonder if my urge to retreat into my bedroom doesn't signal that my life is a little out of whack. After all, I know that true friends lift me out of myself and bring me joy. Have I simply forgotten how to reach out to potential friends? Am I just too lazy to follow through? I always thought it sad that so many men lacked good skills at developing and nurturing close relationships, and now I'm afraid I may be becoming like them. I plan to take a mini-sabbatical from work later this year, which means I should be less busy and hassled. It will be a challenge to see if I can reconnect with some of my old friends as well as make some new ones."

Couples: Make Sure Your Friends Are Really Yours

I have a favor to ask. Make a mental list of your close friends. Now, assuming you are a member of a couple, ask yourself how many of your friends are also coupled. If your answer is "lots" or "most," ask yourself this second question: How often do my partner and I socialize as part of couple-related activities. If you are typical, your answer will probably be frequently.

If so, either you or your mate—depending on which of you survives the other—is at high risk of being seriously lonely later in life. The reason is simple: When the first mate dies, the other very often and very quickly tends to lose close social contact with most close friends who remain coupled. And this is likely to happen even when the couples make a genuine effort to include the newly single person in their activities.

Why do recent widows and widowers and their long-time couple friends have such a hard time maintaining close friendships? There is no simple answer, but here are a few common reasons:

- The newly single person often tries to cope with loneliness by embracing new activities and otherwise keeping busy, while the long-settled couple is content to move more slowly, following old habits.
- The widow or widower needs to be around people who can truly understand and empathize with his or her pain and loneliness. No matter how caring and kind, people who haven't lost a beloved mate simply can't fill this role.
- Whether they admit it or not, many members of couples who are of the same sex as a newly single person become jealous. When this occurs, the friendship can quickly end, or, even if it doesn't, become strained.

Whatever the cause, many people who lose their spouses find that, just when they need them the most, they have also lost many of their old friends. If you doubt this, talk to the members of any social group made up of retired single people; you are likely to learn that at the time their spouse died, the survivor thought she had a good many friends, but by the time she joined the group (often a year or two after her spouse died), she regarded herself as being without a real friend.

What can you and your spouse do to avoid finding yourself in this situation? Short of making sure you die first, here is the advice of my friend Afton Crooks, who has lived through the wrenching experiencing of losing her spouse:

> *No matter how close you are to your spouse, you also need your own good friends, at least a couple of people you are really close to. I don't mean business colleagues or acquaintances, but intimate friends who you truly care about. Obviously, this is particularly true for women, who usually outlive their husbands by a number of years. In addition, it's also wise to keep up a good network of other people whose company you enjoy, people who share your interests.*

Creating and maintaining separate friendships without offending your spouse can sometimes be problematic. A member of a couple that has always socialized as a duo may feel threatened if the other suddenly wants to pursue more personal friendships. The best approach is to discuss the problem with your mate and, if possible jointly, ask an older widow or widower for their insights. Chances are, both of you will be told two things:

1. When one of you dies, the other will rely primarily on his or her own close personal friends for comfort and support, and much less on friends who are members of couples.

2. As we age and the years we have spent with our mates add up, it's important for each of us to reinvigorate our lives with new experiences and thoughts. One excellent way to do this is to make and maintain our own friendships outside of our marriage.

But how do you go about making new friends? Can someone who hasn't made a true friend in many years still do it? Just as is true for a sedentary person who doesn't get adequate exercise, the most important step in dealing with social isolation is to make a determined commitment to take action. Since it's obvious you'll never make new friends—nor reinvigorate old friendships—if you engage in solitary activities such as sitting in front of the TV, reading or spending the day working in your garden, this means you'll need to put yourself in social situations where you will meet compatible people.

Bowling Alone

America used to be a country of joiners—everything from church, grange and Lion's Club to garden society, PTA and Moose Lodge. But recently, this strong national proclivity to forming groups seems to have gone into reverse. Membership in almost every national fraternal organization, most religions and even local bowling leagues is down, often way down.

In his groundbreaking treatise *Bowling Alone: The Collapse and Revival of American Community* (Simon & Schuster, 2000), Robert Putnam speculates that the main reasons for this are:

- the movement of women into the labor force
- people, especially women, have less time to join anything
- mobility—people who don't stay in the same place very long don't become very active in civic endeavors
- demographic transformations—"few marriages, more divorces and lower real wages"
- the ethnological transformation of leisure—televisions, computers and other technologic devices have privatized leisure. Rather than playing games with our neighbors, we watch them on TV.

Whatever the reason, it seems clear that most middle-aged Americans belong to fewer groups than they used to. Unfortunately, the implications of this trend for a "non-joiner's" retirement years are unhappy; unlike older members of the Rotary Club, Shriners or Home Economics Society, who remain welcome at meetings and social gatherings far into old age, many people who retire 15 or 20 years from now will find that when they no longer have a job, they don't belong anywhere.

Of the many possible ways to do this, four stand out:

- Join groups interested in the same intellectual pursuits, hobbies or sports you are.
- Volunteer with a nonprofit group working for a cause you believe in.
- Join a social group or club. Many of these (such as local men's, women's, civic betterment or fraternal groups) contribute to a good cause but are

primarily places where people get together to enjoy one another's company.

- Become active in a church or other spiritual group.

Of course, these approaches aren't mutually exclusive. To stay interested—and interesting—after retirement, most of us will need to pursue at least several different interests (see Chapter 1, What Will You Do When You Retire?). For example, we may want to hike, paint or fly a helicopter in the morning and help out with a church-sponsored food bank for the homeless in the afternoon. But when it comes to making new friends, it's key to realize that how we do our chosen activities matters more than what we do. A photography buff's chances of bonding with others is far higher if she joins a camera club and participates in group field trips than if she wanders the countryside alone.

Hilda, an older hiker who lives in Southern California, offers a good example of how we can combine our deepest personal interests with our basic need for companionship. When she was in her early 50s with her kids off to college, Hilda began to have time on her hands. Having immigrated from Germany as an adult, she had no friends from her school or young adult years to fall back on. And although she had met lots of people during the years her children were growing up, only a couple had become confidants. Confronting both her loneliness and the issue of what she really wanted to do with the rest of her life, Hilda realized that she was happiest when she was exercising outdoors. As a result, she began to set time aside every day to hike along the nearby coastline. But hiking by herself was often lonely, and sometimes scary. As a result, she decided to try to overcome her natural shyness and make some hiking friends.

She started by inviting her two good friends to spend a day on the trail. Both begged off, one claiming a bad leg and the other because she had a full-time job and cared for an infirm parent. Hilda next invited a couple of acquaintances, but again ended up with excuses, not a hiking companion. At this point Hilda realized she needed to be more organized and purposeful in her search for partners. She knew about the Sierra Club and decided to join and get involved in local chapter activities. Although it was an act of some courage for her to go on her first group hike, she was quickly reassured by how friendly and welcoming people were. From that day on, Hilda has never hiked alone. Instead, she happily participates in many day, weekend and occasionally even international hiking trips with what has quickly become a large circle of new acquaintances and a few real friends.

Why It's Wise to Join Early

For a variety of reasons, many people find it hard to become involved with new clubs, nonprofit organizations or even church activities and organizations after they retire. For one, they may simply be out of touch with what is currently going on in their field of interest and therefore have difficulty fitting in and being accepted by people who are more knowledgeable and experienced. After all, the essence of group interaction—and the basis of most friendships—is the ability to contribute, not just to receive. For example, in his 50s and 60s, my dad, who was a canny lawyer and a smart money manager, would have been welcomed by dozens, if not hundreds, of nonprofits eager to put his expertise to good use. Had he become active in a cause he cared about during that part of his life, it's likely he would have contributed a great deal and, in the process, have created a new friendship network. And the fact that ten or 15 years later age had begun to slow him down a little probably wouldn't have caused these groups (or the people he met through them) to abandon him.

Making Friends the High-Tech Way

By encouraging people to be solitary consumers, the first-generation electronic technologies such as radio, records and TV did much to undermine many Americans' sense of community. It is already obvious that another technology—online communication—has begin to reverse this trend.

Once online, older people find a wealth of free information about health, travel and consumer issues of special interest to them. Even more important for many isolated and lonely people, they have a chance to make and easily communicate with friends using electronic mail and chat rooms (many of which are most active in the middle of the night when lots of seniors have trouble sleeping). Even more fascinating, many retired people have established their own sites. Some serve to share expertise about a particular subject—for example, hiking the Grand Canyon, helping new businesses get off the ground or playing better tennis after 70. Others facilitate communication about a particular interest—for example, staying healthy while traveling to difficult places or coping with Parkinson's disease.

You don't even need your own computer to explore the online world. Many public libraries now offer free Internet access—and some basic instructions about how to start. Some community colleges also offer courses on using the Internet.

My favorite sites which focus on the concerns of old people include:

- ThirdAge.com: This informative site contains a load of information about dozens of topics, including family and pets, money and the ever-popular love and sex.
- SeniorNet.com: Helps noncomputer-savvy seniors learn how to master information technologies.

But if we wait until after retirement to become involved with group activities, we may find that some of our skills and energy have begun to erode. Once that happens, it's far harder to gain acceptance either as a volunteer or member of a club or interest group. Even if our minds are still as bright as a new penny, we may begin to see ourselves as being "just too darn old to be worth much" and increasingly reluctant to join group activities. Don't discount this possibility just because you have been gregarious all your life. Even people who were socially adept when they were younger often become insecure and shy as they age. If you have always been a shy person, it's a very good bet you'll be more so later in life.

Shyness was certainly a contributing factor to my dad's increasing inability to make new friends after he turned 70. As it finally dawned on him that he was becoming more and more isolated, he belatedly attempted to become involved in a few helping activities and interest-centered clubs. Sadly, none of these efforts bore fruit, in part because he approached most of them tentatively and withdrew so quickly when he even imagined he wasn't welcome. His long-time church membership provided some social contact, but because he had not really been active in the church community earlier in life, here again he just didn't seem to know how to involve himself deeply enough to form new friendships.

Having talked to so many active, energized retired people who continue to enjoy and be enriched by many good friendships, I understand that my dad—and the tens of thousand of retired people who are deeply lonely near the end of their lives—found himself in this situation primarily because he wasn't fully aware of the danger we all face if we outlive our friends and don't make new ones. I'm determined to at least try to do better. How about you? ■

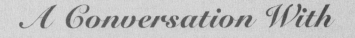

A Conversation With

YURI MORIWAKI SHIBATA

Born in Oakland, California, in 1920, Yuri grew up in the Watts section of Los Angeles. She graduated from the University of California at Berkeley in 1941, just in time to be locked up in a U.S. government internment camp for West Coast persons of Japanese ancestry at Hart Mountain, Wyoming. In camp, Yuri taught English, and after the war enjoyed a career as a teacher of English as a second language. After getting a Master's degree, she became an administrator with the San Francisco Community College district. Widowed in 1981, Yuri retired in 1984. She is the mother of three and grandmother of seven and has recently remarried.

RW: Yuri, I know your first husband, Miki Moriwaki, died very soon after he retired, in 1981. You were just 61 then, and still working.

YS: Yes, Miki only lived nine months after he retired. And actually, I had taken a sabbatical to be with him when he retired.

RW: Why?

YS: I guessed he would have a hard time adjusting. Miki had a very good job and was a highly respected executive. His work was the center of his life; he was immersed in it. He had made no plans for retirement, and had few interests outside of reading. He didn't enjoy activities like fishing or playing golf. He liked being with people, but we had moved to a rural area a year before and had not yet become involved with the community, so I suspected his retirement wouldn't be easy.

RW: Do you think boredom, or maybe I should say not having a sense of purpose, contributed to his death?

YS: No one can know. But I do feel one's mental attitude affects one's health, and I've always been struck by how many men die soon after they retire.

RW: You had already gone back to work with the community college district when Miki died, is that right?

YS: Yes, I had been back at work for two months.

RW: You must have been devastated. How did you even begin to put your life back together?

YS: I knew I needed support. Fortunately, I had two close friends, one of whom I had known since we were in high school, and another I met at work. They helped me tremendously through the early stages, but as wonderful as they were, at some point, they couldn't truly understand what I was experiencing, for the simple reason that they hadn't lost their spouses.

RW: You found that only people who had experienced a similar loss could really help you?

YS: Yes, but it wasn't just help I needed. I knew that I could deal with my own grief better if I could help others in the same situation.

RW: How did you find these people?

YS: I had heard about a second-generation Japanese-American woman who had recently lost her husband. With the help of a retirement organization, we got together and founded a Nisei widow and widower's group.

RW: Nisei means a person is the child of a person who immigrated to the U.S. from Japan?

YS: Yes, my parents' generation—the first to immigrate to the U.S.—are the Issei. I'm second generation, or Nisei, my children are Sansei, third generation, and so on. At any rate, to find more people who needed support, we contacted Japanese-American organizations and placed ads in several Japanese-American newspapers. We started small, but now, 14 years later, we have 60 members, both widows and widowers.

RW: How did doing all this help with your grieving?

YS: Losing your spouse leaves a huge hole in your life—as much as you love your children and grandchildren, your relationships with them aren't the same. It helped me tremendously to help others cope with this loss and to be around people who understood what I was going through.

RW: Yuri, suppose, based on what you know now, someone in their 40s or 50s asked you for advice about preparing for retirement. What would you tell them?

YS: Most fundamentally, I would say this: You never know what is going to happen in life, so developing yourself should be an ongoing goal. That is, be sure to continue learning and growing. For many women, this means not allowing yourself to become a shadow of your husband. If you do, you'll lose a positive sense of yourself, and therefore self-esteem, after retirement age. Of course, it will be even worse if you are widowed.

RW: What else?

YS: Learn to like yourself. The secret of living a decent life is to give to others, but you absolutely can't do that if you don't like yourself. Otherwise, you are too needy. For men, it's important to realize that participating in sports won't be enough to provide a true feeling of self-worth. Furthermore, you must realize that if you retire at 65, in five short years you'll be 70. Your health may curtail physical activities as the years go by. You must think deeper about what you want your life to be about, and act to make it come true. If you don't, life will not have much meaning.

RW: Yuri, you have a pretty good-sized family—three children and seven grandchildren. How do you believe a close family fits into retirement?

YS: If you're fortunate enough to have a family, it's key. After you retire, you need psychological support, which adds up to knowing that you are still important and needed. This is especially important for people who have worked full-time all their lives, since so much of their sense of self-worth is likely to have been provided by the workplace. Loving and helping your family—and feeling needed by them—can fill some of this void.

RW: So, working in midlife to create a close family will be helpful after you retire?

YS: Sure, but that's not why you do it. To have your family work well, you need to give a lot of yourself. But when you are doing it, you aren't thinking of their helping you after retirement.

RW: What about when you retire? Should you make efforts to be emotionally close to your family?

YS: Yes, but you will never succeed by asking for things. I don't believe you should sit around and wait for your kids to do things for you or entertain you. Dependence is always bad. Your job is to learn how to love and help members of your family earlier in life and keep doing it. After retirement, assuming you do this and you keep growing and changing, you will continue to be a vital part of your family.

RW: What else?

YS: Don't sit in judgment of your kids.

RW: That's easy to say, but what do you really mean? Give me an example.

YS: How they spend their money. You may think they are doing something that isn't smart. Keep your mouth shut, but find some way to help them. For example, if as a result of not saving, they come up short for a down payment on a house or some other major purchase they really need, you might quietly help them. Hopefully, they will not only appreciate what you are doing but also gain a little self-knowledge.

RW: You mentioned money—do you have any insights as to how a middle-aged person who is concerned about not having enough money after retirement might plan?

YS: When compared to the larger issues in life, money simply isn't all important. But at a practical level, you want to have some sort of monthly income or enough money saved when you retire—or the skills to get more—so you won't have to worry. For most people, Social Security alone just won't be enough.

RW: I understand that money is important to buy necessities, but you seem to be saying it's important for another reason, too.

YS: Having enough means freedom from anxiety. Beyond that, it also helps you feel independent, and therefore in control of your own life.

RW: I gather your job provided a pension?

YS: Yes, but it's not indexed for inflation, so even with Social Security, I've wanted to keep working part-time. After Miki died, I sold our house and bought another. This got me interested in real estate, and, after retirement, I took the necessary courses to get a license. I've been fairly successful as an agent, which has produced some welcome extra income. But more important than the money has been the chance to work creatively with people to help them find just the right place to live. I'm not a person who is good with hobbies or art—I enjoy working with people—so real estate fulfilled two important needs.

RW: What else would you like to say to middle-aged people if you could do it without seeming to tell them how to live their lives?

YS: Start thinking about retirement in your 40s or 50s. Time will go so fast that, if you don't focus on things you need to take care of, it will be too late.

RW: Such as?

YS: Your health. If you are in your 40s or 50s, you have time to develop good habits. You need to realize that, after 65, a lot depends on whether you have done this. If you have poor physical health after 65, it will be much harder to maintain the good mental health that's essential to enjoying life.

RW: What else?

YS: One thing I have done is senior peer counseling at a local senior center. I was trained by a person connected to the Berkeley Mental Health Department. At any rate, when you work with older people who are isolated and dependent, you see how crucial it is to develop real interests during the middle of your life. A lifetime of just working and saving money won't do it. Too often, people who have been immersed in work reach retirement age without the flexible habits of mind that allow them to start fresh. Sadly, for too many of them, it's just too late. There are people, too, who worked so hard at saving money that, after retirement, they are afraid to spend it. You need to learn how to have fun in life, too.

RW: Yuri, I know that you recently remarried. Can you tell me a little about that, and your plans.

YS: Harry is a retired aeronautical engineer and a wonderful guy. After his wife died, he joined the widow and widower's group I was active in. We have lots of interests in common.

RW: Tell me one.

YS: I guess what I want to say first is that it's not important that Harry shares any particular interest of mine, but that he has an open, inquiring mind. For example, after our marriage, we participated in an Elderhostel program in Hawaii, which we thoroughly enjoyed. We plan to do many more

Elderhostel programs together. These take place all over America and, for that matter, the world. Elderhostel combines travel with education at very reasonable cost. Instead of just going someplace as a tourist, you go to an area to explore and to learn, and you meet many interesting people who are there for the same purpose. It only costs about $300 for room, board, lectures and field trips for five days once you get to a program. It's important to me that, in addition to his enthusiasm about learning and discovering new things, Harry shares my philosophy of life. For example, he cares about real things as opposed to material things. He's interested in nature, the environment, the community and in helping others; he appreciates the beauty in life.

RW: Any final thoughts you want to share?

YS: As people in their 40s and 50s begin to age, they have a choice. They can spend lots of time looking inward and fretting at every new sign of increasing age, or they can look outward at the world and fully participate in life. If they do the latter, they will be far less conscious of, or worried about, the aging process.

RW: You mean, if you are truly interested in the people and things around you, aging will be less of a problem?

YS: Absolutely. Focusing your energy outwards is the key to leading a fulfilling life and relishing your retirement. I'm 75 and I'm looking forward to moving into our new home, traveling and enjoying life with Harry. I'm also planning to take the real estate broker's exam. I've completed all of the coursework. One of these days, I may also want to do some substitute teaching of English as a second language, and recently passed a rigorous examination to update my credential. Incidentally, I don't believe that age should stop a person from learning. There are many wonderful opportunities to keep our minds active. For example, classes at community colleges, adult schools and special programs offered by universities for retirees are widely available at a low cost. Especially as you get older, I feel it's important to set goals. Otherwise, time will speed by and you'll begin to feel that you haven't accomplished anything. ■

Chapter 5

Loving Life

"If a man does not keep pace with his companions, perhaps it is because he hears a different drummer. Let him step to the music he hears."

—Henry David Thoreau

Call it zest for life, call it inner strength, call it optimism—some people just seem to get more enjoyment out of life than others. And this doesn't change after retirement. In our later years some of us will become increasingly bored and boring, while others will discover their most authentic and exciting selves.

Embrace Life, Not Money

What distinguishes energized, interesting, charismatic seniors from others who are depressed, lonely and grumpy? One thing is obvious: It has little to do with how much money they have. Several of the retired people I admire most have very modest savings. Take Howard, who, in exchange for the right to play golf free the rest of the week, works two days a week as an unpaid course marshal at a local public links, driving a cart around to be sure golfers respect the rules. Not only does Howard, who lives on little more than his monthly Social Security check, know and have a good word for hundreds of golfers, he obviously enjoys climbing out of his cart to help find a duffer's ball or teach a beginner the basics of what, at first, can seem an intimidating game.

Or how about Ed, a man in his late 70s, who lives in New Mexico and spends much of his free time as an amateur—but highly knowledgeable—archeologist? Referring to himself as a penniless desert rat, the truth is that Ed has given away most of his once considerable savings to his children and various charities, holding on to just enough to live in what he calls "frugal comfort." Asked why he didn't keep all or most of his money, Ed replied, "I'm too busy doing more interesting things to manage it properly. Also, my kids are at an age when they need it, and I'm at an age when I'm free of needing it."

If having a large investment portfolio won't guarantee that you'll experience a truly fulfilling retirement, what will? In the absence of any trustworthy research, here are my subjective impressions based on my conversations with dozens of vital, interesting retired people:

- **Physical activity.** The overwhelming majority of energized oldsters I've talked to in the course of writing this book exercise a lot—swimming, walking, doing calisthenics, jogging and, in a surprising number of instances, working out with light weights. This is not the same as saying all are in excellent, or even good, health. When pressed, most will admit that they regularly experience chronic pain or illness. But in spite of this—and often as part of a conscious decision not to give in to their physical problems—these retirees insist on working up a daily sweat.

- **A determination to make life better for others.** People who work to improve the world, or at least a little corner of it, seem to maintain a sense of vitality that is missing in those who are intensely self-absorbed. Their "cause" can be the environment, health, education, community economic development or the arts, to mention just a few. And, of course, as discussed in Chapter 4, doing volunteer work offers participants a huge bonus: the opportunity to meet compatible people and make new friends.

- **Romantic love.** Among my own family and friends, I know a fair number of people in their 70s and 80s who are deeply and zestfully in love with their mates—some with a person they have been with for many years, others with a lover met later in life. Either way, compared to the people who are merely rich, those who daily experience love are truly wealthy.

- **A strong family.** When asked the secret of their success, many of the most optimistic older people I know quickly mention their children and grand-children and explain why they feel it's so beneficial to be a real part of their lives. But I'm nevertheless struck by the fact that many of these retirees are so busy with their own activities and interests that they have to consciously make time to spend with their families (and sometimes fend off children, who see their primary role as being babysitters). It's as if these people are wise enough to understand that part of building and maintaining close family ties is to accept that their children and grandchildren need plenty of room to develop their own personalities and live their own lives.

- **True friends.** Not surprisingly, many, if not most, energized seniors have not only maintained friendships with people of all ages throughout their earlier years, but continue to make new friends after retirement. Interestingly, when explaining why they believe it's so important to form friendships with younger people, many of the retired people I interviewed used almost identical words: "They expose me to new ideas," "They jar me out of my ruts," "They keep me on my toes."

- **A willingness to be different.** Trying to conform to the expectations of others all one's life seems to carry with it a heavy price after retirement. It's as if now, when you finally have the freedom to be the individual you really wanted to be all your life, you've forgotten who that person is. As I discuss later in this chapter, people who do well after retirement almost universally develop a strong sense of self earlier in life, even if that means having the courage to be a misfit.

Retirement Role Models

It's simple, really—whether we are five or 55, we humans learn a lot about how to live and make life's major decisions by observing the people around us, especially older people we respect. Thus as kids, those of us lucky enough to have conscientious parents and grandparents almost literally inhale important lessons about life that the children of dysfunctional families must learn later, if at all, by trial and error. And, of course, finding good role models is also a big key to success when we go to school, enter the workplace participate in the arts or become an athlete. Therefore it should come as no surprise that those of us able to find good retirement mentors will have a big leg up on those who don't in the last third of our lives.

Fortunately, by the time we retire we should all know how this benchmarking process works and be eager to identify and learn from people who have proven they know how to retire successfully. When I think about vital older friends whose retirement lives I admire, Gretchen comes first to mind. Born on a ramshackle farm, Gretchen came into her womanhood late in the Depression. As she recalls it, "In my childhood, a new dress was always out of the question. Even a new piece of ribbon to sew onto a raggedy old dress was a once-a-year treat."

At 17, Gretchen, always an excellent student ("How else was I going to escape those darn chickens?"), was admitted to a good state university with a small scholarship. She paid the rest of her bills working as a housekeeper. Marrying soon after graduation, by the late 1940s Gretchen was the mother of two. But just as she was settling into what she describes as a conventional, reasonably contented suburban life, her husband, a high school teacher, began to drink. Before long, he began to drink more. And then, seemingly pleased with his new life as a barfly, he galloped enthusiastically down gin hill until he became a true alcoholic.

That was when Gretchen kicked him out and began divorce proceedings. Suddenly she was again as stony broke as she had been as a kid, the only difference being that she now had two small children of her own to raise. Finding only occasional work as a substitute teacher, Gretchen was barely able to keep a roof over their heads. Even with the help of several steadfast friends, she didn't always have enough money for food. That's when she turned to scavenging. To avoid sending her kids to bed hungry, Gretchen even recovered damaged packaged food items from the big bin behind the local supermarket (something it was a lot easier to do in the '50s before there were so many homeless competitors). And before long she made friends with sympathetic delivery men who gave her perfectly good but outdated cheese, bread and other supplies before they made it into the bin.

After several years of living on, or often over, the financial edge, Gretchen's life began to look up. She started to work regularly as a substitute teacher, and her ex-husband, who still managed to work despite his continued bingeing, was finally coerced by the legal system into paying at least some child support. A few years later, after Gretchen received an unexpected inheritance and surprised herself by making a savvy investment in a small commercial building just before local real estate prices skyrocketed, she was able to rejoin the middle class, and even help pay for her kids' college educations.

When Gretchen was in her 60s—and, thanks to savvy investments and a frugal lifestyle, financially comfortable—she became involved in a number of activities designed to teach homeless people the lessons in self-sufficiency she had learned. Among her activities was working with several local homeless shelters to set up collection routes to gather good food that local restaurants would otherwise discard. In addition, she helped establish a project to create and refurbish toys for homeless children.

Now in her eighties, one of Gretchen's favorite self-help activities is Project Seed, a group of dedicated people of all ages who work together—much like 19th century barn raisers—to quickly build decent affordable houses for low-income families. As a self-described "tiny old lady," when Gretchen shows up at a construction site, younger volunteers tend to smile politely but act as if their main job is to keep Grandma from hurting herself. A few hours later, when Gretchen— who exercises vigorously each day—is still driving ten-penny nails with two hammer strokes, attitudes begin to change. Lots of smiles are still directed at Grandma, but now they are smiles of respect.

Project Seed is just one of Gretchen's current projects. Dividing her energy between helping ill and isolated older friends and acquaintances (often people ten years younger than herself), the project to help feed the homeless and rambling about her neighborhood with her oversize dogs, she is busy, busy, busy. Often she gets impatient at being "so darn old and slow," but before she can sit down and worry about it, she has to cope with a dozen things that need her attention, as well as an 80-pound dog who needs walking.

I asked Gretchen why she is so energized and active at an age when many of her contemporaries are isolated, sedentary and increasingly frail. She immediately pointed to a fundamental lesson she had learned during the tough years of her life: "No matter how impossible things seem, or how lonely I occasionally feel, I know from experience that I have the willpower not only to survive, but to feel good—or at least okay. From way down deep inside, I know I'm a tough, odd and sometimes prickly old bird, and I'm proud of it."

To demonstrate her point, she told me for the first time of her extremely painful chronic problem with arthritic knees, which she has suffered for over ten years. During the worst of these flare-ups, it is difficult or impossible for her to sleep for more than a few minutes, or at best a few hours, at a time, which means she often begins her busy day exhausted. Her point in telling me this was not to ask for sympathy but to make this point: "After all I've been through, I'm not about to let a little pain or lack of sleep slow me down."

Gretchen believes her long-held conclusion that overconsumption is counter-productive to leading a good life has served her particularly well during her retire-ment. She puts it like this: "Especially as you approach 80 it becomes increasingly obvious that it's foolish to keep buying lots of things you'll never need. But if you have spent your whole life getting a large part of your pleasure from shopping, you have a problem—it is probably too late to discover that there are far more fulfilling ways to spend your free time."

While the life Gretchen has created for herself clearly suits her, just as clearly it wouldn't be a good fit for most people. And there is no reason why it should, since among the lessons to be learned in looking at the lives of successful retired people, perhaps the most important is that each of us must find and follow our own path. Some of us will be able to do this by sticking to a well-traveled road or at least a firmly trodden trail, but many others will flourish in their later years only if they successfully blaze a new and possibly difficult trail.

Take, for example, John, another older friend with a true zest for living. In his late 70s, John has diabetes so severe that, just to stay alive, he must self-inject insulin (after first drawing his own blood and testing it for sugar) several times a day. Despite, or maybe partially because of, his life-threatening health problem, John is unfailingly upbeat and enthusiastic about life.

What keeps John functioning so happily despite his health problems? It's not immediately obvious, since he has outlived many old friends, and his poor health restricts his activities so much he has little opportunity to make new ones or, for that matter, even leave his house for more than a few hours at a stretch. If there is a rational explanation for John's evident feeling of well-being, it's most likely his second wife, Maudie, with whom he clearly shares an almost blissful love. Few doubt that John would have died years ago were it not for Maudie's loving energy and unwavering attention to his fragile health. In addition, John has always loved putting his high-level math skills to work solving real-world problems. But how can John do this if he's almost house-bound? His answer has been to develop a consulting business from a corner of his bedroom, contacting his business clients exclusively by phone, fax and email. As one person put it, "After a life of hard knocks, including a long difficult first marriage, John is flatly refusing to die while things are going so well."

Dare to Be Authentic

Why do some retirees cope with life so much better than others? Part of the answer can be found in the list of personal attributes discussed at the beginning of this chapter that many successful retired people seem to share—things like getting daily exercise, working on projects to make life better for others and the determination to create strong friendships and family bonds. But something else also seems to be at work in the lives of many optimistic, zestful seniors. Since I can't quite describe it, I simply call this additional factor "love of life." Over and above—and occasionally even instead of—good living habits, this joie de vivre really does seem to set zestful older people like John and Gretchen apart from so many other retirees.

Unfortunately, understanding that some lucky older people are lifted by their love of life while so many others never experience it brought me no closer to being able to explain why this was true. Or put another way, if there was a straightforward explanation for why a fortunate minority of older people seem to have the knack of living life fully—even though, by at least conventional measures, many had plenty of reasons to live less well—I wasn't smart enough to see it. Finally, realizing that I was at a dead end, I decided to begin my quest again, this time putting aside my own muddled thoughts and asking the successful retirees I interviewed for this book if they could explain why they seemed to enjoy life so much more than some others. My only suggestion was that in addition to thinking about the fairly obvious reasons for retirement success already discussed in this book, such as good friends, good health and a loving family, they also consider more intangible things. Here is my summary of the thoughtful answers I received:

Honor your eccentricity. Throughout most of our lives, many, if not most, of us strive mightily to fit in. Whether we are in fifth grade, in high school, on the basketball team at college or at work, the great majority of us want to be accepted by the people around us. But perhaps somewhat surprisingly, many of the most successful retirees I interviewed claim to have failed miserably at doing this, referring to themselves as "wacky," "weird" or a "lifelong misfit." Indeed, having so many energized seniors tell me how socially inept they had been as younger adults caused me to wonder if the very fact that these people had to come to terms with being "odd" earlier in life helped give them the strength to do well later.

Eccentricity: An Antidote to a Humdrum Life

At first, it surprised me when so many life-loving retirees cheerfully described themselves as "odd," "a little nuts" or even "a true deviant," but when this theme kept cropping up, I took it more seriously. Eventually, I even began asking my interviewees if they believed that odd or eccentric retired people do better than their more conformist peers. The majority answered with a resounding "yes." One friend, Afton Crooks (see our conversation after Chapter 8) explained it like this: "I am the first to admit that I have always been a little odd. You can't help but observe how you fit—or, in my case, often don't fit—into the world. The result is that I gained a sense of humility, or reduced expectations, about life that many conventionally popular people never achieve. Thus I was better adapted to being old in America, a country where everyone over 60 is fundamentally considered to be weird."

Comments like Afton's led me to do a little more research on the subject of eccentricity, I discovered an interesting book called *Eccentricities: A Study of Sanity and Strangeness*, by David Weeks and Jamie James (Villard Books, 1995). Among many interesting conclusions, the authors discovered by administering standard diagnostic tests: "Eccentrics actually have a higher level of mental health than the population at large. Original thinking, it seems, may be better for you than dull conformity."

Develop and respect toughness. When my friend Gretchen calls herself "a tough old bird," she could just as well be speaking for a dozen other active, interesting older people I talked to. Indeed, a common denominator of many of the retirees I identified as living particularly well was a belief that in their earlier years they had lived harder lives than many of their contemporaries. Like Gretchen, they believe that having had to cope with tough problems as children or young adults left them better equipped to deal with old age—a time when living a fulfilling life commonly requires putting all sorts of survival skills to work. A common attitude seemed to be, "Yes, getting old is rough. I look like a prune, my physical problems have increased to the point that pain of one sort or another is common and I am often lonely. So what? I learned years ago that life can be hard and that each day I have a choice—I can give up or I can confront my obstacles and either overcome them or learn to live with them the best I can."

Stay busy. Why do many women do better than men after retirement? One reason my women friends repeatedly emphasized is that they had learned, often the hard way, how to keep busy outside of the workplace. Call it "the revenge of the hausfraus," or "Lucy gets even," but one thing seems clear—after retirement, homemaking responsibilities such as cooking supper, doing the shopping and cleaning out a closet, coupled with time spent helping children and grandchildren, give many women not only a reason to get up in the morning but a way to express love. By contrast, many retired men have far too little to do. While a few learn how to participate in what they grew up considering "women's work," realizing finally that it can be a joy to provide loved ones with good food, a clean welcoming home or loving care for a small child, most don't. Unfortunately, a major consequence of being free of day-to-day chores seems to be that lots of retired men are depressed and, as a result, more likely to experience an early death.

PROBLEMS OFTEN OCCUR WHEN A MAN RETIRES FIRST

As discussed in Chapter 3, these days many women's careers are just peaking as their husbands' wind down. The fact that their mate has become principal breadwinner (and the person who is still valued in the workplace) can be psychologically devastating to many men. My advice to any man who is likely to retire before his mate is to get busy early preparing to live a post-retirement life so interesting that you won't be bothered by the fact your wife is still working.

Welcome pets. Although I was aware that many studies have found that people who live with animals tend to be healthier and happier than those who don't (see "Pets Are Good for You," below), I was nevertheless surprised to see first-hand how many active, interested older people—especially those who live alone—have a close relationship with one or more animals. Cats and dogs, especially dogs who need a lot of exercise, figure prominently in the lives of a surprisingly high number of fulfilled retirees I talked to. Interestingly, not only does a dog serve as a friend and companion, but it helps the older person in several other important ways, including getting exercise and making friends. Just as young kids make friends easily and, as a result, their parents often also become friendly, the owners of your

dog's friends will commonly become at least your friendly acquaintances and sometimes your good friends. For example, when I called one 80-year-old to ask about something related to this book, she put me off until later in the day. She had a date to go dog-walking with a 38-year-old friend she had met a year before, when both their dogs had run off together to chase a deer.

Pets Are Good for You

Dog owners go to the doctor 21% less than people who don't own dogs, concluded UCLA professor Judith M. Seigel, author of a study of 1,000 elderly Californians. She surmised that the dogs were a "stress buffer," which lessened the need of their owners to seek out physicians in times of psychological stress. ("Pet Owners Go to the Doctor Less," *The New York Times*, Aug. 2, 1990.)

If you do get sick, a pet can help you get better faster. One study compared post-coronary survival of pet owners versus non-owners; among the pet owners, 50 of 53 lived at least a year after hospitalization, compared to 17 of 39 non-pet owners. Even eliminating patients who owned dogs (whose health might have been improved just from the exercise of walking the dog), pet owners had a better recovery rate. In a follow-up study, the same researcher found that pet owners' worry about their animals actually speeded their convalescence by providing "a sense of being needed and an impetus for quick recovery."

Ignore your age. I am indebted to an excellent little book by Sharon Kaufman, called *The Ageless Self: Sources of Meaning in Late Life* (Wisconsin, 1986), for the insight that many vibrant life-affirming older people don't fundamentally see themselves as old. Sure, they can tell you how many birthdays they have had and are aware of the physical limitations that come with age, but at a deeper level, they don't believe their age is important to their essential selves. Even though many of their friends and family members act as if they are 110, people in this group continue to feel like strangers in the land of the old. As a 78-year-old friend said, "If I could just break my mirror, I would see myself—inside my own head, that is—as being 40 or 50. And since that's the way I feel, it's the way I try to act. I just don't have much patience with being old. And I certainly don't want to be one of the old busybodies who is forever telling everyone in sight how to live their lives. I'm too busy learning to live mine to be old." ■

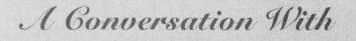

A Conversation With

HAZEL PETERSON

Born in 1914, Hazel grew up in College Hill, a suburb of Cincinnati, Ohio. A mother of four, she worked for 40 years as a leadership trainer for the Girl Scouts of America. In 1985, Hazel and her husband moved to Oakland, California, to be near their children. Widowed in 1992, Hazel currently lives in a small apartment in a senior citizen's apartment complex in Oakland.

RW: Hazel, tell me a little about your background.

HP: Well, as you know, Cincinnati is pretty close to the South, which means, when I was a kid, it was a segregated society. Let me give you just one example of what that was like. I went to school with white children, but even though my name was Banks, and they sat students alphabetically, starting at the front of the room, I was always put in the back row.

RW: Not a great way to teach a child self-respect.

HP: No, but it didn't slow me down. Even as a little girl, I used to say to myself, "You don't know it, but you have a black princess sitting here." Also, I was ready to fight for my rights if someone treated me badly or called me an ugly name. But I was a good athlete and knew how to get along with the other kids, so I wasn't left out. They always wanted me to play.

RW: Later on, did the racial situation improve?

HP: Yes, but not quickly. For example, my husband had to leave the police department after 28 years and go back to school, because no African-American was ever going to be promoted. Later, he became a social worker and then a professor.

RW: These days, I know you're active in senior citizen organizations and activities. Tell me a little about that.

HP: I've always been active physically. I first got involved in senior activities after I had suffered a long, expensive illness and couldn't afford to join a gym. In this area—Berkeley, Oakland and Emeryville—there are a number of centers that offer free exercise programs, as well as lots of other cultural and outdoor activities. I plunged right in, and now I'm on the Council—kind of like a Board of Directors—for the South Berkeley Center.

RW: What does the Council do?

HP: Help plan activities, for one thing. Doing this interests me because, at 81, I know how important it is for me to stay active and interested in life. But I also enjoy the political aspects. For lots of reasons, having good senior programs is important for everyone in society. My children, my friends, you—all will be seniors before you know it. Younger people need to under-stand what it takes for older people to succeed. Yes, of course it takes your own energy, but it also takes help from society. For example, if there were no good senior centers in this area, I would be in trouble.

RW: Hazel, I know you have had three heart attacks and suffer from diabetes. Still you are physically active, live independently and drive a car. Obviously, something inside of you keeps you enjoying life. What really makes you tick?

HP: I like to help others. It does something good for me. It makes me feel good inside. And that's important. Lots of older people don't feel good about themselves. But it's never too late.

RW: Why do you think lots of retired people have such a difficult time?

HP: Lack of self-worth or self-esteem is a big part of it. One reason for this is people feel no one wants what they have to contribute.

RW: What would you say to someone who is thinking about retiring and worried that he or she might end up sedentary and depressed?

HP: Two crucial words: Don't stop! Whatever has made you go during your life, don't stop. Exercise is just one example. At my age, I have aches and pains sure, but I keep participating in dance classes and other physical activities. It helps me and, by example, it helps others. The other day, someone was playing the keyboard at a senior center but no one was dancing. I just got up and did some steps from a line dance called the Electric Slide. Pretty soon, other people loosened up and started to dance. It made me happy.

RW: What else would you tell someone who hasn't retired yet?

HP: It helps to know what you want to do after you retire. If you don't, you're at high risk of quickly losing your sense of self-worth. If you do, you'll begin to withdraw from life, which is no good, since it's so hard to reverse. One big mistake is to center your life exclusively on money, since one thing is sure—lots of money alone won't create a good retirement.

RW: Why not?

HP: Think about it. Money was never the most important thing in your life at any age. Why should it be different when you are old? The trick is to learn to live well on what you have, not to be so fearful that you spend all your energy trying to pile up more. I'm not saying you shouldn't be sensible about money—of course you should, but if you don't get hung up on buying things you don't really need, it shouldn't be that hard.

RW: You live in a pleasant, but small, two-room apartment in a senior center where people live independently. It probably isn't too expensive to live there.

HP: No, it's a HUD rent-assisted project managed by a church. It's a good place for me, since there are lots of nice people living close by, which means there are always many things going on. It's also a place where I can help people—for example, I have a friend in the building who is a paraplegic. I feel grateful for her friendship because she has so much to teach me about living. And I can help her, which helps me feel positive about life.

RW: Before you suffered a series of heart attacks and sky-high medical costs, you lived in a good-sized house with lots more possessions. Some people might feel sorry for you, losing all of that.

HP: Ha! During the year when I was in and out of the hospital and almost died, I just thought of one thing—to get well. I never thought about the money it was costing. You may smile, but I was actually having a good time. And yes, after my recovery, I had to simplify my life. So what? When you're 81, you don't need that many things—it may seem strange to younger people, but money and possessions are not that important anymore.

RW: What is important?

HP: Well, I've talked about activities and interests and exercise. Another thing that's important is your family and friends. I've been fortunate that my four children and my grandchildren are great, and I feel doubly lucky—rich you could say—that they like me and keep me doing things. They feel proud that I'm involved in so many things, which is important to my sense of self-worth.

RW: You and your husband moved to California to be near your kids?

HP: Yes, they were here, and I didn't want them to have to come back to Cincinnati if we needed care. I knew they would have, for sure, which was the problem. I didn't want to disrupt their lives. It's better to live near them, but to stay independent. It's worked out very well. For one thing, it's important to have younger friends as you get older, and my kids' friends have become mine. They call me Grandma Peterson.

RW: You enjoy being around younger people?

HP: Yes. I enjoy listening to them. They keep me fresh socially and politically, and help me understand what's going on in the world. ■

Chapter 6

Reaching Out for Help to Create Your Successful Retirement

"I have never started a poem yet whose end I knew. Writing a poem is discovering."

—Robert Frost, at age 81

It's common for people in midlife to believe that when they retire they will feel free of responsibility and full of possibility, much as they did as young adults. In a word, wrong.

Little about how you experience life in your late 50s and older will be like it was when you were younger. Even if your health and stamina allow you to run ten miles before breakfast, go back to school full time, and travel to dozens of exotic places, you won't be able to recapture your younger self. A good thing, too, since you have already lived the story of your youth, and it really can be more exciting to experience a new plot. But if you're a different person now, you have a big question and answer: Just who are you? Successfully answering this question means that you will meet the great challenge of successfully creating a new identity for your retirement years.

Start by disabusing yourself of any notion that your retirement years will be a long and pleasant glide towards distant old age. Instead, like your earlier life, it is likely to consist of a number of more or less messy—and sometimes scary— personal transitions. If this worries you, think back and remind yourself how many major changes you may have already weathered: Leaving home for the first time, marrying (or forming another close relationship), parenting, changing jobs, dealing with the death of a loved one, to mention just a few.

Chances are, when faced with some of life's major passages, you were delighted for a chance to change at least some aspects of your self—perhaps when you went away to college or took your first full-time job. And you have doubtless also experienced times when the need to reinvent at least some aspects of yourself was thrust upon you—as may have happened if you suffered a serious illness, or confronted the need to stop some type of destructive or addictive behavior.

Oddly and, I think, unfortunately, many of us expect retirement to be a sort of emotional lala land, not a daily effort to come to terms with who we are. Put another way, we don't anticipate, and therefore aren't ready to cope with, the psychological changes that will inevitably occur throughout our retirement years. Even if you decide to work past normal retirement age, the need to change how you look at yourself can't be avoided. The fact that you are now well into the last third of your life—and will need to come to terms with your older self—won't have changed, if for no other reason than at least some of the people you work with will likely begin treating you like an old bat or half-competent geezer.

A Personal Note About Retirement

My concern is that the inner compass that helps me successfully orient myself to my day-to-day world may work less well after I retire, when the many props of a busy workaday child-centered life are removed. Not only is there the possibility that I'll have more time on my hands than I can creatively cope with, but more frightening, fewer people are likely to solicit my opinion, respect my judgment or give a damn about what I do. Although there are welcome signs that as the tens of millions of baby boomers begin to retire they will force society to positively re-evaluate how older people are valued and treated, I don't think my fears are unreasonable. At least since the Civil War, when America's agrarian village-centered lifestyle began to give way to an industrial urban society, prevailing American social attitudes have accorded each generation of older people less value than the one that came before. So although I hope I am being more paranoid than prescient, it's important to me to find ways after I retire to preserve the feeling that I count for something.

Once you accept that a successful retirement will inevitably require you to change how you see yourself, your next step will be to create—or, if retirement is still some years off, prepare to create—your new post-retirement persona. In some moods, on some days, I find this prospect energizing—right up there with the positive buzz I felt when I headed off to college, or became a first-time parent. But I also know that although lots of people do well at college and many take readily to parenting, a far smaller percentage succeed in retirement. Indeed, when I think about the older folks in my social and family network, I can come up with a lengthy list of people who led more or less successful lives up until about age 60 but nevertheless flubbed their last years.

Among the reasons why the personal side of retirement can be so challenging is that successful role models can be hard to find. We are long past the time when supposedly wise elders commonly played a central role in the life of the community, as was common earlier in American history, when older storytellers figured so prominently in village or tribal life. Unfortunately, the mass media that replaced the storytellers have yet to create a rich tapestry of compelling narratives to help us understand and live our older years.

Mass media largely ignores people in the last third of their lives—especially people over 55. Two-year-olds have the Teletubbies, four-year-olds have Sesame Street, and ten-year-olds have Harry Potter. And, of course, teenagers, young adults and folks in their 30s and 40s can choose from literally thousands of written or filmed narratives that universalize the story of their lives, and in the process help them understand who they are. Unfortunately, the same can't be said for people in their mid-50s and older. The fact that there have been a few movies about the very old (*Driving Miss Daisy*, *On Golden Pond*, *Grumpy Old Men* and *The Straight Story* come to mind) only underscores the fact that there is such a dearth of material about what demographers often call the "young old." (The movie *The Bridges of Madison County* and the TV shows *The Golden Girls* and *Murder, She Wrote* are among the few I recall.) The images we do see are either whitewashed—life insurance and mutual fund ads depicting rich and healthy retirees happily playing away their lives with no mention of the physical and mental problems that can accompany aging. Or they are unflattering stereotypes, dementia challenged oldsters doddering around rundown nursing homes. The result is that, in an age when the art of personal storytelling is all but dead, the media offers people over 50 a stark choice: either keep watching or reading the same old plots about much younger people or tune out the media altogether. Even if you don't expect to get life wisdom from Hollywood movies and sitcoms, you still must deal with the fact that the older generation is almost completely invisible in the media that reflect our society.

Left largely to your own devices, how can you begin the process of creating a post-retirement self that will fit you like your favorite old shirt? I begin with lots of questions, including:

- How will I cope with the physical aspects of growing older?
- How will I stay excited about life once many of the preoccupations of my earlier years, such as working 9 to 5 and raising children, are behind me?

- What will I do that keeps me involved in the lives of others?
- How will I avoid—or cope with—the occasional bouts of depression that so often accompany aging?
- How will I stay positive and excited about who I am as gradually my flexibility, desire for sex, and possibly even my mental powers inevitably decline?

But the point is not to provide you with an exhaustive list of my worries (there are more), but to think about crafting a retirement self. How can we stay or become the people who want to maintain good health, have fun, learn new things and help others. If past is prelude, I know that accomplishing even a substantial part of this will mean I'll not only need to change many of the external facts of my life, but also to engage my inner self or spirit. Or put another way, no practical retirement plan will work if my heart is not a believer.

How can you teach yourself how to positively and creatively enter the land of retirement? At least two approaches should prove helpful. The first is to look outward, at how people you admire have grown and changed to meet the challenge of living well in later life. The second is to do some soul-searching about who you are and who you want to be. One good way to do this is by coming together with a small group of people who face the same challenges you do.

When you're depressed, get moving.
During several prickly patches in my life I've found great solace in hiking up to 20 miles per day in the high mountains. Recent biomedical research helps explain why—by exercising vigorously, I was stimulating seretonin, endorphins and other depression-fighting brain chemicals. So when you feel bad, get your carcass up and perambulating. And although no research backs up this further bit of advice—go for activities that make your soul smile.

Find Positive Mentors

When we think about older people you admire, it is easy to think of prominent and successful older people such as Jimmy and Rosalynn Carter, Walter Cronkite, Bill Cosby, Paul Newman, Katherine Hepburn and Lena Horne. And, of course, there is no reason not to find inspiration in the lives of the famous. But since you can't hang out with them to learn their secrets, it makes more sense to identify role models closer to home, among ordinary mortals.

Oddly and, I think, very unfortunately, people rarely ask inspiring older people for insights about how they defined a successful role for themselves in the last third of their lives. Certainly I was the first person to ask most of the fascinating older people interviewed in this book about what they had learned about creating a positive self.

Unfortunately, when you take a look at the lives of older family members and friends, finding good mentors may not prove easy. If you are typical, for every person you can think of who has enjoyed a fulfilling retirement, you will probably identify several who have done less well—people whose main interests include chronicling their illnesses (and often those of all their relatives, including second cousins), complaining about the many ways the world is going to hell, and listing the dubious achievements of their offspring. But even if it takes a little detective work to find a retiree who you really admire, hang in there. Lots of people have entered the largely uncharted territory of extended retirement and done just fine. If your extended family network doesn't produce obvious candidates, look among people in your occupation who have retired in the last five or ten years. It makes no difference whether you teach school, practice law, drive a truck or train horses—surely you know people who have already made the transition to a positive retirement.

When you find older people you admire, arrange to spend some time together —if they are so busy it's hard to make an appointment, you know you have found someone worth talking to. Once the introductory chat is over, don't be afraid to ask your tough questions, whether they be fears about experiencing loneliness, poverty, a decline in sexuality, boredom or death itself. Successful retirees will likely have developed strategies to cope with all of these issues—and probably a bunch more you haven't thought of—and will usually be pleased to pass them on to you. But more important, they will almost surely go beyond the negative to provide you with a positive vision of the excitement and growth possible at a time of life when there are fewer day-to-day responsibilities. Put another way, they will inspire you to craft a positive present, not just get along.

Take your time. Asking people about the life lessons they have learned almost always means listening to stories about their lives. Be prepared to spend some time patiently doing this and you'll be well rewarded. Remember that the people you are asking to share their vision of how to experience a creative and exciting retirement probably have no more experience in explaining their insights than you do in asking for them.

Look Inward

The second approach to preparing for your retirement involves a good measure of soul-searching—something you may not have done in a good many years. As part of this exercise, you need to ask and answer one essential question: Is the inner me well prepared to lead a good last one-third of my life? If you're like me, you may be tempted to answer, "How the hell would the inner me know? It's never retired before."

Since I can't know how I'll feel about myself five or ten years after I retire, the best way I can try to answer this question is to look at how the inner me coped with previous difficult life transitions. To give you an idea of my process, here are the three major life events I focused on:

- my first divorce, when at age 25 I found myself separated from my two beloved young children;
- the exciting and surprising day in my late 20s when I finally stopped denying the fact of my mother's lifetime mental illness and confronted its effect on my life; and
- around age 40 when, to borrow Gail Sheehy's evocative language in her book *Passages*, I had unexpected difficulty making the transition from the "provisional adulthood" of my thirties to my supposedly "flourishing forties" (something I'm happy to report I eventually accomplished).

How did I do? Like many people faced with a life-threatening disease, I first tried to deny the problems, then got upset (mad sometimes) and finally, when these approaches didn't work, became depressed. Although I never quite lost my hold on what passes for functionality in modern America, those close to me know I was a very unhappy camper. In each situation, only when I admitted that I was embroiled in a difficult emotional situation—one that I couldn't simply ignore or tough out—was I ready to make needed inner changes.

But the process of growth and then healing really only occurred when I finally began to talk to others about my anxieties and demons. I know it may sound trite, but breaking through my exaggerated but very real sense of isolation by admitting to others how confused I felt turned out to be the first real step towards surmounting what seemed at first to be huge problems. Listening to and trying to learn from the insights and experiences of people I respected was the next step. Incorporating my knowledge into a new post-traumatic me rounded out the healing process.

Revealing one's most intimate worries, hopes and fantasies to others is, of course, not the only way to begin the process of personal growth. The world is full of a cornucopia of approaches to get in touch with one's innermost self (soul, if you prefer). Yoga, prayer, meditation, martial arts, writing poetry, keeping a journal or writing your autobiography (see sidebar, "Writing Your Life Story," below), are just a few of the literally thousands of approaches. After all, just as some musicians insist that true personal expression means composing everything they play, others express their creativity by interpreting the works of others.

Writing Your Life Story: Another Approach to Personal Growth

It has become popular for retired people to form writers' groups to encourage participants to tell their own life stories. Whether through poetry, autobiography or even fiction, members are encouraged to pay attention to themselves and the importance of their lives. Especially if you aren't comfortable participating in a discussion group, writing your own story—and later sharing it with other group members—can be a great way to focus on your psyche. It not only allows you a way to work through unfinished personal business, but it gives you a formal way to recognize the importance of your own life.

Writers' groups are often offered by senior centers, colleges, elder hostels and other places that cater to retired people. For an excellent article on the subject, see "Turning to Autobiography for Emotional Growth in Old Age," by Sara Rimer (*New York Times*, February 9, 2000).

Participate in a Group Process

One focused way to examine your feelings about aging and retirement involves both looking inward and discussing problems and opportunities with others. Specifically, this involves participating in a small group with others who are also concerned about retirement issues.

Before I explain how this can work, let me briefly explain why I know how effective group discussion groups can be. My first experiences with a group process occurred over a three-year period, starting when I was 28, as part of the Personal Encounter Group (PEG) program sponsored by Stiles Hall, a YMCA associated with the University of California at Berkeley. All told, I participated in about eight separate groups, each consisting of about ten three-hour evening meetings plus a weekend retreat. Half a dozen years later I also participated in a weekly dream analysis group sponsored by the Berkeley Adult School. (As part of this, I did a lot of solitary work which involved teaching myself to wake up several times each night to write down my dreams in a journal.) Each group consisted of about a dozen people voluntarily coming together with no agenda except to share the exciting process of exploring the self. Group members would take turns discussing things that concerned them (a divorce, relationship with a parent, loneliness) with other group members who provided both support and criticism (cut the bs about your divorce and admit you are deeply hurt and mad as hell).

Without exception my group experiences were highly rewarding. Not only did I get to examine a number of my confused feelings at a time when I had a bunch, but I also made friends and enjoyed a sense of community with others committed to a similar journey of soul-searching and personal growth. Making a serious commitment to think about what was going on under my psychic hood seemed to almost immediately induce a feeling of empowerment, which was immediately and positively reinforced by the tough love and insights of group members.

The very essence of any group process is that to achieve success all members must actively participate. You may wonder how this is possible with as many as eight to 12 people vying for attention. One answer is that a well-organized group spends as much time drawing out quiet people as it does reining in voluble ones. Another is that the most powerful personal insights often occur when you are focusing on someone else's drama, not your own. For example, if you clearly see that another member needs to change how she cares for her body, relates to her daughter, and takes responsibility for her own emotional state, you may just as clearly see that you need to do one of the same things. And because you figured this out on your own, you might be more willing to act on it than if someone else had tried to convince you of the same thing.

Sparing you the details of my personal drama, let me just reiterate that group activities had hugely positive effects on how I lived my life and made me a stronger, happier person. For example, confronting the fact that I take direction poorly, I decided to leave my job and start a business. Even more important, I accepted at the deepest personal level that as a divorced father of two, my first job was to assure the well-being of my kids, even when it conflicted with my preferred agenda. Perhaps I would have come to these and a couple of other important insights without the help of others, but I'm convinced it would have taken far longer and been less fun.

My experience of joining with others to face difficult transitions is far from unique. Many teenagers just starting their exciting and scary new life in high school participate in school, church or community-based discussion groups that have many similarities to a more formal group process. And as any parent who has ever hosted a teenage sleepover knows, even more kids form tightly bonded social groups that, although informal, often work brilliantly to help each member create his or her new young adult identity. Teenagers who for one reason or another aren't included often do far less well. And it's no secret that people facing illness or alcohol or drug dependency problems, or wanting to make a big change in their lives, such as losing a significant amount of weight or finding a new career, routinely find that meeting and bonding with people in the same situation is important to achieving success. Yuri Moriwaki Shibata, in the conversation after Chapter 4, reports much the same phenomenon when it comes to helping people deal with the profound grief and sense of emptiness that comes with losing a mate of many years.

You may have one of at least two big resistances to participating in the group process. If you're in your 40s or 50s, you simply don't have the time to systematically focus on the psychological problems of retirement, and are probably stressed by trying to simultaneously cope with work, kids and perhaps aging parents. Fine—take a deep breath (preferably several) and bookmark this page to reread in five or ten years.

If you are approaching retirement or have recently retired, you may feel just too private or shy to participate in a group process. But if you don't have an alternate means of personal expression, the result is likely to be spiritual stagnation, which leaves many older people interested in little more than their aches, pains and operations.

Forming a Geezer/Geezelle Group

The idea of retired people getting together to socialize is as old as human history and continues today in almost numberless ways, including old men playing bocce ball in Padua, Italy, retired farmers getting up with the sun to meet at Mandie's Coffee Shop in Central, South Dakota, or long-distance walkers who meet each day to prowl the corridors of the Mall of America in Bloomington, Minnesota (see Chapter 2 for more on mall walking). But I'm proposing taking the concept of senior bonding one step beyond the friendly companionship of a social group to a systematic discussion of the key personal issues that, as retired people, we will all have to confront.

Because nothing can exist in the modern would without a name, I suggest calling these retirement sessions "geezer" groups. Although many dictionaries define geezer as any feisty older person, it is most often used to describe a male, something that doesn't quite fit my unisex concept. So despite the fact that one of my most erudite feminist friends insists the female equivalent of geezer is "old bat," I prefer the term "geezelle." (I dearly hope I am the first to coin it—it rolls off the tongue so deliciously.) Semantics aside, what I suggest is simple: men and women in their immediate pre- or post-retirement years coming together on a regular basis to talk about who they are, who they hope to be and how they plan to manage the transition. Since all participants will be facing many of the same challenges, opportunities and worries, these groups should be fertile ground for personal growth.

A good first step is to look for a group in your area whose approach you are comfortable with. For example, in many communities, retired executives and professionals have formed organizations. Increasingly, churches, service clubs, university alumni organizations, Y groups and ethnic organizations sponsor organized retirement activities that focus on the personal as well as practical issues that surround aging. But if you can't find a group that fits your needs, you can simply form one of your own. This can be a formal geezer/geezelle group along the lines I describe below or something slightly different. For example, a group of 60ish men I know recently got together to read and discuss poetry— something that most of them hadn't done for decades. Using poetry as their vehicle to look under life's surface, they often discuss personal issues which, of course, often involve aging and retirement.

DON'T OVERLOOK INTERNET RESOURCES

Several Internet sites focus on the interests of older people. Among the sites I like are www.ThirdAge.com and www.Senior.com, all of which offer a variety of discussion groups that deal with issues of personal growth. But as fun and interesting as the virtual world can be, I see its discussion areas as a supplement, not a substitute, for face-to-face discussions. For me, at least, there is something about committing to meeting face to face on a regular basis with others who are more or less in the same boat that gradually builds trust and allows you to bring up your most personal concerns.

If you can't find an existing group that meets your needs, here are some thoughts about how you may want to form your own group.

Choosing group members. You are not looking for playmates or shopping buddies, but people who are interested in exploring personal issues. At least some of the people who you call to play golf, bridge or to organize the church jumble sale may make poor choices. That said, it may also be true that at least some of the people you enjoy spending time with in other contexts may be excellent geezer/geezelle group companions. This is especially likely to be true if the other activity you share has a dimension of personal sharing.

The main criterion for including someone should be that the person is open to discussing retirement and what it will mean in his or her life. It makes little difference if a person is 54 or 68, still working full time, half-retired or completely retired, as long as they are actively interested in this subject. A 55-year-old teacher planning to retire early in a year or two might be a good member, while a 75-year-old judge happy to keep working five days a week for the foreseeable future might not.

Getting started. Often it makes the most sense to begin the process of forming a group by mentioning the idea to two or three people you think might be interested. One good approach is to discuss the possibility in general terms and wait for your friend to show interest. After all, you don't want to gather a group of people whose prime qualification is that you strong-armed them into participating. Once you get a core group of three or four interested participants, chances are each of these people will suggest others. As long as you select the initial group members wisely, you can usually trust them to do a good job recruiting others. Certainly the fact that you may not know some of these people should be an advantage—it's often easier to be open with people you don't have a long history with. But be warned—if you involve a person with poor judgment at the start, you may end up with group members who you don't want to work with.

⚠ GROUPS ARE THERAPEUTIC—THEY'RE NOT THERAPY

It's also important to recognize that discussion groups are neither a substitute for formal therapy nor well suited to helping people who are seriously depressed, who are unable to rein in a serious problem with alcohol or drugs, or who have some other serious medical problem. Far better to keep your focus on more or less normally functioning people worried about retirement issues.

Spouses and significant others. Just say no. This is your chance to explore who you are in as non-threatening a way as possible. You don't need the emotional baggage that comes with even the best long-term relationship. So if you are married or live with someone, simply explain to your partner that you need to do this alone. If he or she feels left out, suggest that this problem is easily solved by engaging in a similar activity.

Single sex or co-ed? There is no one right choice here. You may feel more comfortable discussing at least some personal issues with just women or just men. And if you are coupled and your partner is a jealous sort or your relationship is not on firm ground, it will be best not to complicate your life (and that of your mate) by sharing your innermost thoughts with people he or she may see as sexual rivals. But if you are single, it may be more fun to be in a mixed gender group.

How many members. As with most discussion groups, six to 12 usually work best. I prefer about ten so that even if a couple of members have to miss a meeting, you will still have a decent-sized group.

Duration of the group. Since at least some participants will likely be reluctant to make a long-term involvement until they see whether the group meets their needs, I suggest asking for an initial commitment of eight to ten weekly meetings of two and a half to three hours in length. If things go well, chances are most group members will want to continue. But if they don't—or you simply want to escape what turn out to be several pain-in-the-butt participants—this gives everyone an easy out.

Conducting meetings. Meet in a quiet, private room with no distractions: using one member's home, or rotating among several, can work well. The key is having a comfortable, private place to meet—not turning this into a social occasion. When it comes to seating, functional works better than super-comfortable (you don't want people dozing off) and, if possible, it's best to arrange chairs more or less in a circle. Keep the focus on the here and now by banning phones and pagers. If you include refreshments, keep them to a self-serve minimum so no one has to play the role of host. Alcohol is a no-no.

Subjects for discussion. It can be a good idea to solicit members for discussion topics at or before the first meeting, merging suggestions to create a preliminary list. Chances are a number of participants will suggest talking about similar concerns—health, personal relationships with mates and kids, financial worries, kids' and grandkids' expectations, loneliness and so on. But many other subjects may also be suggested. For example, a meeting of 50-something men I'm familiar with spent a long rewarding evening discussing how their fantasies about women had changed over the years and what that meant for the future.

Once you create your list, narrow it down to some discussion priorities for the first few meetings. There is no need to stick to this list too tightly—as your meetings go forward and your conversations take on a life of their own, you are sure to discover new subjects you want to explore.

> **EXAMPLE:** Beth and Ginger, both about 60, put together a group of nine women all approaching conventional retirement age. By email and phone, they created a list of five possible discussion topics:
> - relationships with kids
> - sex in middle age
> - health and fitness
> - learning new things, and
> - what I want to be like in ten years.
>
> At the first meeting, one member suggested getting everyone's energy up by starting with the X-rated subject. But several others said they felt it would help them to build trust and get comfortable if the first topic was PG. The group agreed and spent a rewarding evening discussing relationships with kids and, in particular, what several members saw as their kids' unrealistic expectations about caring for grandchildren. Several evenings later, sex was on the agenda and by that time most of the shyness that might have inhibited an earlier discussion of this topic had disappeared.

Confidentiality. To create a safe environment in which to share deeply personal facts and feelings, respect for everyone's privacy should be absolute. And that means not discussing what was said with your spouse or partner. Take this issue seriously and have each group member periodically reiterate a commitment not to gossip. If you learn that a member has broken this rule, immediately discuss what happened. If you feel the person can't maintain confidentiality in the future, ask him or her to leave the group.

Leadership. Some groups operate by consensus with no formal leader. This approach can work well with a small group of tractable members, but can be a big time-waster in larger groups. One danger of having a leaderless group is that a couple of group members who are leery of discussing personal issues may waste hours of time gossiping. Another is that a few outspoken members will dominate the group by focusing exclusively on their concerns.

Another workable approach is to rotate leadership, with a different group member operating as meeting and discussion coordinator each week. Again, this approach works best in smaller groups where at least several members have enough group experience to work together to keep things on track.

But it is also possible and sometimes sensible—especially for larger groups—to arrange to have someone with group experience act as a facilitator. One approach is to hire a professional meeting coordinator (look under "meetings" in the Yellow Pages). People who do this valuable work usually help businesses and nonprofits conduct productive meetings. Even though you have no goal other than the personal enlightenment of the participants, an experienced facilitator who understands how to employ proven good meeting techniques can be a big help. But before you parachute someone in, have a number of your group members meet your facilitator and agree that this person really understands and is comfortable with what your group wants to accomplish and has the skills to help you. Also determine what your leader will charge and that all members are willing to pay a share of this fee.

Conduct of the group. The focus of your discussion should be on how people feel in the here and now. That way, participants are encouraged to explore real personal issues ("I'm frightened about how to fill up my time in a meaningful way," not "Let me tell you where I went on my fun trip to Mexico last month"). The job of the weekly leader consists primarily of keeping the discussion more or less on topic, making sure everyone participates and that no one dominates the discussion. For example, halfway through an evening session, the leader might turn to the quietest person present and ask her to discuss her feelings about the evening's topic.

Meeting rules. It's important to have the freedom to say tough, unpopular or controversial things, but it's equally important to do so in a civil, nonthreatening way. Anyone who unreasonably scares or intimidates should be asked to lighten up and, if that doesn't work, to leave the group. ■

Chapter 7

Nursing Homes: How to Avoid Them, or Pay for Them If You Can't

"After the bankers, lawyers and doctors take everything they can, the nursing home grabs the rest."

—Anonymous

For almost a year, I had a bad case of writer's block when it came to working on this chapter. I just plain dreaded discussing and trying to answer key financial planning questions concerning how to pay for nursing home care, such as:

- Should I try to save tens or even hundreds of thousands of dollars more than I'll otherwise need because I might end up in a nursing home?
- Or should I plan to lower the size of my estate later in life by making gifts to my loved ones so Medicaid will pay my nursing home bills?
- Or should I purchase long-term care insurance?

The big reason for my reluctance to grapple with these very practical issues was simple: Intuitively, I believed most people of ordinary means were better off enjoying their lives as best they could for as long as they could, while hoping to drop dead ten minutes before they're no longer able to take care of themselves. And given this view, I found it hard to advise people—even those genuinely fearful of ending up in a lousy nursing home—to save more in midlife in order to be able to afford a little nicer care at life's end.

Then one day the blinders fell off. I realized most people's deepest concerns about needing long-term care at the end of their lives had little to do with money. At bottom, what most of us truly fear is ending our lives alone and confused, surrounded by uncaring strangers. Or put another way, the key question we all want to answer is not, "How do I pay for a decent nursing home?" Instead, what we really want to know is, "How do I reduce the likelihood of needing long-term care in the first place?" Hallelujah! Now that I had finally asked the right question (one which incidentally I wanted to answer

for myself), my writer's block dropped away and I knew I would have no difficulty exploring the subject.

Staying Out of a Nursing Home

Start by understanding that throughout most of recorded history, most people have died in the arms of family or friends, and nursing homes, as we know them, were never needed. And even in America at the end of the 20th century, where people live longer than they used to—with the result that all sorts of once-rare debilitating mental and physical illnesses are common—there are a number of proven strategies you can follow which will greatly reduce your chances of ending your life in a long-term care facility. Indeed, some groups of Americans never patronize them, automatically caring for their own ill or confused elders. This certainly describes the Amish, most of whose communities are clustered in Pennsylvania and Ohio. For the Amish, caring for elderly family members is simply part of the warp and woof of daily life. And the overwhelming majority do so while refusing to accept a nickel of government help—whether it be welfare, Medicaid, Medicare or even Social Security (to which many Amish who work off the farm have contributed for a lifetime).

How do the Amish take care of their dependent seniors outside of nursing homes? Depending on what's needed, family members and close friends, including teenagers, typically set up a daily help rotation, with different people responsible for covering different times of the day. Sometimes this occurs in the older person's home, but more often in a grossdaadi haus—a small retirement house built close by the home of an older child (which may have been the older person's original house). Should seniors—or for that matter anyone else—face extraordinary medical costs beyond their ability to pay, a community-wide alms fund makes the necessary payments.

If you're not Amish or a member of any other close-knit ethnic or religious community, it's fair to ask what relevance any of this has to you. Potentially, lots. Even if you can't count on this type of comprehensive community help, you can nevertheless learn something extremely important from the Amish: People can devise family and social structures which will lessen—or even eliminate—the chances they will die in a nursing home. Let's look at some of them.

Your Chances of Needing Long-Term Care

It's a common misconception that a large percentage of retired people live in nursing homes for an extended period. In fact, according to a study in the *New England Journal of Medicine*, 86% of men and 69% of women won't ever need one. To the contrary, the 1990 census found that:

- Only 5.1% of people over 65 are in these institutions.
- Even when it comes to seniors over age 85, only about 20% reside in nursing homes.

A few years ago, as the number of older Americans began to rapidly increase, some doctors and public policy types predicted that America's population of disabled people would also go through the roof, thereby creating huge problems for both their families and the Medicare system.

But it hasn't happened. According to the federal National Long Term Care Surveys, older people, as a group, are healthier and stronger than they've ever been. In fact, the percentage of older people who have chronic diseases such as high blood pressure, arthritis and emphysema has declined steadily in the last 20 years. For example, in the early 1990s just 20% of men aged 67 to 69 reported that they were unable to work; that figure had been 27% just ten years earlier.

Gender has a lot to do with whether you'll end up in a nursing home. Primarily because on average they live longer and, as a result, can often count on less home-based support, about 40% of women but only 15% of men who enter a nursing home stay there more than a year. But just because you spend some time in a long-term care facility doesn't mean you will live in one for many years. According to the Brookings Institution, a Washington, D.C.-based think tank, of people who do enter nursing homes, only about 25% stay more than one year. The average stay is 19 months.

Guard Your Health

With good diet and exercise, you can hugely reduce the chances you will suffer a heart attack, stroke or other debilitating physical problem, such as broken bones too weak or brittle to heal properly. (See Chapter 2, Health and Fitness.) Since it's physical problems such as those caused by osteoporosis and stroke—not mental diseases such as Alzheimer's—that result in most people needing long-term care, it follows that by taking care of your health you can substantially reduce the chances that you'll end up in a nursing home. For example, osteoporosis, which each year results in over a million annual bone fractures and puts more people in nursing homes than any other single cause, is now 100% preventable, assuming people at risk (about 20 million women and five million men) take very simple preventive actions beginning in their 50s, including getting adequate exercise, vitamin D and calcium.

According to Dr. Roy Shephard in his fascinating article "Exercise and Aging: Extending Independence in Older Adults" (Geriatrics, May 1993), the typical sedentary person faces about 18 years of partial dependency and a final year of total dependency. The same person who takes up moderate but regular exercise training can stay independent for ten to 20 years longer than he or she would have without exercise. Another finding in Dr. Shephard's article is of particular interest to people worried about living too long. Although exercise extends longevity through most of one's life, this phenomenon stops at about age 80; no matter how much you exercise, either before or after age 80, it will not further increase your life expectancy. Obviously, the significant point here is that while exercise will greatly increase your chances of staying out of a nursing home between age 65 and 80, it will not add to them later by increasing the length of your life and therefore your chances of needing institutional help in extreme old age.

Strengthen Your Family Relationships

Even though my dad needed around-the-clock care for six months before his death 12 years ago, he took his last breath in his own bed, surrounded by the people and things he loved. Despite his almost total physical dependence, he didn't end up in a nursing home because my mother was determined he wouldn't. So determined that, for the first time in her life, she deliberately committed a crime. Her legal transgression consisted of searching for and finding affordable nursing care in the persons of three young Irish nurses, who charged $8 an hour. Their rates were low because, after completing their training in Ireland, they were living and working in the U.S. without proper papers. Mom's accomplices in this criminal endeavor were our family doctor, who steered her to a nearby Catholic Church, and several Catholic women who, with the knowledge of their priest, helped put her in touch with the nurses.

My family is far from alone in having provided home care to an infirm older member who, without dedicated help, would surely have been institutionalized. As you read these words, tens of thousands of close and supportive families are doing the same thing. While working on this book, I've talked with many of these loyal people, some who have cared for an older family member for a number of years. You, undoubtedly, could supply your own list.

But face it—no one will receive needed help later in life from a non-functional family. In Chapter 3, Family, I discuss a number of strategies you can follow in midlife to build a genuinely close and strong family, and will not repeat those points here. But I do want to emphasize that, when it comes to worrying about whether you'll end up in a nursing home, it normally makes far more sense to invest your time, energy and love in strengthening family relationships than it does in working longer hours so you can afford to purchase nursing home insurance.

CHILDREN OFTEN NEED TO WORK TOGETHER TO CARE FOR INFIRM PARENTS

Helping infirm seniors stay independent often requires the help, cooperation and shared decision-making of two or more children. Because stress levels are often high in these situations, things will usually go far more easily if siblings already get along well. To allow this to happen, siblings who have less-than-harmonious relationships need to make an extra effort to overcome tensions that often go back to childhood.

Support Community Efforts to Provide Senior Services

The Amish keep their elderly out of nursing homes not only because family members help, but because the entire community is deeply committed to that goal. Similarly, in many American towns and cities, social services for house-bound seniors allow many thousands of seniors who otherwise would end up in a nursing home to live independently. No question, programs such as Meals on Wheels, adult day and respite care, personal grooming services and affordable senior housing can make a huge difference.

And, of course, long before seniors are house-bound, there are many additional things the community can do to help them stay actively independent and thus significantly reduce the chances they will later need long-term care. These include community-based senior centers, senior exercise programs, senior-friendly public transportation and accessible public libraries as well as legal, psychological, medical, dental and nutrition services for low-income seniors. Not only do programs such as these help seniors deal constructively with important problems of day-to-day life, but taken together, they send older people an extremely important message: This community values you and your contributions and wants you to remain an active part of our social fabric.

It follows that after taking steps to improve your health and strength, one of your more effective personal strategies to maintain your independence later in life is to start now to help ensure that good senior support services exist in your community. At a minimum, this means supporting the creation and expansion of these programs. Better yet, why not work with a local nonprofit group to create a needed service for seniors—for example, help start a books-on-wheels program at the public library or help get a senior aerobics program going at the community center?

I know that this sort of personal initiative can be effective, because I have seen it work beautifully where I live in Berkeley, California. Even though, as the home of the University of California and several smaller schools, Berkeley is usually thought of as a college town, about 11,000 of its 100,000 residents are over 65. To help serve them, the city has, among other programs, four senior centers, a free in-home bathing service, Meals on Wheels, an over-60 health center, a number of affordable senior housing programs and an excellent public library system, with five neighborhood branches. As a result of this community-wide commitment to making Berkeley senior-friendly, many older residents, who might otherwise relocate first to a planned retirement community and then to a long-term care facility, choose to remain in their city.

Long-Term Care Insurance

Even though it's possible to significantly reduce the chances you'll ultimately need long-term care, unless you're Amish or a member of a similar group truly dedicated to caring for its elders, you can't eliminate them. No matter how you guard your health, love your family and encourage your community to provide good services for its elders, you may spend time in a nursing home or other long-term assisted living facility.

A year in a nursing or assisted living home currently costs between $40,000 and $70,000. (Some skilled nursing facilities in high-cost parts of the country charge even more, but are usually designed for short-term rehabilitation and are typically paid for, at least in part, by Medicare.) This wide price range is accounted for by several factors, including the type of care needed (nursing care is far more expensive than custodial care), whether the facility is run as a nonprofit or profit-making enterprise (often facilities run by churches or other nonprofit organizations cost less) and the part of the country in which the facility is located (those in the Midwest and South often cost less). Interestingly, paying more does not seem to guarantee excellent care. At least that's what *Consumer Reports* magazine reported in an article entitled "Nursing Homes—When a Loved One Needs Care" (August 1995), which came to the fascinating conclusion that there is "no relation-ship between the price and quality of care you receive." Visits I made to long-term care facilities in 1999-2000 confirmed this conclusion.

What Long-Term Policies Cost

Whenever there's a possibility of suffering a good-sized monetary hit, you can bet the next move many of us make is to call our insurance agent to see if we are covered, or soon can be. So it is with our fear of ending our lives in a nursing home. Realizing we ultimately can't beat the problem of aging with a little cosmetic surgery and a few anti-oxidant pills, lots of us check into buying a long-term care policy. And even if we don't, our insurance agent is likely to call us to flog what the industry has identified as a high-growth, high-profit product.

Although a long-term care policy that provides a decent, but by no means generous, level of long-term care benefits isn't cheap, long-term care insurance is nevertheless affordable for millions of Americans. According to the magazine Smart Money (October 1997), the annual premium for a policy that pays a benefit of $100 per day (with 5% inflation protection) is $892 if you purchase it at age 55 and $1,543 at age 65. Rates are substantially lower if you purchase a policy when you are younger, and much more expensive if you wait until you are over 70. Unfortunately, there seems to be no guarantee that the rates you agree to pay won't go up substantially over the years despite promises like "premiums do not increase with age or health." For example, Conseco Inc. and Penn Treaty American Corp.—two leading players in the long-term insurance business—have repeatedly raised rates for all policy holders in a particular state, claiming economic reasons. The point seems to be that insurers who don't make a profit on long-term care insurance will jack up premiums.

Are Long-Term Care Policies Lousy Deals?

Just a few years ago, the consumer press was full of warnings about the fine print rip-offs included in most long-term care policies. One of the biggest was that dementia-type diseases such as Alzheimer's often weren't covered at all. Today, largely thanks to federal legislation (the Kennedy Kassebaum Act), many of the nastiest features of the older policies have been outlawed. Indeed, good long-term care policies now provide decent benefits for both nursing home or at-home care, with the choice of which route to follow largely left up to you and your family. But, as noted above, one big remaining problem is that most policy premiums are subject to substantial increases and guarantees that this won't happen have been repeatedly shown to be meaningless.

Who Should Consider Insurance?

But the fact that long-term care insurance provides better coverage at a lower price than was true even a few years ago or that millions of Americans can afford it doesn't mean you should purchase it. Given that relatively few people spend more than one year in a long-term care facility, many families can easily afford to self-pay for nursing home care should it become necessary. For example, if instead of buying long-term care insurance when her insurance agent tried to scare her with horror stories about people who ended up in low-end nursing homes, Marsha, a 55-year-old, invested the $892 premium each year and received a 10% after-tax annual return, she would end up with $15,638 by age 65 and $56,198 by age 75. Even allowing for inflation, this would be enough to pay for about nine months of top quality long-term care. But since few people enter nursing homes at 75, it's more reasonable to look at the investment totals ten years later. Assuming at age 75 Marsha stopped making additions to the $56,198 but continued to earn 10% on this investment, she would have $145,764 at age 85.

Of course, saving all this money instead of paying it out in insurance premiums is great if the elderly person never needs to pay for long-term care or extended home health care. And even if she does, but resides in a nursing home—or needs expensive home-based care—for less than two to three years, the necessary funds will be there. But what if she turns out to be one of the relatively few retired people who will experience the much higher cost associated with needing intensive care for a number of years? Not willing to assume this risk, she may be tempted to insure against the possibility—however unlikely—that her assets will be entirely consumed by five or even ten years of long-term care costs. So the question becomes, "Does this make sense?" The answer often largely depends on how affluent you are. Buying long-term care insurance can definitely make sense if your net worth in old age is likely to be roughly in the range of $200,000-$400,000. But for both more affluent seniors and those with little or no savings, buying long-term care insurance is usually a poor idea. And this is true no matter how hard a sell you receive from your insurance agent, who has likely received intensive training in exactly what to say to scare people into signing on the dotted line.

💡 BEWARE OF INSURANCE COMPANY HALF-TRUTHS

Recently I heard a typical radio ad trying to frighten people into purchasing long-term care insurance. The big scare line was that "three out of five Americans will need institutional care, which can cost $50,000 per year." But what was not said was that most of these people will live in a care facility for less than one year and that the cost of their care will be comparatively modest. It makes you wonder if an insurance company exists which tells the whole truth.

Why not buy nursing home insurance if your net worth is over about $400,000? Because even a longish stay in a nursing home is unlikely to be a financial disaster for moderately affluent people. This is true because the yearly income of people with chunky retirement savings will cover much or even sometimes all of any long-term care costs. Start by understanding that a nursing home resident's Social Security income (and pension, if they have one) will usually pay a good part of long-term care. And especially if the person is single (the overwhelming percentage of the people who live in a nursing home for an extended time are elderly widows), any additional money she might otherwise have spent on living expenses can also be redirected to cover long-term care costs with no need to further invade savings. Finally, if the single older person owns a house or condo, chances are it will be sold, with the proceeds invested so as to produce additional income that can be used to help pay for care. In short, even though a nursing home may cost upwards of $50,000 per year, a surprising number of Americans can cover much—or sometimes even all—of that amount on a pay-as-you-go basis, meaning there is no compelling need to purchase insurance.

EXAMPLE: Celia, a widow, enters a long-term care facility at age 86 and lives there until two months before her death at age 90, when after breaking her hip she is transferred to a skilled nursing home. She pays $50,000 per year for long-term care and $16,000 for her last two months, for a total of $216,000. About 45% of this amount is covered by Celia's Social Security benefits and her survivor's benefits from her husband's pension. Since it's clear from the start that Celia will never again be able to live independently, her children (to whom Celia has given a durable power of attorney for financial management) sell her house for $380,000 and invest the proceeds in U.S. government securities. The income produced, plus the income from Celia's other savings and investments of about $250,000, is adequate to pay her nursing home costs without touching her principal.

For people whose very modest savings place them at the lower end of the economic spectrum, it's even more obvious that buying long-term care insurance doesn't make sense. Folks in this economic category simply can't afford it. Or put another way, a middle-aged person struggling to get by on a monthly Social Security check plus a modest additional income from part-time work has lots better things to spend money on than insuring against something that is statistically unlikely to happen 25 or 30 years down the road.

⚠ BEWARE OF PREMIUM INCREASES

Some older Americans who can barely afford to pay long-term care insurance premiums nevertheless sign up. This is almost always a mistake, since despite the assurances of sales people, premiums are likely to increase, sometimes substantially. The result will be that many policyholders on a tight budget will be forced to drop their coverage and thereby lose all the money they have already paid.

As mentioned, long-term care insurance can make sense for people in the approximately $200,000-$400,000 net worth category, especially if their annual income consists of little more than Social Security benefits and the income produced by these savings (for example, they have no additional pension). This is even more true for folks who believe it is a high priority to leave most of their estates to their children or other inheritors. People in this situation are the most logical purchasers of nursing home insurance for two reasons: First, unlike those who have saved little or nothing and who, if need be, will receive financial help from Medicare, people with savings will be required to pay for long-term care. And second, an extended stay in a nursing home really could substantially deplete their net worth (they wouldn't be eligible for Medicare assistance until at least a major chunk of their savings was consumed). Although, as mentioned, it's unlikely any individual will need many years of expensive care, for people who fit this economic profile the peace of mind that comes with insuring against the possibility may be worth the relatively high cost.

How to Find a Good Long-Term Care Policy

As noted, in the last few years, many insurance companies have improved their policies. Still, as with any consumer product, some long-term care policies are better than others. Here are some tips on what to look for:

- Consider policies from good-sized reputable companies rated AAA by *Standard & Poors* or *Moody's* or A+ by *Best Insurance Reports*, information that is available online at www.moodys.com/repldata/insurance/ratings/insfs.html, www.standardandpoors.com/ratings/insurance and www3.ambest.com/ratings/search.html. Since many small companies that issue long-term care polices are poorly funded and, therefore, at risk of cashing in their chips before you do, it really makes sense to do this.

- Be sure the daily benefit the policy pays, when combined with your Social Security and other income, will be enough to pay for decent care. For many people this will be at least $100-$150 per day. Also look for a policy where the benefit amount increases with inflation.

- Before you buy, make sure you know how much premiums will cost in future years. Or put another way, you want a policy that will absolutely guarantee the amount of your yearly premium. Beware of policies that say rates will not change with age or health—many companies simply raise rates for all policy holders, claiming that the increase is to cover higher than expected costs.

- Prefer policies with short non-coverage periods. For example, a good policy provides that you only need be in a nursing home for 20 days before coverage kicks in; a less good one requires 100 days or more nursing home stay before the policy pays benefits. (But, of course, the 100-day policy may still be worth considering if its cost really is substantially lower.)

- Carefully read fine print dealing with home health care. For people with serious medical conditions requiring round the clock care, homebased care can be as expensive as a nursing home. Some policies that are advertised as providing home health care in truth unrealistically limit the amount of care provided as well as how much services can cost, effectively guaranteeing that an inadequate level of care will be provided by people with limited skills.

- Check the periodic ratings published by *Consumer Reports* magazine, which takes into consideration many important issues. Back issues, along with a comprehensive subject matter index, are available at many public libraries. ■

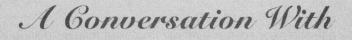

A Conversation With

CECIL STEWART

Cecil Stewart is shown above holding the flag of the Prescott, Arizona Outings Club when he was halfway up Mt. Dhaulagiri in Nepal. Before his retirement, he was a corporate vice president with a Fortune 500 company specializing in food processing and distribution. He lived and worked for many years in the New York City area and then for 17 years in Omaha, Nebraska. Born in 1919, married with three children and five grandchildren, Cecil lives in Prescott, Arizona.

RW: How old were you when you retired from your management job?

CS: Fifty-six. I had planned to retire at 55, but my job was so interesting that I stayed on a little longer.

RW: Where did the idea of early retirement come from?

CS: My father always talked about retiring at 55. He didn't do it, and died of a heart attack at 56. I guess I was influenced by him and by the fact that there were so many things I wanted to do in life. Retiring early was the only way I would have the time I needed to do many of these things.

RW: Does that mean that in your 30s or 40s you had a clear idea of what you would do when you retired?

CS: Not at all. But I knew I was interested in and curious about all sorts of things, and I had a strong sense that there would be plenty to do.

RW: Well, you've now been retired 20 years; has that proven true?

CS: Yes. In fact, I still often feel a sense of frustration that I just don't have enough time to do many of the things I'm interested in doing.

RW: Let's go back 20 years. How did you end up in Prescott, Arizona, and how did you get launched on your retirement?

CS: My parents had moved to Phoenix in 1946 and, visiting them, I fell in love with Arizona. So, when we started thinking of retirement, my wife and I investigated several small cities and picked Prescott. We wanted to be away from a big city, but not live in a dedicated retirement community with nothing but older people. Prescott is both a nice area and a real city—older people are just part of the mix.

RW: When you moved to Prescott, I gather you basically didn't know anyone. How did you fit in?

CS: I taught management part-time at a nearby community college, joined the Rotary Club and got involved in outdoor activities. My wife and I joined the church and she became active in several organizations, including PEO, an international sorority that supports women's education nationally and internationally and contributes to local charities. Prescott is a very friendly place, and we had no trouble being accepted—for example, in less than six months, we had a party with over 50 guests.

RW: What else did you do to stay busy?

CS: Before long, both my wife and I were involved with several nonprofit organizations, serving on the board of directors and so on. Also, we've become involved in a hiking club. This led not only to making friends but to going hiking and camping all over the Southwest. In addition, my wife and I wanted to see the world. We began a series of travels that has taken us lots of places in South America, Africa, New Guinea, China, the former Soviet Union, Nepal, Europe and so on.

Partially as a result of travel, I got interested first in cameras and then video. I've created 18 different visual presentations based on my travels, which I present to organizations interested in travel, hiking, cameras or at the public library. All together, I guess I've put on 250 or so presentations about our travels.

RW: You mentioned video. Do you do your own editing?

CS: Yes. I have good editing equipment that allows me to take the raw film and create a pretty tight show, including voice-overs and background music, to explain what's going on.

RW: If I asked you to list the things that have made your retirement fulfilling, what would you put first?

CS: First, having a good marriage to a strong independent person with whom I share a number of interests. There are many things we like to do together, but we also give each other freedom to pursue individual interests.

Second, the pleasure I get from my three children and five grandchildren. My wife and I are extremely lucky that two of our children have chosen to live nearby, in Prescott, so we see them often.

I guess my third greatest satisfaction is being a real part of the community, in the sense that I know many active, interesting people of all ages who are important to Prescott. I'm proud to be a little part of how the city works.

And I suppose fourth on my list would be my outdoor activities—travel, photography, hiking and the many interesting people I've met doing these things. For example, as part of a Rotary program to India, we lived with Indian families for a month. My wife and I have also developed friendships in Japan, Chile and France, although, oddly, we became good friends with the Frenchman while traveling in Russia. I guess I can sum up by saying it's important to me to be busy doing interesting things.

RW: So far you've listed four major areas of life, but you haven't mentioned money or anything to do with finances.

CS: I've been very lucky not to have to worry about it much. When we first married, my wife and I decided to set up a budget and set aside 10% for retirement.

RW: Did that include money you could expect from company pensions?

CS: Early in my career, I had no pension. But later, when I did become eligible for a good plan, we still saved 10% over and above that.

RW: You stuck to it no matter what?

CS: Yes. And one of the reasons we decided to retire to Prescott from the Chicago area, where we had been living, was that it allowed us to cut our expenses by almost half.

RW: So money hasn't been a problem.

CS: Right. And after retirement, two additional things contributed to this: One, my wife and I are both fairly frugal by nature, and that has continued, so we actually have lived very comfortably without spending a lot. And second, after retirement I had more time to manage our investments, and got into some good growth stocks, which have done well. But as an aside, I would also say that we have many retired friends who are not affluent but who lead very interesting, active lives. Money is important to a good retirement, but by no means all important.

RW: You also didn't mention health on your list. You and your wife both seem to enjoy excellent health. Did you think about taking care of your health early in life so you would hopefully remain healthy after you retired?

CS: Not consciously, but when I hit 40, I saw that I would need to exercise to stay in shape. So I figured out a fairly rigorous exercise program with calisthenics and have carried it on ever since.

RW: You were conscious of getting older and doing something to slow down the process?

CS: I wanted to do so many things in life, and I realized I would have to stay fit to do them.

RW: Obviously, you are very close to your family, and that bond has a lot to do with your feeling good about life. Did it occur to you when you were 35 or 50 that your family would be so important later in life?

CS: No. They were always very important to me and I tried to make the time commitment to do things together as a family, so we would be close, but I really never thought about the pleasures it would bring me when I was older. But now, of course, I'm very conscious of how lucky I am. And I also know that, should my wife or I become ill or frail, my family really can be counted on to help. However, we would never want to be dependent on them.

RW: Is there anything else you would say to a person who has just begun to think about retirement?

CS: Be sure to develop lots of interests outside of work. Too many people stop working and don't know what to do with themselves, and so die early. You need to have a strong sense that the world is a fascinating place and that there are lots of interesting things to do. I'm lucky that, in an average week, my various hiking, community, church, camera and other activities mean I interact with at least 50 people, most of them active and interesting. But of course, I'm not unique—anyone can cultivate lots of interests and learn new skills. As I said earlier, my only real frustration is that I never seem to have enough time to fit in everything I want to do. ■

Chapter 8

How Much Money Will You Need When You Retire?

"I deem myself a wealthy man because my income exceeds my expenses and my expenses equal my desires."

—Edward Gibbon

Articles in the daily press, commentaries by financial planners and "retirement kits" published by mutual fund and insurance companies all tell us that to live comfortably after retirement we will need a big annual income for at least 30 years. Since many of us have no hope of ever saving the megabucks needed to produce this yearly cornucopia, the main effect of these messages is to make us anxious. Fortunately, these "you'll need at least $1 million to retire happily" articles more accurately reflect the biases of the investment industry than they do the spending patterns of real retirees. As a result, they significantly exaggerate the amount you'll really need to save and spend.

If you have any doubt as to whether you can enjoy a fulfilling retirement without being a millionaire, try to remember the last time you read a retirement finance analysis written by a frugal retired person with no connection to a company selling mutual funds or insurance. Probably never. But if you ever do, I predict it will emphasize that the best ways to prepare for a fulfilling life after retirement have little to do with making yourself rich.

A Closer Look at the Retirement Industry

Although possibly exaggerated, you may be thinking that many personal finance articles which advocate saving and investing large sums for retirement are nevertheless basically well-reasoned. Look under the hood. Almost every article or website calculator I've ever looked at starts with the hugely unrealistic assumption that to live comfortably after retirement, you'll need to spend 70%–80% of your highest working years' income. Many follow with a second big fib: That the income you'll receive from Social Security will meet only a tiny fraction of your post-retirement needs. (The more ridiculous articles even predict Social Security's total demise.) And as if telling two whoppers isn't bad enough, lots of commentators continue with a third piece of startlingly poor advice: It's foolhardy to base one's retirement planning on the assumption of inheriting or being given even one penny.

Fortunately, if you correct even one of these false assumptions—for example, you assume that, like most retirees, you can actually get along just fine on 40% to 60% of your pre-retirement income—you will find that your projected financial retirement picture looks far brighter. And if you correct two or more, you are almost sure to feel more relaxed (and less guilty) the next time you order a mocha instead of putting the money in your piggy bank.

If it's really possible to retire comfortably on less money than the financial industry claims, it's fair to ask why supposedly independent financial journalists so often echo the retirement industry's scare stories about the sad fate awaiting poor and unhappy retired people. Or to ask the same question more bluntly, why are we constantly confronted with personal finance articles which predict that Americans who fail to save large sums are at high risk of living out their days munching pet food in a skid row hotel? At least some of the answer can be found by taking a look at who buys the advertisements in personal finance magazines. To do this as accurately as possible, I asked Cheryl Woodard, a prominent magazine consultant (www.publishingbiz.com) and author of *Starting & Running a Successful Newsletter or Magazine* (Nolo), to take a look at who advertised in typical issues of *Kiplinger's Personal Finance* and *Smart Money*. Armed with the latest advertising rates from Standard Rate and Data Services, here is what Woodard found:

> *Over 88% of the ads in the May 2000* Kiplinger's Personal Finance *were for retirement-related financial products and services. Assuming this is a typical issue, and figuring in ad revenue from their website, I estimate that* Kiplinger's Personal Finance *takes in about $34 million from the retirement industry. The May 2000 issue of* Smart Money *contained about 101 pages of advertisements, with about 56% touting retirement industry products and services. (Most of the other ads were for luxury goods targeted at affluent older people.)*

I don't suggest that either of these publications uses their feature articles to push the products of their advertisers. To the contrary, I think both are scrupulous to avoid even the appearance of this type of impropriety. But as someone who has spent most of his adult life in publishing, I can guarantee that no magazine would long survive if it followed an editorial policy that wasn't broadly consistent with the views of its principal advertisers. For example, if I started the *Warner Personal*

Finance Weekly with the goal of reporting on simple living strategies designed to greatly reduce the reader's need to purchase mutual funds and other retirement investments, you can be sure that the financial industry would place their ads elsewhere. Similarly, how long do you think an Internet magazine would stay in business if it consistently ran articles questioning the need to go online?

And it isn't just personal finance publications that have a stake in promoting over-saving. Many of the people who teach financial planning seminars or adult school courses or urge employees to fully fund their 401(k) plans make the lion's share of their income by selling financial services and products to clients. Check this out by making it a habit to look at the teacher's biography included in most descriptions of financial planning courses (or the "About the Author" information at the bottom of retirement advice articles). You'll find that many read more or less like this: "Joan Smith is a registered financial planner with an office in New Delphi, Texas, specializing in retirement planning, and author of *Ten Savvy Ways to Die Rich*."

Be Wary of One-Size-Fits-All Financial Advice

Read closely and you'll see that many articles about investing for retirement begin by claiming that millions of people are at high risk of becoming destitute in their old age. Then, in paragraph two, the author typically goes on to discuss how much income a retiree will need to maintain a second home, travel the world, eat at lovely restaurants and pay dues at social clubs.

A big reason for this schizophrenic approach to retirement advice is that the writer is trying to simultaneously pitch her message to people with vastly different incomes and expectations. In the first sentence, she is discussing the potential financial problems of ordinary working people, some of whom may in fact be at risk of a financially insecure retirement unless they embark upon a sensible savings and investment plan. In the next, she is addressing upper-middle-income people whose only retirement worry will be whether they can finally afford to step up from a Buick to a BMW.

Keep in mind two points whenever you come across a piece of retirement advice:

- There is a huge difference between the income it will take to meet your honest retirement needs and how much you'll need to lead an affluent lifestyle (buy everything you want).
- Assuming you agree that many, if not most, elements of a good retirement really can't be bought, it follows that it only makes sense to save and invest enough to be able to purchase what you really need. Or put another way, it's just plain bonkers to sacrifice important present needs (for example, to live a healthier lifestyle) so you can afford luxuries later.

And now let me briefly address those readers who think it makes sense to scare themselves silly with exaggerated stories about the prospect of an impoverished retirement if it results in their socking away more money. Slow down. No question, it's wise to plan to save enough money to maintain a modestly comfortable lifestyle after you retire; but it's wrong to assume that saving fearfully or blindly is better than not saving at all. Far better to take the little bit of time and energy necessary to follow these three steps:

1. Arrive at a realistic assessment of how much income you'll really need after retirement. (I show you how in the rest of this short chapter.)
2. Calculate how much income you are likely to receive from Social Security and other reasonably assured sources of income such as a pension. (The next chapter will teach you the basics of accomplishing this.)
3. Adopt a plan to close any retirement savings gap. (This is where Chapters 10 and 11 come in.)

If you don't take this rational approach, you are at high risk of making one of three big mistakes:

- Not saving enough for retirement
- Sacrificing your own and your family's present needs on the altar of creating an overlarge or inappropriate retirement fund
- Adopting a schizoid plan that ends up doing a little of both.

How Much Retirement Savings Is Enough?

Retirement planning is best done with a dash of black humor. That's because, no matter what the retirement industry claims, it's impossible to predict with anything approaching accuracy how much you or anyone else really needs to save. For example, unless you are currently in the last stages of a terminal illness or plan to poison yourself next Friday, you can't know how long you will live or how healthy your mind and body will be in your retirement years, both essential facts to accurately determine how much money you'll need.

True, actuarial tables predict that, at 65, the average retired man can expect to live about 20 more years, and the average retired woman, 23. So what? Even if the world avoids a killer flu, a nuclear catastrophe or a colliding comet, all these tables really tell us is that half of us will live to be older than 85 or 88 and half will die younger—some much younger. To make this same point in a more down-to-earth-way, if you live until you're 106 and spend your last 25 years in a pricey nursing home, you will obviously need piles more retirement income than if you are run over by a truck at age 62, three years before you retire. Of course, this is where your sense of humor needs to kick in, since if you fall victim to the accident scenario, every penny you have struggled to save would have been better spent on a trip to Paris.

The question of how much more you will need after retirement is further complicated by your own huge information gap. Since you haven't yet retired, you plain don't know what your month-to-month income needs will be. And because all information you have on the subject is secondhand, you are likely to feel at least somewhat insecure about any conclusions you reach. The result of this "retirement anxiety" is that you are likely to err on the side of saving too much.

Perhaps this point is best made if you compare the process of making retirement-related decisions to planning your first trip to an exotic foreign country. As a result of understandable travel anxiety, chances are you over packed and maybe even overestimated how much money you needed to bring along. No big deal. Bringing along that extra suitcase or a few too many traveler's checks surely did you little harm. Just the same, on your second trip chances are you took along less and were probably relieved not to have to lug that extra bag. Of course, my point is that exactly the same lesson can be applied to retirement. If you got to retire twice, chances are the second time your preparation would emphasize maintaining good health, developing a strong friendship and family network and cultivating new interests, as opposed to concentrating on saving lots of money—much of which you likely won't need.

A FRUGAL RETIREMENT MAY FIT YOU PERFECTLY

Consider the possibility that when retirement time arrives, you may be content to substantially reduce your present rate of consumption. If you doubt this, make a mental list of the retired people you know who you respect most. Then, ask a few of them how much money they spend each month. I'm willing to bet that a number of them live comfortably but modestly.

Many Middle-Class Retirees Don't Need All Their Money

In writing this book, I've talked to hundreds of retirees, and asked lots of people in their 40s and 50s about their parents' retirement financial situations. Although most of the people I interviewed consider themselves to be members of the broad middle class, the great majority thought that they (or their parents) had enough money to live decently. And this was true even though the amount of their (or their parents') annual income varied from about $20,000 to over $200,000.

Again, the fascinating thing was that no matter where the retired people fall in this wide income range, the overwhelming majority reported that they have enough money to cover their immediate financial needs. Even more surprisingly, instead of invading the savings they had accumulated at retirement, many report that they have actually saved more money or, in some instances, given part of their surplus away. And lest you think the people I've talked to are unrepresentative of retirees generally, an article in *The New York Times* entitled "Retired and Still Saving," by Carol Cropper (October 1, 1995), points out that it is common for older people who already have more than enough money to continue to save.

When I asked a number of retirees why they saved lots more money for retirement than they really needed, they responded in a number of ways, including:

- "I (we) just spend a lot less than we thought we would, and so our savings continue to grow."
- "If I want something, I buy it, but I just don't want that many things."
- "Wastefulness appalls me. I get pleasure from not consuming unneeded things."
- "Hey, maybe I'll live to 100, in which case I will be glad I am still a compulsive saver."
- "Giving money to my children while I'm alive—and planning to leave them a comfortable inheritance—is a pleasure worth saving for."

Yet another difficulty with trying to determine how much you need to save for retirement is the fact that the rate of inflation—something even the wisest economist can't predict with accuracy—will affect the future value of money. If recent history is a guide, the value of a dollar (how much it will buy) will continue to drop, meaning that you'll need more dollars in the year 2020 or 2030 to maintain your current standard of living. Of course, you already know that. The big question is how much inflation will erode the value of your retirement savings. For example, if inflation averages 3% for the next 20 years, a dollar in the year 2000 will be worth 54¢ in 2020, meaning you will need to save $90,306 to be able to buy the same amount $50,000 will buy today. No problem, this isn't hard to plan for. But who can be sure inflation will average 3% over the next few decades? After all, during the 1990s and so far in our new decade it has averaged significantly less, but in most recent decades it was higher. In short, any savings plan you make based on a 3% inflation rate will likely be considerably off the mark unless you modify it as you go along.

Estimating Your Retirement Needs

Granted, many variables affect how much money any of us will really need after retirement, including the length of our life, our health after retirement, our future spending habits and the rate of inflation. Against this background of rampant uncertainty, it's fair to ask whether it's even possible to sensibly plan for retirement. I believe the answer is yes, but only if you start with your own common-sense experience of life and keep your planning simple. For example, instead of making lots of guestimates about various inflationary scenarios or considering the pros and cons of a dozen hard-to-understand investments, you'll do far better to start your retirement planning by asking yourself a simple question: How does my family get along financially today?

If your answer is that you're currently living within your income and possibly saving a little to boot, it will be easy to roughly estimate how much income you'll need to maintain a similar lifestyle after retirement. Doing this involves following these commonsensical steps:

Step 1. Guess how long you are likely to live after you retire. (You'll doubtless want to discount the possibility that the Earth will be pulverized, boiled or frozen, or that all the people on it will be annihilated by glutinous creatures from deep space.)

Step 2. Figure out how much you currently spend each year after taxes and savings are deducted.

Step 3. Subtract from this amount any expenditures, such as paying for your mortgage, commuting or helping with kids' education expenses, that you will no longer need to make after you retire.

Step 4. Subtract any anticipated annual savings you will achieve by taking advantage of senior discounts and otherwise purchasing needed items for less.

Step 5. Add the annual cost of items you don't pay for now but are likely to need after retirement. One of these will likely be more expensive medicine. Others might be expenditures for travel or other leisure activities you currently have little time for.

Step 6. Figure how much yearly income you will receive from Social Security, pensions and other assured sources.

Step 7. To determine how much additional money you will need each year, subtract:

- the income figure you just arrived at in Step 6
- from the amount you expect to spend per year as computed in Step 5.
  (Obviously, if your Step 6 number is larger than your Step 5 number, you have no retirement savings gap.)

EXAMPLE: In Step 6 you estimated you will receive $30,000 annually in Social Security and pensions. But in Step 5 you estimated that to live comfortably you'll need income of $45,000 each year. Obviously, to close this gap each year, you'll need to plan to come up with an additional $15,000 (in 2000 dollars).

Step 8. Adjust for inflation the number you came up with in Step 7. (Again, this is the annual dollar amount you'll need to close the gap between your assured income and the amount you would like to spend.)

Step 9. Identify the source, or sources, of the additional money you'll need to produce the yearly income you have just determined to be necessary.

Saving and investing money in retirement plans is one way to provide the money you'll need, but as I discuss in Chapter 9, there are many others.

At this point you may be ready to zone out, figuring that making all these calculations is more trouble than it's worth. Hang in there a little longer—with the help of the short worksheet which appears later in this chapter, you really can come up with a very decent estimate of how much annual income you'll need. And best of all, you can do it in less than an hour. To help motivate you to actually pick up the pencil and invest the hour, this chapter discusses the first five steps in more detail; the rest are covered in the next three chapters.

⚠ IF YOU ARE IN DEBT AND HAVE FEW ASSETS, WORK ON YOUR IMMEDIATE PROBLEMS FIRST

If you are currently awash in debt, before you can realistically plan to save for retirement you need to get your current financial mess under control. For an excellent source of information on your legal situation, see *Money Troubles: Legal Strategies to Cope With Your Debts*, by Robin Leonard (Nolo). And once you fully understand the problems you face, do something about them following the advice in *Credit Repair*, by Robin Leonard (Nolo).

Step 1. Estimate how long you'll live.

No fun here, I'm afraid, since few of us enjoy contemplating our own mortality. My suggestion is that most reasonably healthy middle-aged men pick age 90, and women 94, unless for some health reason you are pretty sure you won't live that long. That's enough longer than the average person's life expectancy at age 65, which is about 20 years for men and 23 for women, to contain a decent safety margin. True, there are currently 52,000 Americans age 100 or over, but your chances of living to this age are so low that, in my opinion at least, it makes little sense to increase one's savings based on this possibility.

Step 2. Determine how much you spend now.

Start by pulling out last year's federal tax return and looking at your after-tax income (any money contributed to a tax-deferred retirement plan will already have been subtracted). Then subtract any money you put into additional savings or gave away (to your kids or to charity, it makes no difference). Your total should more or less reflect what it costs you to live now.

Step 3. Subtract expenses you won't have after retirement.

Now here is some good news. Lots of the expenses you have in midlife will go away later. Indeed, a big reason why many people will have less difficulty than they imagine saving an adequate retirement nest egg is that by their mid-50s their houses will be paid for, meaning that lots of money can be diverted to savings.

Why You'll Need More Money If You Don't Own a House

Close to 80% of Americans will be homeowners before they retire. But if you are a life-long renter, or you will not have paid off your mortgage at retirement, you'll face a bigger job when it comes to saving an adequate amount for your retirement. Instead of enjoying the relatively low-cost housing of their mortgage-free homeowner friends, renters and people who still have mortgages will still need to buy shelter each month. And it's a safe bet this amount won't go down just because they're retired.

One good alternative for life-long renters is to consider the possibility of giving up a relatively expensive apartment after retirement and instead spending less to rent a room from, or share a house with, a retired home-owner. A number of senior groups around the country help broker these arrangements, which can often result in renting pleasant, affordable accommodations, with the bonus of a little human contact thrown in. Another possibility for low-income seniors is to rent in a rent-subsidized senior housing project. (See the conversation with Hazel Peterson following Chapter 5.)

Fortunately, lower housing costs are not the only source of big savings at, or often well before, retirement. As anyone who has ever paid for bikes, braces and a college education well knows, when children grow up and finally leave the nest, expenses go down—often as much as 15% to 20%. No question, this is an area of serious savings, since a teenager who goes to public school costs the typical middle-class family about $8,000–$10,000 per year. While some of the money you no longer spend on your children may still be needed to pay off loans you incurred for their educations, you should nevertheless be able to live comfortably on considerably less.

> **EXAMPLE:** Joan is a single mother raising two children. She earns $44,000 per year and receives $10,000 in child support. By budgeting maniacally, she barely makes ends meet. About 20% of her after-tax income of $47,500, or $9,500, covers the monthly mortgage payment on her small two-bedroom house. Another 5% is used to pay for real estate taxes and homeowner's insurance, which, of course, will not go away even after the house itself is paid for. Since Joan's mortgage will be retired at least five years before she does (and she may want to sell her house and move to a less costly area), she will enjoy a big drop in housing costs when she retires.
>
> A sizable chunk of Joan's remaining income is spent on her two children. Although Joan doesn't track every expenditure, she is sure she spends more than what she receives in child support. Long before Joan reaches retirement age, she plans to have her children out of the nest. So even though child support will stop when the children reach 18, meaning that her income will drop, Joan will still enjoy a significant net savings when her children are on their own. Even without counting other savings her retirement may bring, Joan figures that, by age 65, she will need about $32,000 in pre-tax income, or a little more than 59% of what she receives now.

Step 4. Estimate senior discounts and other savings.

Other expenses that usually go down significantly for retired people include:

- **Transportation.** People who no longer commute regularly often save at least $100–$200 per month, and sometimes more. Remember, if you rely on your car to get to work, you'll not only save a pile in gasoline and maintenance costs, tolls and parking, but your car will last years longer.

This alone will produce big savings, since the total cost of purchasing a new car (especially compared with what you could have earned by investing the money you had to spend) is obviously huge. The U.S. Bureau of Labor Statistics finds that the average person under 65 spends $5,625 on transportation each year, but that an older person spends an average of only $2,863. And after age 80, this amount is likely to be still lower.

- **Entertainment and leisure activities.** Generous discounts for seniors on entertainment, travel, lodging, meals and recreation continue to proliferate and can add up to significant savings. For example, compare how much it costs a 45-year-old to play golf at a public course on a weekend with what it costs for a retired person to play the same course on a Tuesday morning. At many courses, you'll find the senior pays as much as 70% less. Or compare what it costs for a retired person to go to a late afternoon movie to what younger adults pay for a non-discounted evening ticket. In lots of theaters, a senior will pay about $2, while the standard adult price is $7. Savings like this are so significant that they are one major reason why the U.S. Bureau of Labor Statistics estimates that the average person over 65 spends well less than half as much on entertainment when compared to an average person under 65.

- **Savings.** In the last ten to 15 years before retirement, many Americans who have already paid off their houses and fledged their children save 10%-20% of their income, an amount they will no longer need to save once their retirement nest egg is large enough.

Golfer Jim Saves a Bundle

Jim spent most of his career as a well-paid executive for a major pharmaceutical company. When he was 55, Jim's company merged with a larger competitor, and he was given a chance to retire early with a fairly generous severance package.

Before retirement, Jim, an avid golfer, played at a private club near an East Coast city. Not only had Jim paid $20,000 to join (only half of which was refunded when he left), but yearly fees, meals and tips cost him an additional $7,500.

After retiring, Jim and his wife moved to Durango, Colorado, where Jim planned to work in real estate part-time. In Durango, Jim was able to play at a lovely public course (at least as good as his former club's course). A full year's unlimited senior membership card cost him less than $500.

- **House-related expenses.** Many older people move to a smaller house or condo, often in a less-expensive part of the U.S., or sometimes even to a country such as Mexico where costs are a small fraction of those in the U.S. This means property taxes, homeowner's insurance and costs for repairs and maintenance decrease, sometimes substantially. And in many areas of the country, seniors can elect to postpone property taxes until the house is sold or they die, at which point their estate pays them.

EXAMPLE: Jerry and Alice Lincoln owned a small house near Seattle. Although both worked hard (Jerry at a supermarket, Alice at a restaurant), their combined yearly income never exceeded $50,000. Having cheerfully incurred the costs of raising three children, the Lincolns had saved very little by the time they retired. But fortunately, their house, which was paid for, was decently located and worth over $300,000. In part to fulfill a long-held dream to get out of the city and in part to put some money into investments, the Lincolns sold the house soon after their retirement and moved to a small town in eastern Washington. There they were able to purchase a nice piece of land and an almost new double-wide trailer for less than $60,000. Taxes, insurance and upkeep for the trailer were less than 35% of what they had paid for the same items near Seattle.

- **Clothing.** From observing my older friends, it's my guess that most people begin to spend a little less on clothing in their late 60s and then gradually cut back more through their middle 70s and 80s. Corroboration for this observation comes from the U.S. Bureau of Labor Statistics, which in its 1990 survey of consumer expenditures found that the average expenditure of persons under 65 for clothing and related services, such as dry cleaning, was about $1,500. After 65, this expenditure dropped to $755, and after 75 to $434. These savings are usually achieved in two ways:
  - Retired people don't need to purchase a work wardrobe.
  - Having extra time means it's much easier to buy most or all of one's clothing on sale or to otherwise search out good deals.
- **Income taxes.** Although it's impossible to predict what state and federal tax rates will be in the future (and no one knows whether, and under what circumstances, Social Security income will be taxed), it's nevertheless reasonable to assume that if your income drops fairly substantially after you retire, so, too, will your marginal tax rate. In short, you'll keep a substantially higher percentage of what you take in than you do now.

Step 5. Add additional costs you are likely to incur after retirement.

Wouldn't it be great if all your post-retirement expenditures decreased? Although, as we have just seen, overall you'll almost surely spend less than you now do, several types of expenditures may increase. These are the most likely:

- **Adult children may need your financial help.** Obviously, if you have a mentally or physically handicapped child who will continue to need financial assistance as an adult, or you were so late building your nest that your chicks are still in it when you retire, your child-rearing costs will continue, at least for a while.
- **Extensive travel.** Because of discounts, frequent flier programs and the ability to travel at off-peak times, many seniors—especially those who are willing to bypass luxury hotels and restaurants—find they can cover loads of exciting ground at a relatively modest cost. For example, through organizations such as Elderhostel, which sponsors reasonably priced educational travel programs, many seniors are delighted to find that it costs far less to

see and learn about the world than they had budgeted. And by working with one of several organizations that broker house trades, it's even possible to arrange to spend a month or more living in another country with no expense for lodging. Still, it will obviously cost something if you plan to spend your retirement years trotting around the globe. But consider that your urge to travel may not last as long as you do. Despite the message of the famous old song, after you've seen Paris a few times in your 60s or 70s, you may be quite content to stay down on the farm in your later years.

- **Health care.** Depending on your health and that of your spouse, you are likely to spend more for health care as you age. Today, many retirees who are in their 60s and 70s and are in decent health get by supplementing free Medicare coverage with a reasonably priced "medi-gap" insurance policy. But chances are also good that you'll spend more for medicines and unreimbursed medical care than you do now. And medical care may be more costly in the future, as there is a good chance that Medicare benefits will become less generous, especially for retirees who have higher incomes. And if you or your spouse needs long-term care, your expenses will definitely go up. (See Chapter 7 for more on how to think about and plan for the possibility you or your spouse will need expensive long-term care.)

If you haven't already done so, it's time to put the information you've developed in this chapter together in order to make a rough estimate of how much income you'll really need after retirement. If you are typical, you'll probably find that in retirement you can live comfortably on as little as 40% to 60% of your pre-retirement income. But there is no substitute for crunching the numbers yourself, using the worksheet below.

HOW MUCH MONEY WILL YOU NEED WHEN YOU RETIRE?

Current annual living expenses
(after-tax income minus savings and gifts) $ _____

Annual expenses you probably won't have after retirement

     mortgage   –$ _____

     child-related expenses   –$ _____

     work-related transportation   –$ _____

     work-related clothing and other
     expenses   –$ _____

     taxes (based on your lower income)   –$ _____

     other   –$ _____

Additional expenses after retirement

     travel   +$ _____

     health care costs   +$ _____

     other   +$ _____

Income you'll need each year   = $ _____

EXAMPLE 1: Phil and Eve Gold currently spend about $67,000 annually. To arrive at their likely retirement spending, they subtract the $16,000 per year they currently spend on the mortgage, since it will be paid off eight years before they plan to retire. They subtract another $15,000 for costs currently attributable to their two teenage children. Finally, they subtract $5,000 for post-retirement savings they anticipate to achieve by driving less, eliminating work-related expenses and taking advantage of senior discounts. To this total of $31,000 they add $5,000 to cover costs for increased travel and health care. Their total annual anticipated retirement spending in 2000 dollars is $36,000 per year.

EXAMPLE 2: Let's now return to Joan, the single mother of two, who we met earlier in this chapter. Joan's current expenditures are about $47,500. To adjust for the fact that, at retirement, she will have no more child-rearing costs, Joan subtracts $13,000 from the $47,500 and arrives at $34,500. From this amount she subtracts the $9,500 she currently pays for her mortgage, for a total of $25,000. Then, guessing that she can probably save an additional $2,000 per year in transportation and clothing costs, and by taking advantage of senior discounts, Joan concludes that she'll need after-tax income of $23,000 to live comfortably, assuming this will purchase as much as it does in 2000. To this Joan adds $3,000 for travel and $2,000 to cover the possibility that her medical costs will be higher. Although Joan can't predict exactly how much her income taxes will be after she retires, she makes an educated guestimate that income of $32,000 should be enough to pay them and still produce the $28,000 she'll need to live comfortably.

Don't worry, I haven't forgotten about inflation—and you shouldn't, either. Assuming money will buy less in the years ahead, retirees will obviously need more than they would in 2000 dollars to achieve their financial goals. But as I discuss in the next chapters, inflation shouldn't present most retirees with an insurmountable problem since Social Security—a major source of income for most retirees—automatically increases with the cost of living. No question, because some other sources of future income are not similarly indexed, it makes sense to develop good investment strategies so that your retirement savings will grow faster than inflation. But especially if inflation stays anywhere near its current low rate, this shouldn't prove difficult to do. (See Chapter 11 for more on this.) ∎

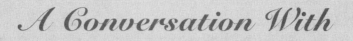

A Conversation With

AFTON CROOKS

Born in 1926, Afton Crooks grew up in Seattle and graduated from the University of Washington. She enjoyed an interesting and challenging career in higher education, mostly as senior administrator at the University of California. Afton retired in 1990, and was widowed in 1992.

RW: We're sitting in a charming little house, built in the backyard of a much bigger 75-year-old house not far from the University of California campus in Berkeley. It's a pleasant neighborhood of young professionals, academics and graduate students. So, Afton, let me start by asking, how did you come to live here?

AC: The house my husband and I had lived in for 40 years on a high ridge above Berkeley, where we enjoyed open space and a wonderful view of the Golden Gate, burned to the ground in the big Oakland fire of October 1991, along with over 3,000 other homes. Two months later, my husband Jim suddenly died.

RW: One day you and your husband were enjoying the first years of your retirement in a home the two of you had created over most of your adult lives, and then, almost overnight, you had nothing but the clothes on your back and a cat.

AC: Yes, and you have to understand that our house was really the center of our universe. We had totally remodeled it over the years, doing much of the work ourselves. We had a large library with many first editions, which my husband found in used bookstores, plus a lovely music collection and a lot of original art. When it was suddenly gone, we moved to a nearby town with friends, but it was too far from what we knew. Finally, we found this lovely little cottage house only a mile or two down the hill from where we used to be. Things were looking up until Jim collapsed and, after massive surgery, died. So, yes, I was left here with a house, mostly unfurnished, and a pussycat.

RW: What did you do first?

AC: I badly needed a place that felt like home, so I immediately set out to create a beautiful environment.

RW: Why didn't you rebuild on the ridge, like so many others? I assume your house was insured.

AC: Before he died, Jim and I decided not to rebuild. In the dry season, the coastal hills are extremely vulnerable to fire. We had escaped through the flames once before, in the 1970s. We just felt it was too much to rebuild only to face another loss. And Jim was frankly concerned about his age. He was a little older than me—too old, he thought, to build a house.

RW: You had planned your retirement and then suddenly your plans were meaningless—what was your survival strategy?

AC: Losing Jim put the loss of the house in perspective. I had a blessed marriage and was very lonely when he died. I told my best friend I felt a lot like I did when I got out of college in Seattle and moved to San Francisco, frightened and starting over. Her response was, "Nonsense, Afton, you've always been independent, always had your own career. You've learned how to cope, and you'll put that knowledge to good use."

RW: Sounds like a wise friend.

AC: Yes, and her advice was fine and good, but I still felt fearful. My life had totally changed, and I had no idea what was in front of me.

RW: What were the three most important things you did to cope?

AC: That's easy: I stayed busy, stayed busy, stayed busy—with immediate day-to-day things, such as furnishing the house and spending huge amounts of time sorting out fire insurance problems, including inventorying and pricing every lost object that had been burned. I also spent lots of time with my friends. I reached out to people as I had never done in my life. I also expanded my work with several nonprofit environmental organizations and got to know my neighbors, especially some of the children. One big decision I made was not to make any major decisions for a year. I just wanted to do things that would get me though life a day or week at a time.

RW: Here in this busy campus neighborhood, you were suddenly living around children.

AC: That's been great. There were four children living in the front house. I appointed myself gardener and, as a result, spent time in the yard with the children. I especially became friends with the eight-year-old boy, named Jason. It was greatly therapeutic.

RW: The biggest thing about your retirement has obviously been surprise—both bad and good. Assuming lots of middle-aged people will experience more changes than they expect when they retire, what would you say if a 48-year-old friend called up and asked for your advice about retirement?

AC: I'm not sure I would be the best person to ask. In the years before I retired, I was frightened at the prospect of my own retirement. I had worked since I was 15, had liked it and didn't particularly want to give it up. Also, I had the example of my dad, who retired badly—he just sat down, gave up and vegetated. But I guess my message to a person who hasn't yet retired would be to develop lots of interests, because you'll need them. I like to hike, garden, swim and bird-watch, to mention just a few of my own interests, and these have helped me greatly to stay active. Recently, I went to the northern Minnesota woods with a friend and hiked several miles a day. And I swim regularly, each year making sure I can still swim as many laps as I am old—I call them birthday laps. This year, I got on a roll and did six extra. But of course, the key isn't what you do, it's to stay mentally and physically active. You can read or garden or do whatever else interests you, but if you're in midlife, don't put all your eggs in one basket, especially if that basket is work-related. Try different things until you find something that fits. When I gave up technical mountain climbing at about age 40, I replaced it with birding.

RW: You had lots of interests before you retired. Could you have developed them later?

AC: I don't know, but it's a mistake to find out. Don't wait until your mid-60s to discover new interests. If you do, you may find you have forgotten how to become interested in new things. Also, make sure at least some of your interests are your own and not tied to your spouse. You absolutely need to be an independent person.

RW: Afton, you've really covered two subjects—interests and exercise.

AC: I guess so. It certainly helps to be in good health, and one should work to maintain it. I've had progressive arthritis for years, which means it's all the more important for me to stay active. For example, I do strength and stretch exercises for 30 minutes every morning. I refuse to give in to it.

RW: Great, but remember, you are still advising a 48-year-old on retirement. What else would you focus on?

AC: Assuming the person was married, I would emphasize that no matter how close you are to your spouse, you also need friends, at least a couple of people you are really close to. I don't mean business colleagues or acquaintances, but intimate friends who you truly care about. Obviously, this is particularly true for women, who usually outlive their husbands by a number of years. In addition, it's also wise to keep up a good network of other people whose company you enjoy, people who share your interests. In my case, involvement with environmental groups is one place where I meet people who I enjoy.

RW: You have mentioned interests, health and friends. What else?

AC: When I was in my late 40s, I began to focus on my future financial security, and I advise others to do the same. In my case, I really didn't have a choice, since I was a child both of the Depression and of a father who had always emphasized financial self-reliance. At one point, I sat down with a financial advisor to figure out what Jim and I would need after we retired. I had an excellent pension plan from the University of California, plus Social Security, but to be on the safe side, we decided to supplement it with additional savings.

RW: Have you needed all the income your pension plan and savings produced?

AC: No. By choice, I actually live somewhat frugally. And remember, when my house burned down, all my assets suddenly became liquid, which is something I didn't plan on. But back to the point, although many wonderful people never have the opportunity to save much and nevertheless do well when they retire, I believe it's important to have as sound a financial plan as possible, one that in the best case will carry you for the rest of your life. It really is a huge relief not to have to worry about money.

RW: Despite everything that has happened to you in the last few years, you seem remarkably at peace with the world.

AC: I don't know about that. But I would say to a 48-year-old that it's crucial during the middle of your life to really learn to live with yourself, to accept yourself, no matter what others think. No one is perfect, and when it comes right down to it, most of us are a little weird at some level—being able to accept this and not try to cover it up makes it easier to find peace of mind as you get older. Unfortunately, many older people have never learned to live with themselves—to accept themselves—which means they are just plain unhappy, And it's worse to be unhappy when you are old. When you are young, you have a chance to break away from a lifestyle that doesn't fit, as I did when I left an upper-middle-class community, where I was supposed to be a wife and mother, to have a career. But if you don't develop inner toughness during your life, it's not going to be easy to do it later on. ■

Where Will Your Money Come From After Age 65?

"All that is gold does not glitter; not all those that wander are lost."

—J.R.R. Tolkien

If you have read Chapter 8, you should have a pretty good idea of how much annual income you'll need after retirement. The next big question is, how will you get it? Most people come by their retirement income in two or more of the following nine ways:

- Social Security retirement benefits
- Employer-paid pensions (defined benefit plans)
- Tax-advantaged retirement savings plans—Keogh, SEP-IRA, IRA, 401(k), 403(b) and Roth IRA
- Working part- or full-time after retirement
- Savings—including, especially, the significant amounts you can save and invest after age 50 if your kids are on their own and your mortgage is paid off
- Inheritances
- Gifts
- Early retirement bonus or buy-out
- Withdrawing equity from your house.

This chapter looks at each of these income sources in some detail.

Social Security Retirement Benefits

The media loves to print dire predictions that the Social Security system is bankrupt, or soon will be, and that anyone who counts on receiving benefits in ten or 20 years is a fool. Prominent politicians often give credence to these doomsday scenarios by claiming Social Security payments will need to be cut radically before the year 2030, when America will have an unprecedented percentage of its population over age 65.

Don't believe it. Short of our entire planet being cooked by global warming, frozen by a nuclear winter or pulverized by a shower of huge comets (other favorite media horror stories), the Social Security Administration will continue to pay benefits to qualified workers in 2015, 2025 and yes, even 2045, just as it has for the last seven decades. This doesn't mean there will be no changes. To reflect the fact that the average person now lives considerably longer than was true when the Social Security system was established in the 1930s, the age at which workers will become eligible for benefits may creep up slightly. It's already scheduled to go to 66 (for people born after 1943), and may eventually increase to 67 or even 68. And, of course, there has long been pressure for Congress to pass legislation allowing people to invest at least a portion of their Social Security contributions in mutual funds and other investments calculated to increase their eventual benefits while helping the system itself remain solvent. But no matter how much tinkering politicians do, benefit levels, which are currently indexed to the rate of inflation, are highly unlikely to decrease.

If you doubt this, consider that, as baby boomers edge closer to retirement and then begin to retire in big numbers after 2010, the percentage of the population vitally concerned with maintaining adequate Social Security payments will dramatically increase. And because of powerful, well-organized groups such as the AARP, older people have proven easy to inform and mobilize whenever Social Security is threatened. Add to this the fact that retired Americans traditionally vote in much larger numbers than do younger adults, and you can see why Social Security is regarded in Congress as a third-rail issue—that is, one too politically charged to touch.

Think back 25 years, to when suggestions that the Social Security system would soon be bankrupt first began to surface. Instead, payroll taxes were raised, and the program was never really in jeopardy. In fact, the Social Security benefits received by a typical American today buy more than they did two or three decades ago. This is because official government measures of inflation, to which Social Security benefit increases are tied, have overstated the increase in the real cost of living. Put another way, prices actually paid by seniors who shop in warehouse stores and otherwise hunt for bargains have gone up more slowly than the official inflation rate, with the result that Social Security benefits go farther than they used to.

Workers Not Covered by Social Security

Some state and local government employees, most federal workers hired before 1984 and railroad workers are covered under separate pension plans and not by Social Security. Of course, if these employees also worked for a sufficient length of time in another job covered by Social Security, they are eligible for dual benefits. For more information, see *Social Security, Medicare and Pensions*, by Joseph Matthews (Nolo).

How Much Will You Receive?

Assuming you are willing to believe that Social Security benefits will still be flowing when you retire, let's move on to the next big question: How many dollars will the Social Security program put in your pocket each month? It's impossible to tell you exactly, since the amount of your Social Security check will depend on:

- how much you earn over all the years you work
- how much benefits increase in future years as a result of inflation and
- the age at which you retire.

For example, you will get a significantly larger Social Security payment if you have had a relatively hefty income for many years than if your earnings were more modest, in part because you will have paid more dollars into the system.

Getting an Official Estimate of Your Benefit Amount

Typically, you need to work about ten years in jobs covered by Social Security to be eligible for benefits. If you meet this requirement, the amount of your benefits will depend on many factors, including your date of birth and the type of benefit (such as retirement or survivors' benefits) you are eligible for. It will also be influenced by your age at retirement. Currently, you can claim some retirement benefits as early as age 62, but normal retirement age is 65 and is scheduled to increase to 66 for retirees born after 1943.

Fortunately, the Social Security Administration (800-772-1213) has finally recognized that millions of Americans are confused as to how much they'll receive in benefits. That's why they mailed a document called "Your Social Security Statement" in spring 2000. If for some reason you never got this estimate of how much money you'll receive each month after you retire, call 800-772-1213, contact your local Social Security office or go to www.ssa.gov/mystatement. Or you can estimate your benefits by going to www.ssa.gov/retire and clicking on calculators. Again, understanding how much your Social Security check will amount to is a crucial first step in budgeting for retirement.

What percentage of your retirement needs will Social Security contribute? For many people planning to live reasonably frugally after retirement, a rough guestimate is 40% to 60%. Support for this estimate can be found from a number of sources, including the Social Security Administration itself, which recently estimated that income from Social Security averages about 57% of total income for senior households—close to 65% if the richest 20% of retired Americans are eliminated.

EXAMPLE 1: David and Kelly have had a combined average annual salary of about $75,000 over many years. They live comfortably, and both manage to contribute to their 401(k) retirement plans. After taxes and retirement savings, they spend about $50,000 per year. Assuming that by the time they retire in the year 2010, David and Kelly's children will be on their own financially and their mortgage will be paid off, chances are they will be able to live comfortably —but not extravagantly—on $35,000 per year, figured in 2000 dollars. After checking with Social Security, David and Kelly find that they will receive about $1,800 per month or $21,000 per year (in 2000 dollars), which means Social Security will provide about 60% of their anticipated income needs.

EXAMPLE 2: Ted is a single man who rents a studio apartment. His earnings as a substitute teacher at a private school, supplemented by work as a tutor, have varied considerably over the years, but have averaged about $35,000 per year. Despite the fact that Ted has never had a huge salary, he is saving and investing about $3,000 per year and expects to have more than $100,000 by age 65. By careful budgeting, Ted's total monthly expenses are currently about $2,000. Since Ted does not own a house whose mortgage he could eventually pay off, he can't look forward to lower-cost housing after retirement, which means his cost of living will drop only modestly after he retires. Even by taking advantage of senior discounts and shopping more carefully, Ted estimates he will need at least $1,800 per month to maintain his present standard of living, and more if he wants to enjoy a little frugal travel or is hit by unanticipated costs.

Ted's Social Security payments will likely approximate $1,100 per month (in 2000 dollars), only about 55% of what he needs. Fortunately, Ted is in great demand as a tutor, both for high school French and Spanish courses and for students who want extra help preparing for college boards. As a result, he is counting on working part-time for a number of years after age 65. Ted anticipates no difficulty in earning up to $1,500 per month, which means he can continue to add to his savings, which he expects to begin tapping when he reaches his middle or late 70s.

Social Security and Working After Retirement

Lots of misinformation circulates about how working after you begin to receive Social Security savages your benefits. Fortunately, the facts are not so grim. In 2000, legislation was passed eliminating the Social Security earnings limit, meaning that a Social Security recipient 65 or older can now earn an unlimited amount without losing any benefits.

Pensions and Other Retirement Savings Plans

Pensions used to be something you got from your employer after a lifetime of steady work. And many people still receive traditional pension benefits. But for many others, a main source of income after retirement is likely to be their own, individual retirement savings plan, such as an IRA or 401(k) account. This section discusses conventional employer-funded pensions (usually called "defined benefit pension plans"), and the next one discusses individual retirement plans.

Employer Pension Plans

A little over 50% of working Americans participate in some type of pension plan. A few of these will provide only minimal benefits, but many people who work for large corporations or federal, state or local governments stand to receive significant pension income over and above Social Security. If you are eligible for a pension, how much you'll receive will, of course, depend on the details of your particular plan. Typically, the most important factors in determining the size of your monthly check are:

- **How long you work for the employer (or employers, if your pension account was transferable).** The more years of employment, the more you get, which means people who opt for early retirement often get less.
- **How much money you make.** Again, the basic principle is simple—the more you make, the larger your pension. Benefits are commonly based on your pay for the last five years of employment.
- **How benefits can be paid.** Some pensions give you a number of payment options—for example, a lump sum, monthly payments during your life or lower monthly payments during your life but continuing for the life of a survivor. It's important to know what your choices are and get expert help if you are in doubt as to which choice is likely to be best for you and your family.

To estimate how much you will receive, ask your employer for a detailed description of your pension plan that explains participation rules, how benefits accrue and become locked in (vested) as well as payment options and claims procedures. If you don't get good answers, talk to your pension plan administrator. Here are the key questions you'll want answered:

1. **How is the amount of my pension determined?** As mentioned, most plans provide that the amount of your pension depends on how long you worked for your employer and how much you were paid over a designated period of time (often your highest-earning years). But exactly how this works and, therefore, how many dollars you'll receive, varies greatly. Make sure you understand how much you are likely to receive under various scenarios— for example, if you work for the company 25, 30 or 35 years and your pay increases slightly, moderately or substantially.

2. **When does my pension vest?** Under most plans, you have no rights to receive a pension until you work for your employer (or another employer, if your pension rights are transferred) for a certain number of years. At that point, the pension vests, which means you have a legal right to receive benefits. Often your right to at least a modest pension will vest after ten years of service, although some plans provide limited vesting after just five years. To receive a good-sized pension, you'll probably need to work for an employer at least 20 or 30 years.

3. **How does receiving a pension affect my right to receive Social Security?** The answer to this question can be extremely complicated. In a nutshell:

   - Many pensions are completely separate from Social Security. You will receive your entire pension check plus all Social Security benefits for which you are eligible. If you have this type of plan and are fairly well-paid, chances are you'll have all the income you need after retirement.

     EXAMPLE: Enid and Walter McDougal both work at jobs that are covered by pensions that are indexed to increase with inflation. Assuming both continue working for another ten years, their combined pension income will be about $38,000 per year. When combined with the approximately $21,000 they will receive each year from Social Security, the McDougals will enjoy more than adequate retirement income.

   - Some private pension plans are integrated with Social Security. This means your monthly pension check will be reduced by all or some of the amount of your Social Security check. Since 1988, however, even integrated plans must leave you with at least half of your pension check.

- If you work for a state or local government, you may get a good pension but no Social Security. For example, the State of California has its own pension system, and some employees do not pay into Social Security. In addition, most federal government employees hired before 1984 and most railroad workers are covered by separate plans. In this situation, you are covered by Social Security only if you have also worked at another job for the required time.

4. **Will my pension be adjusted for inflation?** Especially for public employees, many plans do index the level of benefits to inflation, meaning that as the value of the dollar goes down, your pension goes up. Unfortunately, lots of pensions do not adjust for inflation, which means the purchasing power of the money you receive is likely to decrease if you live for many years after retirement. Assuming you have a non-indexed pension, a rough way to guestimate how much its value is likely to decline between your retirement and your death is to multiply the amount you expect to receive the first year after you retire by 70%.

Benefits for Disabled Veterans

There are two different benefits available to disabled veterans (you can only collect one of them). "Disability compensation" is available to veterans who are disabled as a result of active military service. Benefits range from $100 to $2,036 per month, depending on the amount of disability. A "pension" is available to low-income, wartime veterans who suffer from a permanent and total disability not incurred during military duty. These pensions run about $800 per month ($950 for a veteran with a spouse). For more information on eligibility and other rules, contact the Veterans Administration and refer to *Social Security, Medicare and Pensions*, by Joseph Matthews (Nolo).

💡 GET HELP IF YOUR EMPLOYER DOESN'T PROVIDE ENOUGH INFORMATION

If you don't get the pension answers you need from your employer, you can get information and assistance about your legal rights and how to assert them from the Pension Rights Center, 918 16th St., NW, Washington, DC 20006, 202-296-3776; fax 202-833-2472; website at www.aoa.dhhs.gov/AOA/dir/210.html.

Voluntary Retirement Plans

Increasingly, many businesses, especially smaller companies, choose not to pay traditional pensions. As a result, workers must save and invest on their own, or not at all. Fortunately, a variety of very desirable voluntary retirement savings plans are available to most small business owners and their workers. And these plans offer tax breaks now as well as retirement income later.

401(k) and 403(b) plans. Many companies now offer their workers a chance to participate in 401(k) plans. And people who work for nonprofit organizations usually have a chance to contribute to very similar 403(b) plans. The big incentive to participate is that the money you contribute to your retirement account is not taxed in the year earned. And almost as good, it continues to accumulate tax-free until you withdraw it, any time after age 59$\frac{1}{2}$ (at which point you do owe income tax in your then-current bracket). Over the years, these dual tax incentives combine to allow you to save far more than would otherwise be possible. (See "Growth of a Taxable vs. Tax-Deferred Account," below.) And of course, these plans are even more desirable if, as is common, your employer makes a contribution.

Growth of a Taxable (Non-Roth) vs. Tax-Deferred Account

Assumptions:
- Investments earn 8% annually
- $5,000 is invested annually in the tax-deferred account
- $3,600 (what's left after $5,000 is taxed at 28%) is invested annually in the non-tax-deferred account
- Income on the non-tax-deferred account is taxed annually at 28%, and recipient does not pay state income tax)

 DON'T FORGET ABOUT IRAS AND ROTH IRAS
Many American workers whose employers don't offer other retirement plans are eligible to contribute up to $2,000 per year, tax-deferred, in an Individual Retirement Account (IRA). Although this doesn't sound like much, it's well worth doing since, like other retirement plans, money accumulates tax-free until withdrawal. And for those who are eligible, contributing to a Roth IRA may be an even better idea. While income tax must be paid on money contributed, no tax is due on investment earnings or, assuming you follow the rules, upon withdrawal.

How much money you'll have in a 401(k) or 403(b) account when you retire depends on several factors:

- How much you contribute each year (currently, the maximum is slightly above $10,000 per year)
- How much, if anything, your employer contributes in matching funds
- How many years you make contributions
- Whether you borrow money from your plan
- How well the investments you choose perform over the years.

EXAMPLE 1: You contribute $5,000 to your 401(k) plan each year beginning at age 45 and your employer adds $500 each year. Your investments enjoy an annual return of 8%. At retirement, 20 years later, you'll have $251,690. Even assuming 3% annual inflation over the next 20 years, this amount will have the same purchasing power that $139,355 would have in 2000. And, of course, it's possible that inflation will be lower, as it was during the 1990s.

EXAMPLE 2: Beginning at age 30, you contribute $4,000 a year to your 401(k) plan, with no employer match. With an average annual return of 10% you'll have about $1.1 million at age 65. And if your average annual return is only 8%, you'll still have $689,300. Adjusted for estimated inflation of 3%, when you are 65, $689,300 will have the same purchasing power as $245,000 does today.

Unfortunately, there is a huge difference between excellent and poor 401(k) plans. Good ones not only offer an employer contribution, but allow employees to invest in a good selection of top-quality stock, bond and money market funds, which charge low fees. Poor plans often limit an employee to a few higher-cost investments and charge high fees to administer the money. The worst plans limit employees to investing in the employer's own stock while charging them relatively high fees for this dubious privilege.

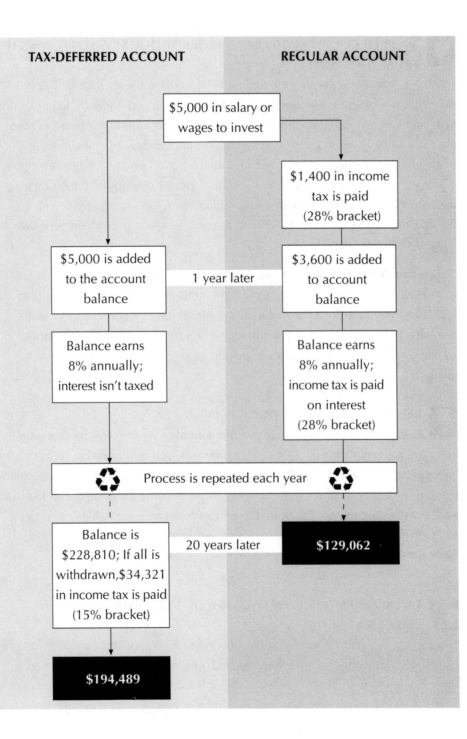

💡 MARRIED COUPLES WHO BOTH WORK SHOULD EVALUATE WHICH 401(K) PLAN IS BEST

The huge disparity between good and bad 401(k) plans means people in solid marriages will want to evaluate which of their plans is best and fully fund that one first. For example, instead of each spouse contributing $5,000 to his or her own plan, it may be better to contribute $10,000 to the spouse's plan which offers better investment choices and lower fees. By contrast, couples who believe their marriages may not last until retirement should always contribute to their own retirement account. Even though pension plan assets are usually divided at divorce, it's always a good idea to keep as many assets as possible in your own name if your marriage is shaky.

IRA and Keogh Plans for the Self-Employed. If you're self-employed, you can contribute to a SEP-IRA or, in higher income brackets, a Keogh retirement plan. Both allow you to make a tax-deductible contribution of a percentage of your earnings to a retirement plan. Contribution limits for these plans are generous, allowing a disciplined self-employed person to save significant amounts fairly quickly.

💡 RELAX IF YOU HAVE ENOUGH INCOME

If Social Security, pension and retirement plan income will be adequate to meet 100% of your income needs after retirement, you don't need to obsess about the information in the rest of this chapter. There is no reason for you to keep piling up more savings, especially if it's at the expense of doing the other things likely to lead to a fulfilling retirement. But if these income sources are unlikely to provide all the income you'll need, the information presented below should help you figure out how best to close the gap.

📖 TAKING MONEY OUT OF IRAS, 401(K)S AND OTHER RETIREMENT PLANS

Both before and after retirement, almost everyone has questions about the rules for removing money from retirement plans. And, of course, we are all concerned about doing this with as little tax as possible. Fortunately, Nolo's retirement center contains good basic information that should be of help. Check it out at www.nolo.com/category/ret_home.html.

Continuing to Work

So many people work after age 65 that, after Social Security, paychecks are the biggest source of retirement income. A Spring 2000 survey by the L.A. Times ("Retirees Reinvent the Concept," *Los Angeles Times*, April 3, 2000), found that a majority of people not yet 65 planned to continue to work—at least part time— past that age. And even more interesting, close to 25% of those who had already retired felt that they had stopped working too soon. You, too, may not want to entirely leave the workplace when you reach age 62, 65 or even 70. Instead, it may prove sensible to consider your older years as just another stage of your working life. Assuming your health remains reasonably good and you have skills— or develop new ones—that are in demand, planning to continue to work at least part-time will have several positive consequences:

- **You don't have to save as much money in midlife.** Instead of needing to put aside enough money to supplement your Social Security and pension income for as many as 25 or 30 years after retirement, continuing to work after age 65 will allow you to substantially reduce this amount.

- **You stay active, busy and connected to others.** As discussed in Chapter 1, What Will You Do When You Retire?, I'm convinced that people who continue to be actively involved in life during their older years are usually more energized and interesting—both to themselves and others— than those who view retirement as a long pre-death vacation. While continuing to work for a paycheck is certainly not the only way to stay busy, it can be a great choice.

When Fishing Isn't Enough

Stan spent 33 years in the U.S. Navy and later worked as a law librarian with the federal government. Retiring at 65 with a solid pension, he looked forward to doing lots of volunteer work and plenty of fishing.

But a couple of funny things happened to Stan on the way to enjoying his retirement. First, his wife, a prominent professor and author, wasn't ready for her own retirement or, as it turned out, Stan's. The idea that Stan would just be hanging around the house for the next couple of decades struck her as little short of weird. Second, Stan found that he missed the busyness and intellectual challenge of work. "The idea of sitting around and watching my body fall apart was just not that appealing," as he put it.

To keep busy, Stan turned to volunteer work. Although his work with several nonprofits was enjoyable, it didn't fill up enough of his time, and he soon realized he needed to do something else. One day, talking to a friend, it occurred to Stan—why not get another job?

Having legal experience, he contacted the publisher of this book, Nolo, about a job. Stan started as a receptionist, planning to stay a few months. Four years later, he moved to the editorial department, where he now helps Nolo editors with a wide variety of research tasks (including the lion's share of research for this book). Stan puts it this way: "Somewhere along the line, I got over the urge to retire. Going to work every day keeps me active and interested and keeps my mind off aging."

- **You make new—and often younger—friends.** The fact that death is inevitable does little to diminish its sting when a close family member or friend dies. Those of us who live to old age will feel this pain many times, finding it increasingly difficult to recover quickly as the years roll on and more and more close friends drop away.

    As discussed in Chapter 4, Friends, the best approach to avoid losing many, if not most of your friends is to make at least some younger ones earlier in life. But unfortunately, because many of our social and community activities tend to group people who are close in age, lots of Americans fail to do this. Enter the workplace, which, thanks in part to antidiscrimination laws, is one of America's few true melting pots of different races, sexes and ages. It's here, and only here, that many older people find it possible to make younger friends. Certainly a person who is still working at age 75 is far more likely to enjoy the company of younger people—and be influenced by their energy and attitudes—than is a 75-year-old who has been retired for ten years. Ernest Callenbach puts it like this: "When you are in a workplace, you get lots of strokes (positive energy) in all sorts of ways. Just the fact that people pay attention to you is pleasurable. And no matter what your age, there is always a little low-level flirting that goes on, which is also fun."

Income From Savings and Investments

Americans are constantly chastised by the investment industry for not saving nearly enough for retirement. The implication seems to be that the average family can't wait to blow every paycheck at the mall, with absolutely no concern about the future. Nonsense. Despite what the ever-richer and ever-greedier mavens of the investment business would have you believe, the truth is that, as a group, Americans between the ages of 35 and 55 are saving far more money for retirement than any other generation in our history. For example, according to a 1995 EBRI-Gallop survey, fully 77% of people in this age group have set up a retirement savings plan. The result is that when the average baby boomer retires, he or she will be better off than the present generation of American retirees, which by all measures is already the richest in history.

Why Many Experts Are Wrong

How much should you be saving for retirement? Start by understanding that most estimates you read, which often claim you'll need as much as a million dollars (or even more), are malarkey. For example, a recent article in a prominent magazine started by discussing how scary it can be to look forward to an impoverished old age. But rather than discussing the real problems low income people have saving a retirement nest egg, it immediately began to paint a picture of a supposedly typical upper-middle-class couple (let's call them Jack and Jill) in their late 30s. Worried about their retirement, Jack and Jill consult a financial planner (let's call her Caitlin). Caitlin, who barely seems to notice the two Js already own their house and have two well-funded 401(k) plans (which, if maintained, would produce about $1 million at retirement), as well as other investments, encourages them to increase their savings rate.

How could any so-called retirement expert justify pushing this already well-provided-for couple to save more? Instead of having Jack and Jill focus on how much income they will really need in order to live decently after retirement, Caitlin asks them to visualize their ideal retirement scenario. As it turns out, this includes a Mercedes for Jack and a Jaguar for Jill, plus a Jeep Cherokee for their occasional jaunts on bumpy roads. And that is just the beginning. The three vehicles are to be garaged in a fancy two-story condo next to a golf course. For recreation, the couple will take two luxury European vacations per year and three domestic trips, always eating at top-of-the-line restaurants. In addition, this pampered pair also imagines purchasing plenty of toys and luxuries.

To afford all this, Caitlin correctly concludes that Jack and Jill will need to climb a big retirement savings hill, putting aside a total of $2.1 million. In what I'm sure the article's author considered a touching conclusion, the Js decide to follow Caitlin's advice and go for it, even though this means reducing current spending and increasing their already long work hours (Jack as a lawyer and Jill as a therapist).

When I was done chuckling at this idiocy, I wrote a letter to the editor, suggesting that the article should have been titled, "Retirement: How Jack and Jill Jumped From the Gutter to Paris in One Big Bound." I went on to point out that this couple was already on course to save far more for retirement than they would ever really need. And given the fact they both already worked at least 50 hours a week, their best approach would be to work less and spend more time with their kids. The magazine, which contained dozens of ads for mutual funds, life insurance and annuity plans, never printed my letter.

How Much Extra Do You Really Need to Save?

Although it may be hard to believe, the truth is that for many people, especially those who will receive a decent pension or a good-sized inheritance, or have already adequately funded a Keogh, SEP-IRA, 401(k) or 403(b) retirement plan, there is no compelling need to save more. If sensibly invested, the money they can already count on, when added to what they will receive from Social Security, will meet their reasonable needs.

> **EXAMPLE:** Robin and Mandy are in their late 40s. Their house is almost paid for, and their kids will finish college in five years. In addition to Social Security, each of them should receive a decent pension, Robin as a bookkeeper at the city library and Mandy from her job with a major corporation. And partly as a result of an inheritance, they already have over $200,000 invested in a balanced portfolio of stocks and bonds. Although they plan to save more over the next few years, both are conscious of the wonderful opportunity they have to work a little less and develop other interests. Accordingly, Robin has arranged for a six-month unpaid leave of absence from work, and Mandy to cut back to four days a week.

Of course, many of us aren't this fortunate and do need to save for retirement. The question remains, how much? In broad outline, the answer is easy: Ideally, you will need to save enough to produce annual income that will close the gap between what you'll receive from Social Security, pensions and other assured sources and the amount of income you will need to live comfortably.

Fortunately, there is a reasonably easy four-step process to figure out how much this is. I recommend that you follow this approach and not try to generate an even quicker answer by entering a few numbers in one of dozens of online retirement calculators before clicking enter. One reason is that most online calculators use unrealistic assumptions (for example, that you'll need 80% of your preretirement income every year after retirement). Another is that popular calculators often arrive at very different results without explaining why. For example, the article "Calculating Retirement? It's No Simple Equation" (*The New York Times*, February 7, 2000), found that, using the same facts, T. Rowe Price's Retirement Worksheet found that an investor in mid-life would wind up $1.1 million short of a comfortable retirement, while Charles Schwab's Retirement Planner put the shortfall just under $200,000 and the Motley Fool's Foolish Calculator actually concluded that the same investor would end up with over $669,000 more than she needed.

Step 1: Calculate the amount of supplemental monthly retirement income you will need

If you have read Chapter 8, How Much Money Will You Need When You Retire?, you have a pretty good estimate as to the total amount of retirement income you'll need. And if you have read the sections of this chapter dealing with Social Security, pensions and retirement plans, you know how much of this amount you can already count on receiving. The difference between these two numbers is your retirement income gap. When you divide your annual retirement income gap by 12, you arrive at the amount of additional monthly income you'll need to meet your anticipated expenses.

Let's say you conclude you will need $42,000 per year to live decently when you retire, and that you will receive $20,000 from Social Security and $10,000 from a pension. Your income gap will be $12,000. Dividing by 12, this means the supplemental monthly income (SMI) you'll need will be $1,000.

Total annual retirement expenditures	42,000
Annual Social Security payments	– 20,000
Annual pension payments	– 10,000
Annual retirement income gap	12,000
	÷12
Supplemental monthly income (SMI) needed	$1,000

Step 2: Adjust for inflation between now and retirement

While Social Security and many pension plans are adjusted for inflation, you must calculate the effect of future inflation on your SMI. Use Table A below to adjust for inflation based on a conservative guestimate of 3% per year. (The inflation rate was actually significantly lower during the 1990s, so you may want to use 2%.) Multiply the inflation factor by your SMI to get the amount you will actually need when you retire. For example, if you have 20 years until retirement, your inflation factor is 1.81. Multiply this factor by your SMI (in the above example, this would be $1,000 times 1.81). That gives you the amount ($1,810) of SMI you will need each month in 2020 dollars.

Years until retirement	20
Monthly supplemental retirement income	$1,000
Inflation factor from Table A:	X 1.81
Adjusted SMI	$1,810

Table A: Adjusting for Anticipated Inflation

Number of Years to Retirement	Inflation Factor *	Number of Years to Retirement	Inflation Factor *
5	1.16	25	2.09
10	1.34	30	2.43
15	1.56	35	2.81
20	1.81	40	3.26

*Based on a 3% annual inflation rate

Step 3: Calculate how much you need to save

Next you need to determine how much savings you will need to generate your SMI for as long as you expect to be retired. In order to do this, you need to make several assumptions.

- First, you must make a guestimate as to the annual return on your investments after you retire. For the purpose of this discussion, let's say this will be 8%. (If you are more optimistic or pessimistic, use a different number.)
- Next, you need to make an assumption about the rate of inflation during your retirement years. Let's use 3% (again, you may prefer to use a lower number).
- Next subtract the estimated annual inflation rate from your expected investment return to find the approximate expected real annual return after inflation: 5%.
- Finally, you need one more guestimate: how long you will be retired.

Based on these assumptions, Table B will tell you how many dollars you will need to put aside for each dollar you want to withdraw each month. For example, let's assume you plan to spend 25 years in retirement, and expect to get a real (adjusted for inflation) annual return on your investments of 5%. Table B tells you that you'll need $171.77 in savings when you retire to withdraw $1 each month for 25 years. Since, for purposes of this example, you've already determined that you'll need $1,810/month in supplemental income, multiply 171.77 by $1,810 to arrive at a figure of $310,900. This is the amount of savings you'll need to fully meet your goal.

Expected annual return on investments	8%
Expected annual inflation	– 3%
Expected real annual return	5%
Years of retirement	25
Amount from Table B	171.77
Supplemental monthly income needed	X 1,810
Required savings	$310,900

Table B: Amount You Must Save to Generate $1 Per Month

Number of years you plan to with-draw $1 per month	Annual rate of return on investment				
	5%	6%	8%	10%	12%
15	$136.98	$119.10	$105.34	$ 93.83	$ 84.15
20	$152.16	140.28	120.35	104.49	91.73
25	$171.77	155.98	130.43	110.96	95.90
30	$187.06	167.63	137.19	114.90	98.19
35	$198.97	176.26	141.73	117.29	99.45

 NOLO'S ONLINE STARTING BALANCE CALCULATOR

If you have Internet access, you can use one of Nolo's online calculators to make these calculations for you. Go to http://nolo.com/calculator/calculatorret_start.html and follow these instructions:

- Enter the day you'll retire (or start needing your SMI) in the box after "Start date."
- Enter your supplemental monthly income in the box after "Monthly withdrawal amount."
- Enter the number of months you'll need to make withdrawals in the box after "Number of withdrawals." For instance, let's assume you'll spend 25 years in retirement. Multiply 25 x 12 for the numbers of months.

Worksheet: How Much You Need to Save for Retirement

Years until retirement   _____

Years of retirement   _____

Total annual retirement expenditures   _____

Annual Social Security payments   − _____

Annual pension and retirement plan income   − _____

Annual retirement income gap   = _____

÷   12

Supplemental monthly income (SMI) needed   = _____

Inflation factor from Table A: X _____

Adjusted SMI   = _____

Expected annual return on investment   _____

Expected annual inflation   − _____

Expected real annual return   _____

Factor from Table B   X _____

Required savings   = _____

Factor from Table C   X _____

Annual investment in Tax Deferred Plan   = _____

Less Employer's Contribution   − _____

Your Annual Contribution   = _____

- Enter your expected real annual rate of return in the box after "Interest rate."
- Press the "Compute" button.

The number you'll see on your screen will be the amount of savings you'll need to fully meet your retirement goal.

Step 4: Calculate how much you will need to save per year to meet your savings goal

You can use Table C, below, to figure out how much you need to save per year in order to reach your savings goal. For example, if you intend to invest over a 20-year period in a tax-deferred account you estimate will yield 9% annually, you need to multiply the factor in Table C (.0195) by your goal of $310,900. The result, $6,100, is the amount which needs to be invested each year. If your employer makes a $500 contribution per year, you will need to put in $5,600 annually.

Table C: Amount You Need to Invest Annually to Have $1 in the Future

Years to retirement	Expected rate of return on investments				
	7%	8%	9%	10%	12%
5	$0.1739	$0.1705	$0.1671	$0.1638	$0.1574
10	$0.0724	0.0690	0.0658	0.0627	0.0570
15	$0.0398	0.0368	0.0341	0.0315	0.0268
20	$0.0244	0.0219	0.0195	0.0175	0.0139
25	$0.0158	0.0137	0.0118	0.0102	0.0075
30	$0.0106	0.0088	0.0073	0.0061	0.0041
35	$0.0072	0.0058	0.0046	0.0037	0.0023
40	$0.0050	0.0039	0.0030	0.0023	0.0013

NOLO'S ONLINE DEPOSIT CALCULATOR

If you have Internet access, you can use one of Nolo's online calculators to make these calculations for you. Go to http://nolo.com/calculator/calculatorinv_month.html and follow these instructions:

- Enter the day you'll start saving toward retirement in the box after "Savings start date."
- If you already have a nest egg, enter that amount in the box after "Starting balance."
- Enter the number of years you'll be saving before retirement in the box after "Number of years."
- Enter your expected annual rate of return in the box after "Interest rate."
- Enter your retirement goal in the box after "Savings amount."
- Press the "Compute" button.

The number you'll see on your screen will be the amount of savings you'll need to invest each month to fully meet your retirement goal.

After analyzing your own situation with the worksheet below, you may conclude you will be able to meet or exceed your savings goals fairly easily. But if it looks difficult or impossible to put aside the amount you think you'll need, don't despair. If you are currently under 45, or even 50, it's important to realize that you still have time to save a good-sized nest egg. And, thanks to the wonderful ability of money to grow when interest and dividends are reinvested, you don't have to save a huge sum in any one year.

Inheritance

How much money will Americans who are now over 65 leave behind when they die? More than $10 trillion, according to a 1994 study by Avery and Rendell of Cornell University. And given the rapid rise of the stock market and real estate prices since then, this number is surely closer to $25 trillion today. Although it's hard to wrap your mind around a number this big, it will probably help to understand that if this money were inherited equally by all the children of people now over 65, each would receive close to $250,000. Of course, this won't happen; people in affluent families will inherit much more, and those in very poor families little or nothing.

Just the same, chances are good that you and most other middle-class Americans will eventually inherit some money. It will probably amount to considerably more than you now guess. As a result, for a significant number of Americans ensuring a financially comfortable retirement is as simple as investing your inheritance and letting it grow until it's needed to supplement your Social Security and other retirement income. It follows that it's important to have accurate information about how much money you are likely to inherit. (Also see the next section, which discusses the trend towards transferring significant amounts by gift.)

Despite the fact that millions of Americans will inherit or be given a large amount of money, a substantial percentage act as if this weren't true. If pressed, many say something like this: "My parents or grandparents will probably leave me some money eventually, but I just don't want to think about it, because it means thinking about the death of people I love. And anyway, you never know what will happen—Dad might marry a bimbo and blow all the money or Mom might need years of expensive nursing home care which could easily use up all the money I might otherwise inherit."

Comments like this underscore the big problem with factoring a possible inheritance into your retirement planning: Any estimate you make is really only a guestimate. And, unfortunately, for a variety of reasons many of us have no idea how to even go about making a decent guess. Typically, our guesses are poor for one of the following reasons:

- We don't know how much our parents (or other likely benefactors) are currently worth.
- We don't know how to estimate how much our parents are likely to spend—over and above their income—during the rest of their lives.
- We don't know how long our parents (or other likely benefactors) will live.
- We worry about changing family relationships—the remarriage of a parent, for example—which could add a big element of uncertainty to our guestimates.

For some readers, not knowing how much they are likely to inherit makes little practical difference—they would live their pre-retirement lives the same whether or not they expected to receive a substantial amount. But for many others, ignoring their inheritance prospects can result in terrible decisions both about their current lives and their retirement finances.

EXAMPLE: Steve, a tenor with a respected opera company in a mid-sized city, was in his middle 30s with a wife and three young children. Although his salary was relatively modest, Steve supplemented it with income from private students and teaching at a summer music camp. Combined with money his wife Julie earned by working two days a week as a bookkeeper, Steve and Julie were living fairly comfortably within their income. But then Steve and Julie read several financial planning articles, which convinced them (scared them into believing) they needed to immediately start a retirement savings program. They also concluded that they should begin to save for their kids' college educations. While putting money aside to meet one of these goals might have been possible, they didn't have nearly enough income to do both. Not surprisingly, this caused them to worry. And the more they worried, the poorer they felt.

Finally, concluding he would never make enough as a singer to meet his financial responsibilities, Steve resigned from the opera and entered dental school. He was lucky. Despite his late start, he did well as a dentist, and was able to help his kids finance their educations. By age 50, Steve and Julie had begun to save enough each year to guarantee themselves a comfortable retirement nest egg.

Unfortunately, Steve never got nearly the satisfaction from dentistry that he had from music. And as the years passed, he and Julie came to accept that they had panicked and, as a result, made a bad decision. This was confirmed when, a few years later, Steve's father, Philip, died and left him over $900,000. Clearly, it had never been necessary for Steve to quit his career as a musician.

When considering whether Steve really needed to make a career change, why didn't Steve and Julie take into consideration the money they would almost surely inherit from Philip? When I asked, Steve answered like this:

Although I always loved and respected Dad, we didn't see eye-to-eye in a number of areas. And until shortly before he died, we had trouble talking to each other about anything serious. The result was that although I knew Dad was financially comfortable, I had no idea he had over a million dollars and that, even after inheritance taxes, I would inherit anything like $900,000. Also, despite the fact that Dad wasn't in the best of health, I hoped he would live until age 98 (he actually died at 78) and use up all his money.

Julie later added a bit more information that Steve hadn't volunteered: "In Steve's mind at least, his dad was a sufficiently quirky guy that there was always a chance he might leave his money to someone else, or to charity."

In hindsight, had Steve and his father been able to communicate better about finances when he decided to go to dental school, Steve might have learned facts like these:

- Philip really was well-off.
- That as an only child, Steve stood to inherit almost all of Philip's property and that no garden-variety family tension or occasional disagreements would change this.
- Philip had purchased a long-term care insurance policy that would have covered most of the costs had he needed to live in a nursing home or similar facility. (Chapter 7 discusses whether nursing home insurance policies make good financial sense—for Philip the answer would probably be no.)
- Philip was not spending all the income he received from his Social Security, pension and investments, meaning that the longer lived, the wealthier he became.
- Philip was already planning on helping to pay for his grandchildren's educations and had often wondered why Steve didn't ask him for financial help to buy a better house.

Would this information have caused Steve and Julie to make a different choice? Probably. Knowing that money would eventually be available for their kids' educations and, if necessary, to cushion their retirement, chances are good Steve would have stuck with his first love, music. After all, his career as a singer was going well, and he and Julie were earning enough to support their family.

Sadly, many children of financially comfortable people face similar situations, involving one or more of these elements:

- A history of less-than-perfect family communication going back to teenage or young adult years.
- A completely understandable desire on the part of the children to be independent.
- The fear in the minds of many parents and grandparents that a child who realizes the family is financially well-off may demand financial help too soon and as a result never learn self-sufficiency.

- The fear in the minds of many parents—especially fathers—that if they don't keep their kids guessing about their inheritance, they will lose power over them.

Talking to Your Parents

In my opinion, it's silly to allow these sorts of considerations to prevent you from factoring the amount of your likely inheritance into your retirement planning. Especially if you are likely to inherit a goodly sum, your ability to sensibly plan your financial future depends on breaking through the wall of family silence to get the facts straight. If you have siblings who are also concerned about their inheritance prospects, one approach to doing this is to propose a family business meeting. The idea is for all family members—parents, children and perhaps even older grandchildren—to disclose their current financial situation (assets and liabilities) before considering important future expenses. This analysis should start with the financial needs of the older generation (after all, it's their money you are talking about) but also take into consideration the educational needs of grandchildren and the long-term retirement savings needs of the children.

BE SENSITIVE WHEN ASKING YOUR PARENTS ABOUT THEIR FINANCES To initiate a process that will lead to full financial disclosure, it is often best to schedule several family meetings, so that no one feels immediately pressured to reveal more information or make more commitments than is comfortable. It will often help parents open up about their finances if children make it clear that the big reason they're asking is because they're trying to plan responsibly for their children's education and for their own retirement. One good way to get the ball rolling at the first meeting is for the children to disclose their own financial situation, especially if their personal books show they have learned to be good managers.

Assuming your parents or grandparents are willing to disclose their finances, or have already done so, ask whether they plan to leave the bulk of their property to their children more or less equally. Most will, but it's also common for a parent to provide a little extra for a child with health or financial problems, or to leave a bit less to a child who has already received a disproportionate amount of financial help.

EXAMPLE: Ben and Sara are the only children of Edwina, a widow in her early 70s. Edwina, who recently sold the family pharmacy business, is not a person who gabs at the supper table about how much she made when she sold her stock in Microsoft. So although her children are pretty sure she is financially comfortable, they have no idea how much she is really worth and what her estate plan is. Ben and Sara, who are both married with two young children, are doing reasonably well financially, but each faces life choices that could be far better made if they had some idea of how much they might eventually inherit.

Sara is wondering whether she should go back to work full-time to save for the kids' college costs and her own retirement or whether she can continue to work three days a week and spend more time with her children, with the expectation that Edwina will help with college expenses.

Ben, who lives in a big city with poor public schools, would like to send his children to a private school, but is concerned it would mean he couldn't fully fund his 401(k) plan, shortchanging his retirement savings.

Finally, after several false starts—Ben always becomes shy to the point of being tongue-tied around his mother—Sara and Ben write Edwina a friendly one-page note. It raises some of their personal worries and asks if Edwina will take a few hours to discuss finances with them when they all get together over the Christmas holiday.

When Ben, Sara and their families arrive at Edwina's that Christmas, they are pleasantly surprised. As soon as the children are off to bed, Edwina serves them coffee, pecan pie and a complete list of her assets, joking that this should really give them food for thought. It is immediately apparent to Ben and Sara that Edwina owns property worth about twice the amount they had guessed.

Edwina tells them she has decided to give both Sara's and Ben's children $10,000 every year for the foreseeable future, with the twin goals of decreasing her eventual estate tax burden (for more on estate taxes, see the section "Gifts," below) and providing enough money so that all the kids will be able to afford the college of their choice. Edwina goes on to say that, at her death (which she laughingly says she intends to forestall as long as possible), she plans to divide her property equally between them, after giving about 15% of her estate to several charities she has supported for many years.

When the discussion is over and the tension has dissipated, Sara asks why Edwina hadn't shared her estate plan with them earlier. Edwina laughs and says she was waiting for the two of them to grow up enough to ask.

Despite the best efforts of children to open lines of communication, some parents simply won't talk about money. If you face this situation, your best approach is to make an educated guess about how much you are likely to inherit and then reduce that amount somewhat, to be certain any error is on the conservative side. Since many older people have a substantial part of their net worth tied up in their fully paid-for house, estimating your parents' net worth often involves no more than checking how much comparable houses are selling for and then dividing that amount by the number of likely inheritors.

INVEST INHERITED MONEY WELL

If you receive an inheritance and spend it poorly—whether on cars, clothes luxury vacations or a poorly conceived business scheme—it will obviously produce no retirement income. And while it's a far better approach to put your inheritance in a certificate of deposit at your bank, this approach nevertheless guarantees that the money will grow only slightly faster than inflation erodes its value. By contrast, if you invest a $100,000 inheritance in a mixture of high-quality stocks and bonds which increase at an annual rate of 8%, it will be worth $215,892 in ten years and $466,096 in 20—a nice retirement nest egg, even after inflation is taken into account. (See Chapter 11, The Savvy Peasant's Investment Guide, for more on investments.)

NOLO'S ONLINE FUTURE VALUE CALCULATOR

If you have Internet access, you can find out how much your inheritance or other investment money will grow by using one of Nolo's online calculators. Go to http://www.nolo.com/calculator/calculatorinv_fval.html and follow these instructions:

- Enter today's date in the box after "Present date."
- Enter the date when you will cash in your investment in the box after "Future date."
- Enter the current value of your investment in the box after "Present value."

- Enter your expected average annual rate of return in the box after "Interest rate."
- Press the "Submit Query" button.

The number you'll see on your screen will be the amount that your investment will be worth on the date you cash it out.

How to Think About Inheritance Uncertainties

Even assuming you learn how much your parents (or other persons from whom you expect an inheritance) own, and confirm they plan to leave a significant portion of their property to you, you still won't know how much you will eventually inherit. As discussed earlier, lots of things can happen to your parents' money between now and the time of their death. Here is a brief guide which should help you think about the most likely ones:

- **Your parents will spend all their money.** In fact, if your parents are over 60 and financially comfortable , it's highly unlikely they will spend all—or even most—of their money before they die. As people get older, even big spenders tend to become more fiscally conservative, making income from Social Security, pensions and investments stretch a long way. If your parents are already over 70, the chances go way up that they will spend less than their annual income, with the result—absent the need to spend big bucks on long-term care—that they are likely to gradually become wealthier.

- **Medical or long-term care costs will eat up your inheritance.** If your parents' net worth is less than approximately $400,000 and their annual income less than $30,000, their wealth could be significantly depleted if either or both suffer a long-term, high-maintenance illness such as Alzheimer's and, as a result, spend years in a nursing home. (But as discussed in Chapter 7, a long stay in a nursing home is statistically unlikely, and by purchasing long-term care insurance your parents can be sure they don't die broke.) And the chances that an older person (or couple) will use up all their assets becomes increasingly remote as the value of their property exceeds about $400,000, since in this situation their annual investment earnings, added to their Social Security income, will defray a major portion of any long-term care bills with little or no need to invade principal.

- **A divorced or widowed parent will remarry and leave the bulk of family money to the new spouse.** Most parents who are not deeply estranged from their children are extremely anxious to honor their children's expectations that they—and not a new spouse—will eventually inherit most family assets. At the same time, a person who remarries later in life typically wants to provide any necessary financial help for her mate. (Of course, in many remarriages both spouses are financially comfortable, meaning there is no need for one to leave property to the other.) Although detailed estate planning is beyond the scope of this book, there are several good legal planning devices that parents can and often do use to meet the needs of both their children and their new spouse. Very briefly, here are a couple of the most common.

- **Prenuptial Agreements.** If both new spouses are already financially comfortable and thus have no reason to leave property to one another, they can easily confirm this "keep all property separate" plan by signing a contract either before or after their marriage. To reassure children that this has really been done, it is often a good idea to give them a copy of the contract (and possibly also a copy of Mom's or Dad's will or probate-avoiding living trust).

- **Marital Life Estate Trusts.** If one of the new spouses is affluent and the other much less so, the couple may want to engage in more extensive estate planning. This is especially true if the poorer spouse is much younger or healthier than the other. In this situation, one good plan that balances the needs of both the affluent spouse's new partner and children works like this: The new couple prepares a written pre- or postnuptial agreement, stating that the property of each will be kept separate. Then, to be sure the less affluent spouse (let's assume it's the wife) has enough to live on if she is the survivor—and at the same time reassure the children of the husband that they will inherit the bulk of the property—the husband creates a trust called a "marital life estate" or "AB" trust. (See sidebar below, "The AB Trust Explained.") When the husband dies, this trust contains sufficient assets to allow his widow to maintain a reasonably comfortable lifestyle, with any additional property going immediately to the children by will or probate-avoiding living trust. At the wife's death, the property in the life estate trust also goes to the husband's children.

The AB Trust Explained

A legal device known as a "marital life estate trust" or "AB trust" allows one spouse (or, in slightly different form, a living-together partner) to provide financial security for both a current spouse and children from a previous marriage. With such a trust, you can designate property for your spouse to use (a house or car), or receive income from (a bank account or investments), during her lifetime. At the death of the surviving spouse, the assets themselves go to named beneficiaries, usually the children or grandchildren of the person who established the trust.

For example, it would be fairly typical for one spouse in a second marriage to establish a trust to provide the other the right to live in a house and receive a reasonable amount of income for the rest of her life. The result would be that the children from that spouse's first marriage would inherit some property when the parent died and the rest (in this case, the house and the other income-producing assets) when the surviving spouse dies.

For more information about marital life estate trusts, as well as other options for people in second marriages, see *Plan Your Estate*, by Denis Clifford and Cora Jordan (Nolo).

Gifts

Although it may surprise you, the amount transferred by lifetime gifts from one generation to the next amounts to about 20% of all U.S. wealth and one-third of all transfers from one person to another. Inheritances make up most of the rest. (These figures come from a 1994 article by William G. Gale and John Karl Scholz in the *Journal of Economic Perspectives*.)

Most gifts are made by older people to their children and grandchildren, motivated by a desire to help them with major expenditures such as buying a house or educating children. At the beginning of the 20th century, when the average life expectancy for men was about 48 years, leaving property at death usually achieved this goal. Today, it rarely does, since by the time both parents die, children are often well into middle-age and even grandchildren have often reached adulthood.

Two advantageous federal tax rules also serve as powerful motivators for affluent people to make gifts. To understand how they work, you must first understand that in 2000 the federal government levies a tax on estates (property left at death) worth more than $675,000 (the tax-exempt amount gradually increases to $1 million by 2006). The estate tax rate begins at 37%, and increases to a whopping 55% for estates over $3 million. Gifts made during life are also taxed under this same system, but with several big exceptions. One of them allows any person to give up to $10,000 per year, per recipient, entirely free of estate and gift tax. Another allows one person to directly pay another's school and medical bills free of tax. Still another exempts 100% of money or assets given to charity.

Together, these tax exemptions allow you to transfer a large amount of money tax-free. For example, a husband and wife who each give $10,000 annually to their two children for ten years would transfer $400,000 free of estate and gift tax. If, in addition, they paid the yearly private school fees for several grandchildren, they could transfer a lot more—let's guess an additional $200,000. By comparison, if no gifts were made and the same $600,000 were taxed at death, between 37% and 55% of it could end up in the federal treasury.

As significant as this is, it's only part of the tax benefit of making gifts. If instead of giving the $600,000 away, the parents keep it until their death, chances are it would more than double—with the result that over twice as much tax would be owed. (Of course, how much it grows is a factor of how long the surviving parent lives and how the money is invested.) Or put another way, the tax savings that can be achieved by transferring the $600,000 prior to death and letting it grow in the kid's accounts is truly huge. In addition, assuming parents are in a higher tax bracket than their children, the income taxes payable on the interest and dividends generated by the $600,000 will be considerably less if paid by the children.

Enough tax law. When it comes to gifts, the question you face is, obviously, whether anyone is likely to give you any money in the first place. If your parents or grandparents are fairly affluent but have not yet begun an annual gift program, you may want to help them understand the tax advantages of this approach by having them read up on the subject. Again, an excellent source of information is the chapter on gifts in *Plan Your Estate*, by Denis Clifford and Cora Jordan (Nolo).

Receiving a series of $10,000 yearly gifts can obviously be a huge plus when it comes to helping the recipient plan for retirement, but only if the money is invested wisely. As discussed in Chapter 10, How to Save Enough—Even If You Think It's Impossible, one good choice is to start by paying off credit card and other high-interest debt as part of a long-term plan to live debt-free. If you've already done this, increasing the amount you contribute to tax-sheltered retirement plans and, once these are maxed out, paying off your mortgage early, are also good retirement investment strategies.

Early Retirement Incentives and Buy-Outs

In the last decade, loads of corporations interested in downsizing their payrolls offered long-term employees the right to retire early, often with severance packages that include hefty lump-sum payments. Sadly, too many people, including experienced executives and managers, spent all or most of this money on nonessential items instead of investing the bulk of it for retirement. And, in a search for something to do, many executives who were not psychologically ready to retire squandered much or sometimes all of their buy-out money by purchasing poor-quality franchises or starting businesses in fields in which they had little experience.

If you receive a large lump sum, consider the wisdom of a different approach. Simply invest your nest egg in a mix of high-quality stocks and bonds and get another job, even one that pays less. Think of it this way: Many people in their late 40s and 50s who have already purchased all or most of their houses and their children's educations don't need to earn lots more money to guarantee a financially comfortable retirement. All that's really required is to invest their lump sum sensibly and let it grow over the next ten, 20 or 30 years.

Despite the often-repeated stories about how hard it is for middle-aged workers to find a new job, the truth is otherwise—it is often remarkably easy for skilled workers in their late 40s and 50s or even 60s to find quality work, especially if they are willing to take a moderate cut in pay. In fact, experienced workers are in such high demand in many fields that a significant percentage of people who have been laid off as part of a major corporation's belt-tightening are able to find more interesting work in less than six months.

EXAMPLE 1: At age 54, when the well-known computer company she worked for merged with a larger company, Dayna was offered an early retirement package totaling $160,000. When combined with the $140,000 she had in her 401(k) plan and the fact that her upscale condo was paid for, Dayna felt she had already saved most of what she would need for retirement. After taking six months off, Dayna applied for a job with a small educational software company, specifying that she wanted to work a four-day schedule. At first, the software outfit was skeptical about hiring Dayna, since the salary they offered was considerably less than what she had been making. But when Dayna convinced them that she had enough money in the bank and genuinely wanted to work for a small company whose product she believed in, the deal was done.

EXAMPLE 2: At age 53, Marty, a lawyer for a major corporation, was given a chance to take early retirement. He decided to add the entire $130,000 he received as a retirement incentive to his existing savings. Instead of looking for another job as a lawyer, Marty, an excellent amateur skier, decided to work with a resort to create an over-50s ski and snowboarding school. Without investing any of his own money, Marty created an exciting new career. True, he earned a lot less than he did at his former job, but with his retirement assured and his wife still bringing home income as a teacher, Marty could afford to work at a job he loved.

Withdrawing Equity From Your House

It's an excellent pre-retirement strategy to purchase and pay for a house while you are working. If you do, the amount of money you'll need to save for retirement will be substantially less than if you rent or still have a mortgage.

But if you haven't been able to save much and will live primarily on Social Security income, owning a house means that the lion's share of your assets are tied up in one place. Or, put another way, you may find that you are house-rich but short of money to go to the grocery store. Fortunately, this needn't be a big worry, since with a little planning there are several good ways your house can provide you with additional income.

Help for the House-Rich and Cash-Poor

A number of states have adopted property tax postponement programs for people over 65. These allow older people on fixed incomes to put off paying property taxes on their residences until their death, at which point the taxes are paid before inheritors take their inheritances. For information, call your local property tax assessor's office.

Rent Out One or More Rooms

Especially if you live near a college, resort area or community that is growing fairly rapidly, it may be fairly easy to bring in substantial monthly income by renting one or more rooms. And it will probably be even easier in the future, since a number of senior organizations are beginning to establish programs to match older people who need good affordable housing with other retirees who have space to rent. To be sure, many people shy away from the idea of renting space in their homes out of fear of losing privacy or getting a troublesome tenant. But by using the good planning and screening techniques developed by many senior organizations, it really should be possible to comfortably rent surplus space.

Move to a Less Expensive House

If you purchase a significantly smaller, less costly house or condo, you can bank a significant amount of the equity in your original house and use the income it produces (and eventually part of the principal) for living expenses. This is easy to do, given the federal law which allows married couples who file joint returns to pocket $500,000 of profit from a house sale tax-free and single people to similarly exclude $250,000 from taxes (assuming in both cases that the house has been the owner's principal residence for two out of the last five years).

> **EXAMPLE:** Dot and Harry, a married couple, own a nice house within commuting distance of a good-sized midwestern city. When Harry retires at age 67, they sell the house they have lived in for 20 years for a net of $420,000 after sales costs. They then purchase a nearly new condo on the outer fringe of a resort area in southern Colorado for $125,000. Dot and Harry owe no federal capital gains tax and thus are free to invest all their net proceeds, which total $295,000. They plan to withdraw a little of their nest egg each year to supplement their Social Security income. Assuming that they will invest in a mix of stock and bond mutual funds that produce an annual return of 8%, this means their money will last at least 25 years.

Sell Your House and Become a Renter

Selling your house or condo instead of renting your living space can be a good strategy for those who want to live in a smaller space, free of responsibility for maintenance and repairs.

EXAMPLE 1: Shae, age 72 and single, sells her four-bedroom house, which she purchased for $200,000 ten years ago for $400,000. Because of the tax law, which allows her to exclude $250,000 in capital gains, she is able to invest the entire $400,000. Shae invests in a mixture of growth-oriented mutual funds and U.S. government securities providing an average annual return of 8%. The result is that her annual earnings and appreciation, before tax, will be almost $32,000. Combined with Social Security—and even allowing for inflation—Shae estimates that she'll have more than enough to rent a decent apartment and live comfortably.

EXAMPLE 2: Allison is close to 70. Several years ago, her lovely Florida house, full of a lifetime of possessions, was destroyed by a hurricane. Not interested in rebuilding (and actually enjoying having less stuff), Allison collected her insurance settlement, sold the real estate and invested her money. An avid mountaineer, she then rented a small but lovely apartment in Boulder, Colorado. Currently, her rent is less than half of the monthly income she receives as a result of having invested the proceeds from the destruction of her house and the sale of the land. Not only does the extra money allow Allison to travel, but she has been able to help her daughter and son-in-law purchase a house.

Get a Reverse Mortgage

If selling the family house and moving to a smaller place is unpalatable, and you want to stay in your own house until the day you die, you may want to consider a "reverse mortgage." As you may know, the idea is simple: An older homeowner trades some or all of her equity in her house in exchange for a monthly payment from a bank or other lender. The payment can be in cash or in the form of a line of credit that can be drawn on as needed. After the homeowner's death (or if she voluntarily moves out), the house is sold and the lender repaid (plus interest, of course). Whatever is left over goes to the homeowner's inheritors (or the homeowner, if still alive).

For example, the Federal National Mortgage Company (Fannie Mae) offers the "Homekeeper Mortgage," designed to let qualifying homeowners over 62 borrow up to $240,000 worth of their equity in the form of an adjustable rate reverse mortgage. Prepayment is required when the borrower moves, sells the property or dies.

Especially for retirees who have substantial equity accumulated in their houses but need money to live on day to day, a reverse mortgage can be a good fit. Homeowners have the opportunity to work out a plan that will let them withdraw substantial amounts of money for years and still not be close to the reverse mortgage maximum, which is often about 80% of the owner's equity interest. And of course, there is also a good chance that, short of a deep and lasting recession, the house's value will increase over time, meaning that the amount one can draw against is also likely to go up.

> **EXAMPLE:** Edna, age 78, owns her house outright. The house is worth about $500,000, but Edna's savings are almost exhausted and her Social Security income barely pays enough to cover her personal expenses—with nothing left over to cover the costs of maintaining and insuring her house. Edna's two children have offered to provide whatever income she needs, but even though they will recover it when they ultimately inherit her house, Edna is determined not to be a burden. She eventually solves her liquidity problem by participating in the Federal Housing Administration's reverse mortgage program. Edna immediately borrows $10,000 so that she can replace her deteriorating roof, and then arranges to receive a payment of $1,000 per month. Even allowing for loan costs and interest, and assuming Edna lives into her mid-90s, she will not come close to exhausting her $500,000 equity (which may even increase if the value of her house goes up faster than the amount of her modest withdrawals).

⚠ REVERSE MORTGAGES ARE A BAD DEAL FOR SHORT-TERM NEEDS

Loan origination costs and up-front fees for appraisals, insurance and management mean reverse mortgages can be a relatively expensive way to borrow money, especially if you plan to own the house for only a relatively short period. In this situation a better alternative is often to borrow needed money from a solvent child who can be repaid when the house is sold. But these one-time reverse mortgage costs are much less of a factor for younger seniors in decent health who expect to live in their homes for many years and thus spread these costs over a decade or more.

More About Reverse Mortgages

Reverse mortgages are relatively new, and more varieties are being invented regularly. In the past, making accurate comparisons was tricky, but now the U.S. government requires all issuers of reverse mortgages to disclose total mortgage costs—including interest and all fees and closing costs—as a percentage of the loan.

For a list of lenders that offer reverse mortgages (and to get help in finding one that will fit you like a glove, not a handcuff), send a self-addressed business-size envelope to NCHEC, 360 N. Robert St., #403, St. Paul, MN 55101, or visit the "sources" page at www.reverse.org. Good information is also available on reverse mortgages from AARP's website at www.aarp.org/hecc/basicfct.html.

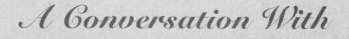

A Conversation With

BABETTE MARKS

Babette Marks grew up in the 1920s and '30s on a small poultry ranch in Southern California, surrounded by animals. She worked her way through the University of California at Berkeley, graduating with a B.A. and M.A. in Fine Art. As a divorced mother of two children, she was a secondary school teacher for many years. Retired from teaching at 51, she later owned and ran an antique and collectibles shop. Babette is now 78 and lives in El Cerrito, California.

RW: Since you stopped teaching almost 30 years ago, you've done lots of volunteer work helping needy people and animals. How did you get started?

BM: While I was still teaching school, I got started helping with an evening tutoring program for kids in North Richmond, a nearby low-income community. Then, later, when I stopped teaching, I got more deeply involved helping out with a Head Start program for preschoolers. One thing just led to another. When homelessness first started being a huge problem in the early 1970s, I helped set up a surplus food network by talking to stores and restaurants about donating food they would otherwise have thrown away. With contributions from food chains like Safeway, this was obviously a way to get enough food to make a difference.

RW: And you've also worked with animal projects?

BM: Yes, in several ways. Perhaps the most exciting and fulfilling has been working with the Lawrence Hall of Science, a sort of kid's science museum in Berkeley, helping smaller children interact with animals. This later led to my also becoming involved with an intergenerational program that focused on having older people introduce small animals to children in grade school. One senior is at a table with six to eight kids, so it becomes a very individual, intimate experience for kids and adults alike. And hopefully, the kids learn to respect and care for living creatures. Most of my other helping activities have also had to do with animals—for example, working at the Bird Rescue Center for six months, following the big oil spill in San Francisco Bay, in 1971. I learned to be empathic with animals probably because, as a child, I was often ignored by my family.

RW: Do you use your volunteer work as something primarily designed to keep you busy, or does it have a larger purpose?

BM: Sorry, but I don't analyze myself much—I just do things. But at the risk of overusing the word, I know I have lots of empathy and that I have to put it someplace. The place it seems to express itself best is with kids and animals. Once I get involved with one helping activity, one thing just seems to lead to another. I see where an unmet need is and move in that direction. But I never see my activities as a way to fill time. I'm already overbusy most of the time. I just see that something needs to be done and try to do it.

RW: You mentioned not fitting into your family. How exactly did you learn to compensate by bonding with animals?

BM: Growing up on a poultry ranch, we had animals everywhere, including a horse, goats, rabbits and dogs and cats, as well as turkeys and chickens, of course. My parents were very dour, and being outgoing and gregarious, I not only never fit in, but I often offended them by not being the quiet, respectable little girl they wanted. As a result, I identified and made friends with the animals, especially those who were injured and/or sick. In a way, my childhood career was taking care of sick animals, and I guess I've been at it ever since.

RW: As part of your helping activities, I know you've made quite a few younger friends. Suppose a few who are now in their 40s and 50s invited you over for supper and said, "Babette, you're a role model for us. What should we do to prepare for retirement?"

BM: I don't know that you can really do that much to prepare that will be meaningful. What's kept me sane (and I use that term loosely) has been to stay involved with lots of interesting younger people, people who constantly invigorate me with their ideas and energy. Without good younger friends, an older person just stagnates. I have at least eight or ten real friends who are now in their 40s or 50s. Incidentally, I got close to several of them when, in their 20s, they faced a crisis and just needed a roof over their heads, and they stayed with me.

RW: What else has helped you lead such an interesting, energized retirement?

BM: This may surprise you, but I think a big part of it has been the fact that I know I'm weird—or eccentric, if you prefer that word. In some ways, I think my kids might have wished I were a bit more conventional when they were growing up in the 1950s. We lived in a half-finished barn of a house, complete with a few nude paintings from my art school days. In addition, I made most of our clothes, and we bought almost nothing. I remember some neighborhood women disapproved of my running around in shorts when I was working on the house or repairing the car. But since I was a Cub Scout den mother, Girl Scout Leader and a Sunday School teacher, they really couldn't openly criticize my lifestyle. After all, I was helping with the kids far more than they were. And then, for many years, I drove an old police car I bought at a CHP auction. (This really made points for me with all the teens.)

RW: It would make a terrific movie: "Bizarre Babette Meets Ozzie and Harriet." But when it comes to retirement, are you saying that being a little weird earlier in life helps you later on?

BM: I've never tried to be weird. In fact, at times I've tried not to be. But as I went along in life, I've just had to face that I was born a bit dingy (my daughter's pet term). It has made me the odd person out from the time I was a kid. But that's okay. Many friends told me years later that they were attracted to me because I wasn't afraid of being different. My teachers called me a Free Spirit.

RW: But what about now that you're older?

BM: I was getting to that. My childhood experience of being unacceptable in the eyes of my parents and siblings helped me in the long run, since it taught me not to care much about how others saw me. Instead, I learned to look inside and come to terms with myself. Now, in my old age, when few oldsters really fit into America's youth-dominated culture, I'm pretty well adapted. I don't analyze it that much, but I know it's a positive thing that I can happily see myself as a little old bag lady retrieving discarded food to feed raccoons, or whatever other oddball thing I'm doing. The point is, my weirdness has helped me to live an authentic life, even if it's a bit eccentric. Unfortunately, lots of unhappy older people I've known have never figured out who they were or are and are trying to be what they think they ought to be. I read something once that really sums up how I feel about coming to terms with yourself. It was, "You are what you are. And the most religious thing you can do is to be it as kindly as you can."

RW: You've always been in pretty good physical shape and seem to enjoy good health. How important to a successful retirement do you think it is to take good care of yourself when you're younger?

BM: I walk a lot—at least four miles per day and often as many as eight. I do some sit-ups and other exercises. The key to a feeling of well-being for an older person is not to be sedentary. If my roof needs a patch, I get out my ladder and do it. But I'm not so sure about the good health part. Like most older people, I have plenty of aches and pains. For example, my lower back is often very painful and I frequently can't sleep due to severe headaches. But so what? Aches and pains aren't interesting, and they are certainly no reason to slow down. If you feel lousy, you just keep going and get through the day. No big deal.

RW: What else would you talk to your younger friends about?

BM: Younger people really need to learn to open their hearts to a world beyond themselves. I have no idea how you do it, but developing a caring attitude toward the world around you is crucial.

As you get older, this spirit of caring helps you cope. Face it, most people need something to be responsible for, or to. My dog plays this role for me. Every day, whether I feel good or awful, I need to walk my dog, so I do it. A relationship like this is obviously particularly important if you are single. Volunteer helping work can play much the same role. If you promise to show up, you do, no matter how easy it could be to make up an excuse and stay home.

RW: What about money? We've been chatting most of the morning about all sorts of interesting subjects, and we've hardly mentioned it. Do you think people in their 40s and 50s should be worrying about saving a lot of money for retirement?

BM: In my opinion, it's just not that important to pile up money. You'll most surely fail if you try to create the image of an affluent retirement lifestyle and then try to get enough money to live it out. The truth is, despite the propaganda of the retirement industry, most people now in their 40s and 50s will have more than enough money if they will just adjust their lifestyle to what they have, which, of course, is already much more than most people in the world will ever have and probably far more than their own grandparents enjoyed. It's downright sad that millions of people are sacrificing their lives to get luxuries they don't need.

RW: Are you saying that by focusing on money, lots of people in midlife are doing precisely the wrong thing?

BM: Well, I'm sufficiently off the norm that I can't say much about what others should or should not do. But I feel sorry for men—and now I guess many women—caught in the traditional business rat-race. They're at much risk of losing themselves. They are supposed to make money, so they forget about what they care about and instead do something that's practical. Then, when they retire and finally have all the money they need to do what they want, they have forgotten what that is. It's truly sad when people get so programmed to earn a living that they totally forget who they are. Maybe I'm being unfair, but it seems that these are the people who pile up in those retirement communities.

RW: You obviously don't spend much money.

BM: Well, I actually inherited a little, so I could if I wanted to. But no, I spend very little, mostly because there is not much I want to buy. My house is paid for, so that leaves only house taxes and insurance, and, of course, food for myself and my dog and cat. Since I walk everywhere and often take public transit, I rarely even put gas in my car. All told, I guess I live on quite a bit less than $1,000 a month. The truth is, life is so full of things to be interested in, I don't have time to spend money. ■

Chapter 10

How to Save Enough—Even If You Think It's Impossible

"There's no money in poetry, but there's no poetry in money, either."

—Robert Graves, at 67

➡ SKIP AHEAD IF YOU NEVER USE CREDIT

This chapter discusses how average Americans can save a bundle by avoiding paying too much interest on credit cards, car loans and mortgages and produce a comfortable retirement nest egg by investing their savings. If you don't buy anything on credit, skip ahead to Chapter 11.

In this chapter, I present a simple plan that can help many middle-income people—even many who are currently deep in debt—achieve financial security when they retire. And if your retirement plan is already in decent shape, you'll find that if you follow the strategies discussed here, your financial situation will further improve.

Unlike many personal finance writers, I don't believe the best strategy to increase your retirement savings is to put yourself on a strict budget (although for some people reducing unneeded consumption can also make sense). Here's why:

1. I respect your judgment. You probably have a pretty good reason for making most of your current expenditures, including those that aren't absolutely essential, such as the occasional restaurant meal, movie or vacation. Sure, with a bit more financial self-discipline and a determination to live more simply you can undoubtedly spend less and save more, but you don't need me to tell you that.

2. Strict budgets, like strict diets, usually don't work for very long. And when you abandon one, it's extremely likely you'll go on a spending binge. That's why it's almost always better to adopt a moderate approach and stick to it.

How can I magically show you how to save adequate money to fund a secure retirement without cutting back greatly on what you spend? The solution to this apparent paradox can be stated in a sentence: Live debt-free and sensibly invest the money you would have otherwise spent on interest. For many American families in their 30s, 40s or even early 50s, just embracing this simple concept will provide enough money to fund a comfortable retirement.

The wonderful thing about making a commitment not to pay interest and to invest what you save is that your interest dollars never bought you anything tangible in the first place. If instead of buying on credit you saved your money and paid cash, you could have bought exactly the same goods and services just a little later. It follows that if you alter your spending habits a little and invest the money you currently pay out in the form of interest, you can almost painlessly make yourself financially comfortable. Feathering your own nest, instead of those of banks and other credit grantors, requires that you do just three things:

1. Break the credit habit. This means go cold turkey on making new purchases on credit, except where absolutely necessary, such as buying a house (and even with houses it often pays to reduce your long-term interest burden by prepaying your mortgage—as discussed later in this chapter).

2. Pay off all existing interest-bearing debts as soon as possible.

3. Save and carefully invest the money you used to pay in the form of interest.

EXAMPLE: Terri buys a jacket, paying $50 cash. Jake buys the same jacket using a credit card that charges interest at an 18% annual rate, and pays $4.58 each month over 12 months. Jake will have spent $55, or 10% more for the jacket. The reason, of course, is that he has foolishly chosen to borrow money from a bank at a punishing rate of interest simply for the privilege of owning the jacket a little sooner than if he had saved the money.

You may be thinking that it's small potatoes to save a few dollars by paying cash for a jacket. What difference will it make to your long-term financial picture if you pay an extra $5? Very little, of course. But if instead of looking at credit transactions one—or even several—at a time, you look at them over a number of years, the blinders will fall off and you will understand two crucial things:

- By buying lots of small items on credit, and paying only the minimum amount required each month, you can end up paying at least twice the actual cost of the items. It's like voluntarily subjecting your purchases to a huge and unnecessary tax.

- If, instead of doing this, you choose to live debt-free and conscientiously invest exactly the same amount you used to pay in interest, you will easily save enough to more than adequately supplement your Social Security (and any other retirement income), and all but guarantee a financially comfortable retirement.

⚠ DON'T PAY INTEREST JUST BECAUSE SOMETHING IS ON SALE
Sure, it can be hard to resist buying on credit when you're short of cash and see something wonderful on sale. But even if the item really is terrific, don't give in. If you just say no and instead wait until you save up the money to pay cash for the item you covet, chances are excellent you'll be able to find it—or something very similar—at another big sale. And who knows—if you put off making the purchase for a few months, you may even decide that you don't really need the item.

Of course, understanding that it's wise to live debt-free and having the willpower to do it are animals of very different colors. The rest of this chapter sets out some practical strategies that may help you change your credit habits.

Credit Card Interest: How the Poor Pay the Rich

According to VISA International, the average American holds three-plus credit cards and charges more than $3,000 per year. The typical household holds five different credit cards and charges $6,000 per year. Of course, many millions of people charge much more.

According to the U.S. Federal Reserve Board, in 2000 consumers owed over $800 billion on their credit cards (another $600 billion is owed for auto loans). Almost 70% of credit card users don't pay their bills in full each month. In fact, the average payment is only about 15% of the outstanding balance. This, of course, means tens of millions of people pay interest on the unpaid balance, which currently amounts to over $500 billion. With interest rates which can often be as high as 18%–21% or more, this means just carrying this debt costs consumers tens of billions of dollars per year, which brings me quickly to the most important message of this chapter. If instead of paying this huge interest bill, Americans saved even half this amount, the vast majority could retire to affluence.

Credit card interest rates are so high that many states have had to pass legislation to exempt revolving charge accounts from traditional "usury laws," which prohibit charging interest at rates higher than 10%–12% per year. Think about it: If your Uncle Harry charged as much interest for a loan as you probably pay to VISA or MasterCard, he would be guilty of criminal behavior. For an example of just how insidious buying on credit can be, here is a contemporary fable adopted from *The Pocket Change Investor* (see sidebar, "Reexamining Your Relationship to Money," for order information).

> **EXAMPLE:** Dayna charges $2,000 on a credit card carrying an annual interest rate of 19.8%. Feeling financially strapped, she sends in only the minimum payment each month. To fully retire the debt following this approach will take Dayna 42 years and cost a total of $9,637.

NOLO'S ONLINE CREDIT CARD REPAYMENT CALCULATOR

If you have Internet access, you can find out how long it will take you to pay off your credit cards, based on your current balance and the additional charges you make every month. Go to http://www.nolo.com/calculator/calculatordc_credit.html and enter the information requested.

Reexamining Your Relationship to Money

This book discusses financial issues only as they relate to sensible strategies for retiring well. Unfortunately, I don't have the space for an in-depth discussion of the sometimes negative role money plays in the lives of many Americans. Although most people handle their finances reasonably well, others clearly need an attitude adjustment. Particularly if you feel that no matter how much money you earn, you are always broke, you will greatly benefit if you consider changing a few of your basic attitudes toward earning and spending money. For people who are in perpetual financial difficulty, the goal is to move from a life in which money is seen as scarce—and getting enough is a source of anxiety—to a life in which the same amount of money is viewed as being plenty to comfortably meet your needs.

Fortunately, others have done good work in this area. I particularly recommend that you pick up a fascinating book, *Your Money or Your Life: Transforming Your Relationship With Money and Achieving Financial Independence*, by Joe Dominguez and Vicki Robin (Viking). (Or look for it at your local library and save a few dollars.)

Your Money or Your Life asks and helps you answer questions like these:

- Do you have enough money? Will you ever?
- If you lost your job tomorrow, would your world fall apart or finally make sense?
- Are you at peace with money?
- Is your life whole? Do all the pieces—your job, your expenditures, your relationships, your values—fit together?

Once you have decided to change your spending habits, your chances of sticking to your resolution to resist the lure of the shopping mall will go up if you arrange to receive regular reinforcement. I recommend a very reasonably priced quarterly newsletter called *The Pocket Change Investor* (Box 78, Elizaville, NY 12523, $12.95 per year). The subtitle says it all: "The Secrets of Getting Ahead—Even If You Have a Pile of Credit Card Bills, Hefty Mortgage Payments, Loans Out on a Clunker or Two, and a Bad Case of the 'I'm Tired of Living Payday-to-Payday Blues.'" Yes, this publication does cost a few bucks, but it's one of the few things you'll ever buy that will save you money in the long run.

Credit Cards: Robin Hood in Reverse

Many of us love the story of Robin Hood because, for once, money is transferred from the purses of the rich to the pockets of the poor. In real life, of course, it's almost always the other way around—the wealthy figure out lots of ways to deploy their assets to get richer while everyone else huffs and puffs to get by.

Credit cards are a perfect example of one of these Robin-Hood-in-reverse schemes. Large banks at the top of the income heap borrow money from their depositors and others at extremely low interest rates, lately averaging about 3%–4%. They then lend this money at higher rates, making their profit on the spread between their cost of borrowing and their income from lending. No problem so far—that's what banks are supposed to do.

Major corporations and financially savvy people with lots of assets borrow money from the bank—or sometimes by selling bonds—at an interest rate that is only a few percentage points above what the bank pays its depositors. Let's assume big business pays 7% interest.

Smaller business people with decent credit, but not as much clout, must pay significantly more—perhaps 9%. But of course, like big businesses, they can deduct all the interest they pay as a business expense on their federal and state tax returns.

After going through several more categories of customers who pay increasingly higher rates of interest, we finally reach the average working stiff who uses a credit card and doesn't pay her bill in full each month. On average, this luckless customer pays the bank or other credit grantor an annual interest rate of about 18% (the usual range is from about 10% to 24%), and it's not tax-deductible.

In short, banks have found a large group of customers so unsophisticated and gullible (think of them as the peasants of Sherwood Forest without Robin to guide them) they will cheerfully pay the bank over four times what it costs the bank to borrow the money in the first place. As you might guess, this means banks and other large lenders enjoy a hugely profitable business.

Looking at Your Credit Habits

Why do so many Americans who are so broke they can't afford to pay cash for their purchases agree to pay interest of 18% or more annually above the price of what they buy? After all, many of these same people have saved little or nothing for retirement and worry about being impoverished later in life. Leaving aside the small number of people who really are psychologically addicted to shopping, I believe the answer can be traced to the fact that most Americans receive a lousy education on credit, debt and other consumer basics—so bad that they plain don't realize how much it costs to carry a credit card balance or how fast their savings could grow if they swore off buying things on credit and invested their interest savings.

Here is a quick test of your consumer credit IQ:

- When was the last time you added the cost of anticipated credit card interest to the cost of a purchase?
- Would you still have made the purchase at the higher price?
- How much credit card interest did you pay last year? If you had saved and invested this same amount (which, after all, bought you nothing), how much would you have after five years?

Chances are you have never asked or answered any of these questions. Surely, if you had, you would understand just how impoverishing it is to routinely pay interest at an annual rate of 18% or more.

Let's take a minute to examine what would happen to a typical family if they stopped paying credit card interest. Assume that Winston and Jennifer Lee are a middle-class couple who use their revolving credit cards to charge $6,000 of merchandise per year, resulting in interest charges of about $900. Your first thought may be that $900 isn't much—surely not enough to contribute significantly to the Lees' retirement savings needs even if they invested it wisely. Think again. The chart below illustrates what would happen if, instead of paying credit card interest, the Lees annually saved and invested this amount in a mutual fund, starting at different ages and keeping the investment until they retire at age 65. It also assumes their money will grow at a rate of 8% per year, and that they reinvest all dividends and interest without paying tax, as would be possible if they put the money in a tax-sheltered retirement plan.

How the Lees' Small Investment Grows Big

Age the Lees start to invest $900	Value at age 65	Age the Lees start to invest $900	Value at age 65
25	$233,151	45	$41,186
30	$155,085	50	$24,437
35	$101,955	55	$13,038
40	$65,795	60	$5,280

Yes, the Lees' potential savings really are impressive. And even more impressive, they achieved them without working one more hour, earning one extra dollar or even making one less purchase.

Fine and good for solidly middle-class folk, you may be thinking, but isn't buying things on credit a necessity for many lower-income families, who simply can't afford to pay for needed items immediately? In a word, no. Buying on credit may be a convenience, a habit and, for a few people, an addiction, but it's very rarely necessary. Here's why:

- The majority of credit transactions don't involve real necessities, such as food or medicine. Instead, most credit card purchases are for things like clothing, jewelry, restaurant meals, recreational equipment, travel and toys (both for kids and adults)—purchases that could, with a little discipline, be put off until the cash necessary to purchase the item was saved. As proof, consider that most people, no matter what their income level, charge a significant amount of their year's credit card total just before the Christmas holidays. Sure, it feels good to give your children and loved ones a pile of nice gifts, but if you call the great majority of holiday expenditures necessary, you really are kidding yourself.
- Credit card issuers know that people with lower incomes pose a higher risk of default and therefore make it relatively harder for them to get unrestricted credit cards in the first place. When credit is granted, the interest rate is often a staggering 24% or more. Using credit this expensive so greatly increases the costs of buying things that the closer you are to the ragged financial edge, the less—not more—you can afford to use it. Put more

bluntly, if you're short of money in the first place, the significant percentage of your total disposable income you must pay to use credit cards is almost sure to make you enough poorer that you won't be able to pay your bills, with the result that your credit privileges will be cut off. And if, as is likely, you can't quickly repay what you have already borrowed, a collection agency will sue you and attach your wages. About this time, you are likely to join the over one million Americans who each year declare personal bankruptcy.

EXAMPLE 1: Doris, a single mother, is proud of her 12-year-old daughter, Bonnie, who not only does well in school, but is also a great kid. With the holidays approaching, Doris, remembering her own childhood holiday excitement, wants Bonnie to have all the school supplies and clothes she needs and, if possible, several much-coveted luxuries as well. Bonnie, who learned to expect a big, exciting Christmas before her parents divorced, has begun to prepare her wish list, which includes CDs, soccer shoes, overalls, a fancy ski jacket and half a dozen other items. In an effort to fulfill all these pre-teen yearnings, Doris, who is barely getting by on the income from her job as a medical technician supplemented by child support payments, puts $545 worth of purchases on her VISA card, which charges interest at 18% per year. Assuming Doris makes a $50 monthly payment, it will take her one year to pay this debt off, with her total expenditure being $600. And, of course, if Doris makes only the minimum allowable monthly payment, she'll pay the credit card company a lot more.

EXAMPLE 2: This time, instead of taking her credit card to the mall, Doris sits down with Bonnie at the end of October and explains her tight financial situation, and why it won't be possible for her to afford lots of holiday gifts. After Bonnie gets over some garden-variety 12-year-old disappointment, the two of them identify what Bonnie really needs now and what would be nice to have but can be purchased later. Doris ends up paying cash for $50 worth of books and school supplies, and, as a surprise, the CD Bonnie most desires. Bonnie, at her mom's suggestion, does a little extra babysitting for a neighbor and buys herself the badly needed new overalls and soccer shoes. Several of the other items are purchased each month during the year as cash becomes available. No interest is paid, and Doris ends up saving the $55 she would have paid in interest and proudly adds it to her 401(k) plan—an amount that is matched by her employer. Invested in a mutual fund estimated to return 9% per year, Doris's $55 (plus her employer's matching contribution) will grow to $948.54 over the 25 years before she retires.

True, $948.54 won't make a big dent in Doris' retirement needs. But remember, this amount was produced just by refusing to use plastic to purchase one year's Christmas gifts. If followed throughout the year, this same approach could easily result in Doris being able to save $3,000 or more. And since Doris has many years before retirement, it is easy to see that if she sticks to her resolution not to buy things on credit and to invest her savings, she has the opportunity to create an impressive nest egg.

Practical Ways to Break the Credit Habit

In theory, eliminating credit card interest payments should be relatively easy. Simply lock up your credit cards for the months it will take to pay off the outstanding balance and get far enough ahead financially that you'll be able to pay cash for needed purchases. From then on, charge things only when you are sure you can pay your bill at the end of the month. Unfortunately, for people who already have a large outstanding balance, there is preliminary work to be done. Here are a few suggestions that may ease your job of paying off your existing balances and breaking the credit purchase habit.

- If you owe enough to make the interest savings worthwhile, apply for a credit card with a lower rate of interest (make sure it lets you transfer your existing balance without a fee).
- Once your outstanding balance is paid off, get rid of all your credit cards and instead carry a debit card for those times when it's inconvenient to pay cash. Debit cards, issued by many banks, immediately subtract the cost of a purchase from your bank account, at no cost to you. This means if your bank account is empty, you will be unable to make additional purchases. A similar strategy involves using a secured credit card, which allows you to charge only up to the amount you have deposited with the financial institution.
- Discuss your resolution to pay off your current credit card balances and stop using credit for future purchases with any friends who are also prone to pay with plastic. Several may be interested in joining you. If so, plan to

get together or chat by phone or email regularly to compare progress. Just like losing weight or cutting down on drinking, a little support can make it a lot easier to break the credit habit and begin a retirement savings program.

- If you think your resolve is strong enough, you can keep one or two credit cards and use them only when you are sure you can pay your bill in full at month's end. To help ensure you keep your resolution, put a piece of easy-to-remove tape across your credit card and use the card only after you remove the tape. This little reminder should slow you down enough that you have a chance to consider whether you really are sticking to your plan.

What to Do If You Are Already Over Your Head in Debt

There are several strategies you can employ to cope with overdue debts:

1. Pay them off gradually, concentrating first on those carrying the highest interest rates.

2. Work with the nonprofit organization Consumer Credit Counseling Service or a similar group to help restructure your debts and reduce or stop ruinous interest payments while you pay them over time.

3. If debts are so high that you are contemplating bankruptcy, contact the creditor, explain your problem and ask to have the debt rescheduled at a lower rate of interest.

4. Negotiate with the creditor or collection agency to cancel the entire debt in exchange for one big payment that is considerably less than the total owed. If you are successful, ask a close family member or friend to lend you the needed sum, interest-free.

5. Declare bankruptcy—either Chapter 7, which wipes out most consumer debt but may require your giving up "secured assets" (possibly even your house), or Chapter 13, which allows you to reorganize your debts into manageable payments without losing any property.

For more information about these and other strategies, plus sample letters you can write to bill collectors, see *Money Troubles: Legal Strategies to Cope With Your Debts*, by Robin Leonard (Nolo).

Using a Home Equity Loan or Borrowing From a 401(k) Plan to Pay Off Credit Card Debt

As most people know, interest rates on mortgages and home equity lines of credit are usually much lower than credit card interest rates. In addition, interest paid on most mortgages and home equity loans is income tax-deductible, while interest paid for credit card debts and car loans is not. Given this great disparity in cost, lots of people respond to ads for home equity loans and use the money they borrow to pay off credit card debt. But is this really a good idea? It can be, but usually only if you repay the home equity loan within about two years. Unfortunately, if like most homeowners you extend payments over a much longer period, you'll be out of pocket even more money in the form of interest than if you had taken a year to pay off your higher-interest credit card debt.

As an alternative to borrowing against your house, it can be even a better deal to borrow from a 401(k) (or 403(b)) retirement plan to pay off high-interest credit card debts. Not only is the interest rate you must pay likely to be lower, but since you are borrowing the money from yourself, your interest payments go right back into your own account. But of course, as with any borrowing, there is a downside; in addition to paying various fees, money borrowed from a retirement plan does not earn a return, which means at retirement your retirement savings will be lower than if you hadn't borrowed.

Plan to Avoid Car Payments

Now we reach an even more emotionally charged subject: automobiles. It's no secret that many of us love our cars so much that we are willing to spend a significant portion of our take-home pay to buy or lease a pricey new one. And on top of that, there are the stiff costs of insuring, registering and maintaining our expensive new steed. Although we know that car costs represent a large chunk of our budgets, few of us bother to figure out exactly how much. And fewer still understand that if we are willing to alter our car-buying behavior somewhat, we can own a very decent vehicle for as much as 70% less.

This huge savings is achievable if, instead of buying a new car on credit, you pay cash for a moderately priced two- or three-year-old model. The car itself will cost about half of what you would pay for a new one, and the rest of your savings will come from not paying interest and enjoying lower insurance, sales tax and registration costs.

Saving significant amounts by not buying your cars new may sound great until the next time you enjoy a ride in a friend's shiny new sedan or spot an irresistible model in your neighbor's driveway. Then, like the toad in Kenneth Graham's classic *The Wind in the Willows*, you are likely to fall madly in love with the idea of piloting your own shiny new motorcar down the high road. If so, you will be just another victim of new car fever—certainly one of the world's most mind-altering diseases. Having caught this bug a time or two myself, I know better than to try to talk you out of it. For many Americans, a lifetime is way too short to drive a previously owned vehicle. But just because you prefer to buy your car new doesn't mean you must finance the car and end up paying a fortune in interest. Far better for your long-term economic health to put off your purchase for the time it takes to pay cash.

> **EXAMPLE:** Daria, age 25, has her eye on a new car that costs $18,000. If she put down $1,000 and financed the rest, she could pay it off over three years; at 10% interest, her total payments would be $20,747. If, instead, Daria didn't purchase the car but deposited the amount of the down payment in a money market account paying 5%, and then each month added to it the amount of that month's car payment ($549.54), it would take her about 2.5 years to save enough to pay cash for the car (assuming Daria paid federal income taxes of 28% and no state income taxes). And if, after she bought the car, she kept investing the same amount every month for the next six months (the length of time she would still have been making car payments) in a tax-deferred retirement account such as a 401(k), and left it there for the 37 years remaining until she retired (at 8% annual interest), Daria would not only have the car, but $57,700 to boot.

But suppose, unlike patient Daria, you can't wait two-and-one-half years to get another car, but need one much sooner. Here is a plan that will enable you to purchase a used car fairly promptly and a new one after three years and still save a bundle.

> **Step 1:** Instead of going out and buying a new car on credit, wait six months. Do it even if this means driving your rattletrap a bit longer, carpooling, using public transportation or, perish the thought, biking

or walking. (C'mon, don't turn up your nose. You probably need the exercise.)

Step 2: Save the amount you would otherwise have used for the new car down payment and other up-front purchase costs, such as delivery fees and the difference in registration and insurance costs between your present car and the new one.

Step 3: Each month, add to your new car fund the amount of the car payment you don't have to make. At the end of the six months, chances are you'll have between $3,000 and $6,000.

Step 4: Use this money to buy a decent used car for cash.

Step 5: Continue to save exactly the amount you would have spent each month on payments for the new car you didn't buy, subtracting the amount of any repairs—but not maintenance costs—for your used car. (This is fair, since if you had purchased a new car, repair costs would be covered by your warranty.)

Step 6: After about three years, buy a new car for cash.

EXAMPLE: Assume you purchase a new car for $18,000, to be paid monthly over three years at 10% interest. If you make a down payment of $1,000, your total payments will be $20,747. Now assume that instead of buying a new car on credit, you instead deposited each monthly payment in a money market fund receiving 5% interest and kept at it until you had enough money to purchase your new car for cash. Assuming you are in the 28% tax bracket, it would have taken you about 29.5 months. Assuming, finally, that you went on to invest the entire amount of your car payment for the next 6.5 months in a 401(k) or other tax-sheltered investment earning 8% and didn't touch it for 20 years, your balance would be $18,000. (And, of course, if your employer matched some or all of your contribution, it would be higher.)

The really great thing is that if you are stubborn enough to follow this plan, you may never have to buy a car on credit again. You now have a new vehicle that should last many years, allowing plenty of time to accumulate enough savings to purchase your next one for cash. Once you no longer have to make monthly car payments, and instead are able to invest this money, you should become a lifetime convert to paying cash for your cars and, over time, save enough in unpaid interest to fund a good chunk of your retirement.

Leasing a Car: Almost Always a Rotten Deal

Think of it this way—a car lease is like a high-interest car loan with a huge balloon payment at the end. When the lease runs out, you must either buy the car (often for more than it's worth) or end up with no car and no money. And to make matters worse, many people, mesmerized by ads touting an "affordable monthly payment," end up paying significantly more for the vehicle than if they had negotiated a good purchase price. Even compared to buying a new car on credit, leasing one is usually a bad deal. Chances are if you buy the car it will cost less in the first place and will last for at least several years after you get done paying for it.

⚠ THE MONEY YOU SAVE BY PAYING CASH FOR YOUR CARS: DON'T SQUANDER IT

Turning the money you save by not paying interest on car loans into a significant retirement fund is easy, as long as you faithfully invest the money you save. Remember, I'm not suggesting you work more hours, cut back other spending or give up the idea of owning a new car. All you need to execute this plan is the backbone to change the way you buy your new cars and to invest the resulting savings.

How to Buy a Decent Used Car for Cash

The car purchase scenarios we just looked at are fairly rosy. They show that people with comfortable middle-class incomes can save a pile of money by not paying interest on a car loan and still buy a new car when their old one wears out. Unfortunately, this isn't a realistic possibility for millions of Americans, whose incomes are already so stretched they may never be able to purchase even one new car.

Fortunately, the principle of just saying no to paying interest can also be effectively applied to the purchase of used cars. And because the interest rates charged on used vehicle loans are almost always higher than for new ones, you will still achieve a significant savings, even though the amount you borrow is lower. If you are cash-strapped, it may be tougher to save the full amount needed to buy your first used vehicle for cash, but it is also far more important that you do so. The reason is obvious. Since, by definition, you'll have far less money to spend during your life than will higher-income folks, you can even less afford to pay out big chunks of it in the form of interest.

But what if you don't have the $5,000 necessary to purchase your first decent used car for cash? It's time to engage in some creative financing. Start by seeing how much you can scrape together by selling unneeded items, using classified ads and garage sales. Next, see if an older family member will lend the needed money interest-free (or better yet, give you a used but serviceable car they no longer really need).

> **EXAMPLE:** Instead of buying a $5,000 used car on credit, Michelle scrimps and saves for six months, raises money at a garage sale and gets an interest-free pay advance from her boss, which she will repay over six months. Once she has the car, Michelle decides to put aside the $110 she is saving each month by not paying interest on a car loan. (She assumes she would have borrowed $4,000 at 14% interest, repayable over four years.) After she repays her boss, Michelle puts the money in a money market account in which she earns an after-tax return of 5%. After four years, she sells her car for $2,500 and combines this amount with $2,500 from her savings to buy another one, leaving about $2,500, which she transfers to a mutual fund that averages an 8% annual return. Again Michelle invests what she doesn't have to pay out in interest payments at 14% and, after four years, she replaces her car. As you can see, before long Michelle's determination not to pay interest will have resulted in her having saved a meaningful nest egg.

Don't Buy a Lemon

Saving money by buying a used car works if you buy one in sound mechanical condition. Here's one good approach that will raise your odds of making a good choice. Get a copy of Consumer Reports' *Annual Guide to Used Cars*, which rates models based on their long-term durability (or often lack thereof). Once you find a used car that Consumer Reports says is likely to be reliable, negotiate a tentative price with the seller. It's usually wise to start by offering about 25% less than the asking price.

Don't finalize the deal until you have the car thoroughly checked out at a trustworthy local garage (it's best to line this up in advance). Ask the seller to pay half this cost. If possible, be present while the mechanic runs the tests, to be sure they are done carefully. If a significant but fixable defect is found (worn brake pads, for example), ask the seller to lower the price by the amount of the repair.

 NOLO'S ONLINE AUTOMOBILE AFFORDABILITY CALCULATOR
If you are considering buying a car on credit, and you have Internet access, you can find out how much you'll pay in interest over the course of a car loan. Go to http://nolo.com/calculator/calculatordc_car.html and enter the information requested.

Prepay Your Mortgage

If you are like the great majority of Americans, you will own at least one—probably several—houses in your lifetime. If you still doubt whether eliminating interest payments can really produce enough money to allow you to retire with adequate savings, consider how much you could save if you didn't have to pay interest on your mortgage. Let's say you buy a house for $187,500, making a 20% down payment and taking out a $150,000 fixed-rate mortgage carrying 8% interest for 30 years. Before you own the house free and clear, you'll pay more than $396,000, which is a huge sum, even allowing for the fact that inflation will mean dollars you repay in ten or 20 years will be worth less than they are today. If, like lots of people, your house is more expensive and your mortgage bigger, you'll pay even more interest—as much as a half-million dollars on a house costing $300,000.

But isn't the true financial picture less bleak, since mortgage interest payments are income tax-deductible? True, but that's not the same as saying it's good to owe money on your mortgage. Think of it this way: Who is financially better off, a person who owes nothing or a person who pays $1 to a lender and gets back roughly 15¢ to 39¢ (depending on her tax bracket) when she pays her taxes? The answer, of course, is the person who isn't in debt in the first place.

Because houses are so expensive, most people can't completely duck mortgage payments. But fortunately, by paying your mortgage off early, you can save much of the amount you would otherwise pay in interest. And if you invest what you save, you'll have made a terrific start on saving what you need for a financially secure retirement.

> **EXAMPLE:** Yoshiko prepays $50 per month over the monthly amount due on her 30-year, fixed-rate $150,000 mortgage, at 8% interest. This means she pays off the loan in 25.5 years instead of 30 and saves $44,150.

Why does paying a few extra dollars result in a mortgage being paid off so much faster? Simple. By paying down part of the principal of your mortgage now, you prevent interest from mounting up on that money for as many years as you have left on your mortgage. And the earlier you begin prepaying, the more you save.

The chart below shows how increasing your monthly payment on a 30-year fixed-rate mortgage will affect the time it will take to pay it off. For instance, if you pay an extra $50 each month on an 8% mortgage with a $1,000 monthly payment, you will repay the loan in 25.1 years. (This table is based on the extra payments being made from the beginning of the loan. If you already have a mortgage, the earlier you start making extra payments the sooner it will be paid off.)

Prepayment on a $150,000, 30-year fixed-rate mortgage @ 8%

Amount of extra payment	No. of years to payoff	Amount of extra payment	No. of years to payoff
$ 50	25.5	$300	15.7
$100	22.4	$350	14.7
$150	20.2	$400	13.8
$200	18.4	$450	13.0
$250	16.9	$500	12.3

NOLO'S ONLINE EXTRA PAYMENT CALCULATOR

If you have Internet access, you can find out how much faster you can pay off your mortgage with one of Nolo's online calculators. Go to http://nolo.com/calculator/calculatorre_extra.html and enter the information requested.

KEEP A FEW DOLLARS IN RESERVE

It's not wise to put every cent of your savings into mortgage prepayments, since it can be time-consuming and sometimes impossible to get at this money in case of emergency. For example, if you lose your job, you'll still need money to pay your monthly mortgage payment. If you can't do this, you'll need to sell the house or risk foreclosure. (The fact that you have prepaid mortgage principal for years won't help you; this money can't be converted to future payments.) Far better to set aside, in an emergency fund, enough cash to tide you over for a few months; money market funds offered by stockbrokers are one decent choice. If your job offers one, a 401(k) or 403(b) retirement plan is usually an even better way to go, since money you contribute is tax-deferred and, in case of emergency, easy to borrow back.

Fortunately, it's easy to prepay most mortgage loans. Simply send in an extra payment each month along with your normal mortgage payment or, if you can't always afford this, make an occasional extra payment. When my wife and I first began prepaying our mortgage, we sent in a fairly modest extra amount. Then, as we saw how much we were saving and how much faster our loan was being re-paid, we increased the amount of our extra payment several times. The result was we paid off a 20-year fixed-rate mortgage in less than eight years. This in turn freed us to invest the money we would otherwise have spent on mortgage interest payments. Since we are now receiving interest (and appreciation on some invest-ments) rather than paying it, our savings have begun to grow fairly quickly.

⚠ PAY OFF OTHER DEBTS BEFORE PREPAYING YOUR MORTGAGE

Interest on credit card debt, personal financial loans and car loans is not tax-deductible. And chances are good that interest rates charged are much higher than for a home loan. It follows that before you prepay your mortgage, you should first pay off these other loans. One possible exception to this rule involves student loans, which often carry a relatively low rate of interest and can, in some circum-stances, be rescheduled with no interest payments.

Comparing Mortgage Prepayments to Other Investments

Suppose, instead of making extra payments on your mortgage, you pay it off over its normal term and invest the amount you would have prepaid in other ways. Fine; there are many good investments, and you may be able to achieve just as good a return—possibly even a better one. (See sidebar, "Which is Better, Prepay-ing Your Mortgage or Investing in a Retirement Plan?", below.) Unfortunately, however, a great many people who might add an extra $50 or $100 to a mortgage payment find it impossible to save and invest the same amount.

If you are disciplined enough to invest any surplus funds you don't use to prepay your mortgage, the next question, is how much must you earn on your investments to better the return you would achieve by prepaying your mortgage? In a *Wall Street Journal* article ("If You've Got Money to Squirrel Away, Sometimes There's No Place Like Home"), Jonathan Clements concluded that, depending on an individual's tax bracket and rate of interest on the mortgage, most people would have to earn close to 8% on their investments to equal what they would save by simply prepaying their mortgage. Although in the last few years it has often been possible to do this, Clements goes on to point out that because repaying your mortgage is risk-free, it compares favorably to other types of investments such as mutual funds, which carry a significant level of downside risk.

Which Is Better, Prepaying Your Mortgage or Investing in a Retirement Plan?

What about investing extra money in a tax-sheltered retirement plan, such as a 401(k), IRA or Keogh plan? Is doing this better than prepaying your mortgage? There is no definitive answer, since it greatly depends on the performance of the investments you choose as part of your retirement plan. Some 401(k) plans are so employee-unfriendly that they are best avoided—for example, plans that provide no matching funds from your employer and either force you to invest in the stock of your employer or offer a poor selection of high-fee investments.

But on balance, the edge goes to retirement plans, since the money you contribute lowers your taxable income and therefore the amount of your income tax in the year you contribute it. Also, in case of emergency, you can borrow against the money in a retirement plan, paying interest to yourself, not a lender. By contrast, depending on your credit rating at the time you wish to borrow, the equity in your house may be less readily available, and there will almost surely be more loan fees. Finally, if you have college-bound children who will be applying for financial assistance, it is also important to know that money invested in retirement plans is not counted when judging aid eligibility, while money invested in home equity increases your family's net worth and therefore decreases the amount of financial help your kids qualify for.

Where Will Money to Prepay Your Mortgage Come From?

Once you understand the significant long-term savings achievable by prepaying your mortgage, you may be motivated to try to pay $25, $50 or even $100 extra each month, even though you are also contributing the maximum to a tax-sheltered retirement plan at work. For some readers, this won't be onerous. But if your family finances are already stretched to the limit, it will obviously be tough to pay more than required. Here are a few suggestions for coming up with a few extra dollars:

- **Save $1 a day.** This suggestion may sound corny, but it's nevertheless true that lots of people who never have money left at the end of the month can manage to put a dollar into a cookie jar each day. If this describes you, deposit your extra $30 in your bank account at the end of the month and immediately add it to your mortgage check. Paying just $30 extra per month on a $100,000 30-year mortgage payment at 8% means you will pay it off in less than 26 years. If for the next four years you then put the amount of your entire mortgage (in this case, $763.76) into a tax-free retirement plan anticipated to return 8% per year, you will have $38,372. If you leave it there for another ten years, you'll have $82,842. And if you don't touch it for yet another decade, it will grow to $178,849.41. This is a tidy sum, even allowing for the likely decline in the purchasing power of the dollar over the years.

- **Ask your parents for a gift.** Many readers have no hope of receiving financial help from their parents, and may even need to help them. But if your parents are financially comfortable, consider asking them for some of the money needed to prepay your loan. Especially for older parents whose assets add up to more than the 2000 federal estate tax threshold of $675,000, it makes great sense to give gifts (up to $10,000 per year per recipient) to people who will ultimately inherit it. (See the discussion on gifts in Chapter 9, Where Will Your Money Come From After Age 65?)

💡 PARENTS OFTEN COUNT HOUSES AS A GOOD INVESTMENT

Some parents are hard to approach about money—and many adult children are so determinedly independent that they don't want to ask for help. Nevertheless, the huge double benefit to the family of saving both on death taxes and mortgage interest payments is a compelling reason to at least raise this possibility. In my experience, parents who understand why prepaying your mortgage is such a powerful idea (lend them a copy of *The Banker's Secret*, rather than trying to explain it yourself) are often pleased to offer financial help even if, in the past, they have been less than enthusiastic about lending you money for what they saw as frivolous purposes.

Don't Buy a House You Can't Afford

Too many Americans struggle to qualify for the nicest, most expensive house possible. Although this may be good for family ego, it is often a terrible mistake. Not only does it mean these people will have to work too hard to make the mortgage payments and consequently spend too little time with each other and their children, but it almost guarantees that the family—no matter how high its income—will feel financially insecure. If a job is lost or a family-owned business does poorly, it may be impossible to make mortgage payments, to say nothing of paying a little extra to reduce interest expenses. Far better to buy a less expensive house than you can comfortably afford (this also lowers your insurance and property tax payments) and have extra money for other purposes—one of which may be to pay off your mortgage early in order to almost effortlessly create a comfortable retirement nest egg.

- **Ask your parents for an interest-only loan.** Parents with modest savings may be glad to help you prepay your mortgage (or better yet, help you increase your down payment and thereby reduce your loan fees). At the same time, they may worry that in the future they might need the principal back. One way to deal with this concern is to have your parents lend you money at a reasonable rate of interest, with no payments of principal or interest due for several years. Be sure you prepare and sign a written agreement, or the IRS may not treat it as a bona fide loan.

For example, assume your parents lend you $10,000 to add to your down payment, with the result that you take out a 30-year loan of $140,000, rather than $150,000. If each month you pay the lender the entire $1,100 payment that would have been due on the $150,000, you'll pay off your loan in 23.6 years (6.4 years early). If later, when the loan comes due, your parents don't need either the interest or principal, they can simply make you a gift of that amount. If sometime in the future your parents need financial help, you should be well-placed to voluntarily provide it, since once your mortgage is paid off, you will have been able to increase your savings. Even if your mortgage isn't paid off, you'll have plenty of equity in your house to borrow against. And if, as is often the case, your parents don't ever need their money back, they can simply use their will to forgive the debt.

Adding Up the Savings

Now let's put the information in this chapter together to see what happens if, over a 25-year period, an average family commits itself to living as free of debt as possible. Instead of buying clothing, meals, gasoline or a vacation and paying interest for several months or more at a rate of almost 18% per year, they wait until they can afford to buy the same things for cash. Keeping track of the interest savings they achieve, our sensible couple first use this extra money to pay off other debts such as car and student loans. Their next priority is to fully fund their tax-sheltered 401(k) or other plans. After this is accomplished, they plan to use any additional savings to begin paying off their home mortgage early.

EXAMPLE: Tom and Elizabeth, both teachers who participate in pension plans as part of their jobs, purchase a house for $300,000, borrowing $204,425 on a fixed-rate mortgage with an 8% interest rate. Their payments are $1,500 per month. Normally, Tom and Elizabeth maintain an average outstanding balance of $2,000 on their credit cards at 18% per year, paying $360 in interest yearly. Three years into their mortgage, Tom and Elizabeth decide to change their habits and charge nothing on their credit cards until they can pay their bill in full each month. It takes them about two years to pay off their balance at $100 per month. When they finally do, they add the $100 to each month's mortgage check. (If Tom and Elizabeth did not have employer-funded pension plans, but instead were eligible to contribute to a 401(k) or 403(b) retirement plan, fully funding these plans would normally come before prepaying their mortgage.)

Tom and Elizabeth also decide to go cold turkey on car payments. To accomplish this, they decide not to purchase a new car right away, instead depositing half of their avoided car payments (about $150 per month) in what they label their new car savings account. They use the other half to prepay their mortgage, starting the same month as they did with the extra $100 discussed above. This results in a scenario in which the house will be all theirs in less than 24 years. Long before this happens, their new car account will be fat enough to allow them to trade in one of their old ones and purchase a new model. Once their house is paid off, they decide to put all the money they have been paying for their house (about $1,675) into a retirement savings fund. Over ten years, at an annual appreciation rate of 8%, this grows to $165,700. ■

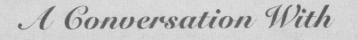

A Conversation With

PETER WOLFORD

Born in 1919 in Berkeley, California, Peter grew up loving music—a love he expressed initially as a pianist, then on woodwinds (saxophone, oboe, bassoon), then as an orchestra leader in high school. He got his first job after graduation as Purser's Assistant with the Dollar Steamship Lines; a few years later, after attending the College of Marin, Peter worked in a dance band and the Sheriff's Office, where he contracted tuberculosis and was in and out of residential treatment facilities for five years. Under doctor's orders not to play the saxophone, he learned to play the organ. Faced with an out-of-tune organ, he taught himself the art of organ tuning and later learned to tune and rebuild pianos. His big break came in 1946, when he got a job tuning the pianos at San Francisco's Golden Gate Theater, then a top-level vaudeville hall where Duke Ellington, Frank Sinatra, Bing Crosby, Count Basie, Lionel Hampton and many other famous bands appeared. Later he added the San Francisco Conservatory of Music, CBS Records and Fantasy Recording Studio, as well as a number of popular night clubs, to his clientele. These days, Peter has reduced his workload somewhat but is still tuning pianos three days a week in Marin County, where he and his wife of 49 years, Marguerite, live.

RW: Peter, you've worked for yourself, tuning pianos, for over 50 years and you're still at it. You must like what you do.

PW: I certainly do. Remember, I had tuberculosis as a young man, before antibiotics came along and knocked it out. In the early 1940s, no one wanted to hire a person with my medical history, so I had to kind of invent a job for myself.

RW: You were obviously successful.

PW: I enjoy what I do. It's not a run-of-the-mill job. I keep meeting new and interesting people. I'm a people person, and piano-tuning allows you to create bonds with people—sometimes real friendships. When I tune someone's piano, I like to think I bring them a little harmony in more ways than one.

RW: You are obviously enjoying your retirement—or I guess I should say non-retirement—years. Based on what you've learned, what advice would you give to someone like me, who is thinking about how best to prepare for retirement?

PW: Most important—keep learning new things. Really challenge yourself. Don't get in a rut.

RW: Can you give me an example from your life?

PW: Well, I've done lots of things. We were in yachting for over 25 years, kept bees, I played the bagpipe for over 20 years in several bands, studied navigation and so on. But as I began to get older, I started to worry a little about my memory. This was after I stopped playing the pipes, in about 1983, and no longer had to memorize all the pipe music. To train my mind,

I first started doing crossword puzzles, and later I went back to studying German.

RW: That's quite a mix.

PW: Yes, but that's only part of it. As if out of the blue, I heard a voice speak to me and say, "Learn Morse Code."

RW: How old were you?

PW: About 64.

RW: Did you learn all those dots and dashes?

PW: Yes. I got out the encyclopedia, and two weeks later ran into an experienced ham radio operator friend who invited me to a novice class. I was immediately hooked. I studied and passed the government exam for a Novice Class license and, in so doing, joined the Marin Amateur Radio Club, where I met the nicest group of men and women with whom I have ever been associated. Later, I passed the Tech and General Class licenses, became the club president, taught code classes and, after ten years, passed the Advanced and then the Extra Class licenses. With the latter, I can use all of the amateur bands, not just specific portions.

RW: Learning Morse Code must be great for the memory.

PW: Yes, when you're sending and receiving 20 or more words per minute, you have to be fairly quick. When it comes to your mind, I really believe it's a question of using it or losing it. But ham radio is also fun at a personal level. Currently, I'm the editor of our monthly newsletter as well as the Membership Chairman.

RW: What other retirement advice would you give a younger person?

PW: Be enthusiastic in what you do. Learn not to dwell on negativity or illness. As my wife Marguerite says, "If you name it, you claim it." Instead, just take what comes and get on with your life as well as you can.

RW: What about money? We are sitting and talking in your nice home in a reasonably affluent area. When you were younger, did you think a lot about saving for retirement?

PW: No. Marguerite and I did some sensible things, but we didn't really worry about it too much. For example, years ago we acquired a small apartment house on Russian Hill in San Francisco, managed it and later, when we sold it, bought an annuity, having paid off our own mortgage many years previously. Now, with our Social Security and me still working, we get along fine. And that's true even though we allow ourselves a few small luxuries, such as buying a prepared meal most evenings. Recently, we converted my workshop underneath the house into a studio apartment, which we rent out. Later, if one of us becomes frail and we need help, it will be a place for a live-in helper.

RW: Do you have many friends?

PW: Yes, we have quite a few friends who are important in our lives. Most are around our age, but we've been lucky to make quite a few close younger friends of the baby boom generation. You see, with my medical condition, we decided not to have children, since for a while, I really didn't know if I would be alive to see them grow up. So maybe to make up for that, we've become very close to some of the children of our friends—people we've known all their lives. In fact, I taught one of my closest friends and several of his children the piano service trade, so they were also my apprentices.

RW: That's another way your work has created friendships.

PW: Yes. I've had 27 or 28 apprentices over the years. Also, Marguerite and I are close to our two nephews. And then, of course, our dog is a great ice breaker. I meet lots of people dogwalking.

RW: Do you exercise every day?

PW: Since I turned 65, I've been walking about 2.5 miles a day, most days. This compensates for sitting at the computer.

RW: What else do you do for your health?

PW: My wife and I are sensible. We have a scotch before dinner and a small glass of wine with dinner and we eat a balanced diet. But to tell you the truth, we don't worry about physical health all that much.

RW: I get the feeling you believe good health has other dimensions.

PW: Absolutely. The spiritual side of life is very important. How you feel inside has a lot to do with your overall well-being.

RW: Can you elaborate a little?

PW: In a sentence, I guess I'd put it like this: I believe, as human beings, we are here on earth to learn to give unconditional love.

RW: Really? Unconditional love to everyone? That's a lot to learn, isn't it?

PW: Yes, which is why I believe that, at a spiritual level, the idea of reincarnation makes sense. I don't mean that you'll come back as a cow or a bug—it's more to do with consciousness. It takes lots of time—lots of lives—to learn to love yourself, which, of course, is the key to learning to love others. Once you can accept and love yourself, you can accept other people the way they are.

RW: Really accept them, warts and all?

PW: Sure; it doesn't make any difference. And it's when you can do this, you can avoid anger and confrontation and learn to give them unconditional love.

RW: Last, let me ask you about your marriage. You refer to your wife, Marguerite, very fondly. Obviously, she's very important to you.

PW: Yes, having a soul mate, as I do, is wonderful. Marriage is a real commitment; to make it work and grow, you need to find and nurture at least some activities you enjoy doing together. Once it was suggested that I start spending time at an exclusive all-male retreat facility. No way, I thought. I didn't get married to go off and leave Marguerite home by herself. ■

The Savvy Peasant's Investment Guide

"Money is a singular thing. It ranks with love as man's greatest source of joy. And with death as his greatest source of anxiety."

—John Kenneth Galbraith

There are hundreds of ways to invest a retirement nest egg. No matter which of them you choose, your goals should always be the same: To keep your savings safe so they will be there when you need them, to keep them growing so they will more than outpace inflation, and to invest them in ways that profit-draining taxes and fees are minimized.

Surely you have received dozens if not hundreds of sales pitches from brokers and others importuning you to buy stocks, mutual funds, bonds, annuities, real estate and possibly even commodities, precious metals, art and other collectibles. And of course, every time you read a personal finance article or book, or visit any one of the hundreds of websites specializing in investments, you're sure to be presented with the pros and cons of at least a dozen retirement savings opportunities. Chances are you will find much of this advice confusing and contradictory, and at least some of the people who provide it aggressive and untrustworthy. Against this unhappy background, this guide presents several comparatively simple ways to invest for your retirement, which meet the twin goals of safety and growth.

How to Invest Like a Savvy Peasant

I use the term "savvy peasant" to evoke the image of a person too busy to spend lots of time untangling Wall Street gobbledygook, but who nevertheless has more than enough financial smarts to invest money wisely. When it comes to planning for retirement, the savvy peasant is content to get rich slowly but surely—that is, to invest her nest egg in ways calculated to grow faster than the rate of inflation while at the same time minimizing the risk of suffering a big loss. Here are a few of any savvy peasant's basic axioms:

Don't be too greedy. Throughout most of American history it has been fairly easy to achieve solid, inflation-beating investment returns over the long term, but all too easy to lose big if you try to double or triple your money fast. The savvy peasant wants to save for a comfortable retirement, not start a second career as a speculator.

Purchase only investments you thoroughly understand. Although it should go almost without saying, people with common sense—and that certainly includes our friend the savvy peasant—do not purchase investments whose risks and rewards they don't fully grasp. For example, you probably know how bank accounts, certificates of deposit and mutual funds work, but may have little knowledge about futures trading, currency hedges, buying on margin or taking a short position in an Internet stock. No problem, as long as you fess up when you are in over your head and stick to what you know.

Make up your own mind. It is almost always a mistake to invest on the basis of a tip from a friend, relative or, especially, an investment salesperson who will make a profit (commission) as a result of your purchase. Commissioned investment salespeople have a built-in bias towards convincing you to frequently buy and sell investments (which puts money in their pockets)—a strategy that, given our tax system and the fact you must pay fees or commissions to the advisor, is almost doomed to failure. Even worse, they often receive extra compensation if you purchase a particular type of investment that their company happens to be pushing.

Also, despite what you may have read elsewhere, there are at least three reasons to be wary of investment advice sold by financial planners who, instead of taking a commission on each transaction, charge you a management fee—usually

based on a small percentage of the dollar value of your portfolio. First, even though this approach is supposed to produce more objective advice (since the expert does not earn commissions by talking you into buying and selling investments frequently), conflicts of interest are common. An article in *Money Magazine* confirmed what lots of people have long suspected: As many as one-third of supposedly independent advisors secretly take commissions (payoffs) for selling particular types of investments. ("The Big Bad News About Fee-Only Financial Planners," by Ruth Simon, December 1995.) Second and even more troublesome is the fact that it can be very hard to determine if a particular advisor is any good—often harder than learning how to invest your money yourself following the principles discussed in this guide. Certainly, it's wise to take any statements the advisor makes about her own great investment record with a large grain of salt.

Finally, there is no compelling reason to employ a financial advisor in the first place. If you follow the advice in this guide and invest in a good mix of stock and bond mutual funds (especially low-cost tax-minimizing index funds), you will very likely do better than you would if you paid someone to manage your investments.

FINANCIAL ADVISORS MAKE MORE SENSE FOR THE WEALTHY

If you have more than enough retirement savings and absolutely no interest in managing your stash, you can afford to purchase financial advice. But before settling on an advisor, painstakingly check out a prospective advisor's references, credentials and track record. Membership in respected professional organizations, as indicated by the designation Certified Financial Planner (CFP), Certified Public Accountant—Personal Finance Specialist (CPA-PFS) or Chartered Financial Consultant (ChFC), is some indication of experience and, possibly, competence. In addition, always ask the planner for both Part I and Part II of Federal Securities Disclosure Form ADV, which contains information about a financial planner's background and qualifications and discloses any legal or financial problems in the planner's past. But most important, ask to talk to several of the advisor's long-term clients. With a couple of phone calls, the advisor should be able to arrange this. If for any reason she isn't able to, look for a different advisor.

Know your own comfort level. All investments more sophisticated than a bank account and other cash equivalent investments, such as short-term U.S. government debt, are likely to fluctuate substantially in value (and, of course, putting money in a bank account carries with it the risk that it won't earn enough to keep up with inflation). It's best not to invest money in volatile investments, such as stocks and bonds, if you will be freaked out by a sharp loss. The reason is painfully simple. People who have little or no experience with risky investments are likely to panic and sell when markets take a big drop—a reaction that almost guarantees a far worse result than if they had stuck long term to more conservative investments.

⚠ DON'T FALL IN LOVE WITH THE STOCK MARKET

You have undoubtedly read and heard "experts" who claim that, when investing for retirement, the stock market is the only smart place to invest 100% of your savings. Bosh. It's possible for the stock market to drop like a stone and stay at the bottom for an extended period. For example, if anticipating his retirement in ten or even 20 years, your grandfather had put his money in the stock market in 1929, he would have been one sorry old coot, since market averages didn't exceed their 1929 level until 1953. And the Great Depression wasn't the only time stock performed badly over a number of years. Since 1926, there have been seven periods in which investors saw the value of their stocks go down over five consecutive years. Even in the October 1987 crash, where the market recovered in two years, many if not a majority of small investors lost money when they hurriedly sold stock near the bottom of the market. And as I write this, we have just experienced several years of market volatility severe enough to cause any savvy peasant to think twice about investing all his retirement eggs in this particular basket.

Diversify your investments. No investor is smart or lucky enough to be right all the time, and relatively few end up winners even most of the time. Knowing this, the savvy peasant never puts more than 10% of her eggs (assets) in one basket (investment), especially if that basket is inherently risky, as is always true if you invest in one—or even a few—stocks. As discussed later in this chapter, a mix of investments, including cash equivalents, stock and bond funds—especially low-cost index funds—is usually the best choice.

Maximize tax-advantaged investments. 401(k) plans, Keoghs, IRAs and SEP-IRAs all allow you to put money aside for retirement income tax-deferred. Depending on whether you are self-employed and have established a Keogh or SEP-IRA, or you work for an employer who has established a 401(k) plan (or a 403(b) plan if you work for a nonprofit) or invest in an IRA or Roth IRA on your own, the details of how, and how much, you can invest each year will vary considerably. But the basic idea is the same—in addition to investing money that would otherwise be subject to income tax, your nest egg will grow tax-free until withdrawal. And if your employer matches some or all of your contributions, it will obviously grow even faster. This means if you reinvest interest or dividends and even move money from one mutual fund or stock to another, you need pay no federal income tax until the money is eventually withdrawn (after age 59$\frac{1}{2}$, without penalty).

Money contributed to your retirement plan should (just like the rest of your assets) be spread over a sensible mix of reasonably conservative investments. It's especially wise to avoid investing a major portion of 401(k) money in the stock of the company you work for; if that company does poorly, you could simultaneously be out of a job and suffer a major loss of your retirement nest egg.

If you participate in a high-quality tax-sheltered retirement plan for many years, you should be able to accumulate all the money you need to supplement your Social Security, with no compelling need to save more. For example, a 30-year-old who puts $4,000 into a 401(k) plan every year will have close to $1.1 million at age 65, assuming his investments earn 10% annually ($690,000 assuming an 8% annual growth rate). Of course, if, as is likely, inflation continues to be a fact of life, this money will buy less in 35 years than it does now. Assuming an annual inflation rate of 3% (inflation has actually been lower for a number of years), $690,000 will be worth only $245,000 in today's dollars in 35 years. But this is still a pretty good retirement nest egg, since starting at age 65, it will allow you to withdraw $1,846 per month for the next 25 years.

NOLO'S ONLINE IRA SAVINGS CALCULATOR

If you have Internet access, you can find out how much money you can save in a tax-free 401(k) or IRA. Go to http://nolo.com/calculator/calculatorret_ira.html and enter the information requested.

And if you are eligible (your adjusted gross income is less than $110,000 for individuals and $160,000 for couples), it makes great sense to also invest in a Roth IRA. Although investors can't tax-deduct their original contributions, earnings accumulate tax-free and no federal income tax is due when the money is eventually withdrawn.

NOLO'S ONLINE ROTH IRA SAVINGS CALCULATOR

If you have Internet access, you can find out how much money you can save in a Roth IRA. Go to http://nolo.com/calculator/calculatorret_roth.html and enter the information requested.

PAY OFF YOUR DEBTS BEFORE YOU INVEST

Don't start shopping for investments until you stop paying interest on high-interest debt. Especially if you are paying credit card interest at a rate of 18% or more, your best investment is to begin to live debt-free.

Don't Overlook the Current Quality of Your Life

I strongly urge you to consider your retirement investment strategy as part of—not separate from—the other aspects of your life that will have a profound effect on your retirement. Check out whether you really are doing this by asking yourself the following questions:

- How physically fit am I?
- How solid are my relationships with family and friends?
- Do I find time for activities that are likely to interest me and keep me busy later in life?
- Do I work over-long hours, face a grueling commute or for some other reason have inadequate time or energy to fulfill personal or family needs?

If you have a serious problem—or even if you have room for improvement—in any of these areas, consider ways you can restructure your life, including working fewer hours. Obsessing about saving and investing more money makes no sense when you need to face up to one or more of these very real threats to your present and future happiness.

Basic Investment Principles Reviewed

Start by accepting the fact that money and risk always march together. Even if you avoid all types of investments and instead put your nest egg under the mattress, you're taking a risk; someone might steal it, or your house might burn down. And assuming you avoid these hazards by putting your stash in a safe-deposit box, you still run the real risk that over the years inflation will substantially erode its purchasing power.

The second key investment concept you'll need to grasp also involves risk, but this time there is a potential upside. Put simply, in exchange for risking your dollars by investing them, you will be promised a variety of rewards. But before going further, it is essential that you fully grasp investing's first commandment: The bigger the risk you are willing to take, the bigger your possible gain or loss. For example, if you buy a stock in a company pioneering a new technology (hydrogen-powered cars, for example), you will be taking a big risk that for any one of at least a dozen reasons the company will fail. But if you guess right and the company's technology quickly gains mainstream acceptance, you'll likely make a huge profit. By contrast, if you think alternative fuels are mostly hype and invest your money in the stock of a large, established petroleum company, chances are you'll gain far less if you're right and most folks stick with gas-powered cars for the next 20 years (since the big company's stock already reflects its current success, it will go up in value only if the company does well in a mature market). On the other hand, if you are wrong and lots of people really do embrace alternative fuel vehicles, your loss will likely be much smaller, in part because the big company produces lots of other profitable petroleum products (home heating oil, for example). In addition, if the big company sees its gasoline business declining, it has the resources to diversify (perhaps into producing an alternate vehicle fuel such as hydrogen).

How can a relatively inexperienced investor best cope with these types of risks—risks, incidentally, which are inherent in all stock market investments? Although there are several very decent strategies, probably the best is to divide your money between several categories of well-researched and thought-out investments (for example, stocks, bonds and money market funds), each of which promises to grow over time somewhat faster than the rate of inflation. And within each category, to further diversify your holdings by spreading your money across a number of individual investments. Of course, because this approach is so sensible, it is just what many well-run stock or bond mutual funds do when they purchase the stock or debt of established companies.

Here now is a quick review of the risks and rewards of the types of investments readily available to the average investor, presented roughly in order of increasing risk.

Bank Savings Accounts

Banks, credit unions and savings and loan accounts have one big advantage: They are insured by the federal government for up to $100,000 per account. By simply setting up accounts in different financial institutions, you can obtain insurance coverage for an unlimited amount. Nevertheless, because these accounts pay low interest rates, you run a substantial risk that your savings won't even grow fast enough to keep up with the rate of inflation. In short, putting your money in a savings account is a lousy way to invest. Even a not very investment savvy peasant can easily grasp the fact that if the cost of living goes up an average of 2.2% each year for the next 20 years and your bank pays you 2% interest on your deposits, your savings will purchase significantly less two decades hence than they do now. Of course, bank accounts do have the advantage of giving you quick and easy access to your money in case of emergency—but so do other types of investments that pay a higher rate of return.

Bank Certificates of Deposit

You can easily and simply increase your rate of return by purchasing certificates of deposit from your bank. In exchange for tying your money up for an extended period (for example, six months, one year, two years or ten years), you'll receive a guaranteed rate of interest considerably higher than is paid on a savings account while still enjoying U.S. government insurance coverage up to $100,000. (The longer you commit your money, the higher the interest rate.) Shop around for the best CD interest rate; they vary significantly from one bank or savings and loan to another.

Is there anything wrong with just putting all your money in CDs and ignoring riskier, harder-to-understand investments? If you are highly risk-averse, CDs can be a fair place to put a portion of your nest egg. That way, no matter what the stock markets do, your money will be safe. But for most long-term investors, the rate of return, which recently has been in the 5%–6% range, will be too low to result in an adequate retirement nest egg once inflation is considered. U.S. government bonds, especially those with fluctuating interest rates (see U.S. Government Bonds and Notes, below) provide equivalent safety and, over time, will almost always prove to be a more profitable investment.

Money Market Accounts

Money market accounts, offered by a number of stock brokerage and mutual fund companies, pay a significantly higher rate of interest than bank savings accounts, and usually slightly more than bank CDs. One big advantage is that, like a checking account, your money is readily available, without an early withdrawal penalty (which makes them a great place to stash money you may need soon). Although not insured by the federal government, most money market funds are managed extremely conservatively; their funds are invested principally in short-term U.S. government securities (discussed below), and they charge very low management fees. In addition, a number of investment companies provide built-in private insurance from reputable companies. Thus, on balance, money market accounts—like bank CDs—are considered to be conservative investments, which nevertheless produce a rate of return somewhat better than the rate of inflation. But because the rate of interest they pay is lower than other reasonably conservative investments, money market funds are not the best choice for the bulk of your long-term retirement savings.

WHEN THE STOCK MARKET TAKES A BIG DROP, CASH CAN BE KING
Holding a portion of your portfolio in a cash equivalent form such as a money market fund isn't necessarily a stodgy way to invest. For example, if an overvalued stock market drops precipitously, any cash you have put aside will be able to purchase significantly more shares of a particular company than if you had invested in the same company when the stock market was at its peak.

U.S. Treasury Bills

U.S. government treasury bills offer a superior alternative to bank CDs, and if you are willing to tie up your money for a short period, to money market accounts. Treasury bills are generally issued in denominations of $10,000 or more, although smaller denominations are sold at times. They are available for three-, six-, nine- and twelve-month maturities. They do not pay interest as such; instead they are issued at an appropriate discount from their face value (depending on current interest rates), but pay their full value at maturity. The primary advantage of U.S. government securities is their safety. An added benefit is that profits are free of state income tax. Short-term government securities may be purchased directly from the U.S. government, from a stockbroker for a small fee or by investing in a bond fund that specializes in this type of investment. (The Vanguard Group is one good source for this type of investment. Contact them at 800-635-1511.)

U.S. Government Bonds and Notes

A bond is an I.O.U. that obligates the entity issuing it (in this case, the federal government) to repay money you have lent it, plus agreed-upon interest, at a certain date. The primary advantage of U.S. government bonds (somewhat confusingly, the term "note" is used for shorter-term U.S. bonds) is that they are backed by the U.S. government. Bonds can be a good choice for the conservative investor, especially those in states with a high income tax, since income is free of state tax.

Treasury notes can be purchased to mature (be paid off) in one to seven years. Treasury bonds are available with maturities of five years to 30 years. Interest rates tend to be higher the longer it will take for a bond to mature, thus rewarding the investor for the increased risk of tying money up for an extended period. For example, a U.S. bond that matures in 15 years might currently pay interest at the rate of about 6.5% per year—that is, about 4% more than the current rate of inflation. But a bond that matures in two years (again, called a "note") might pay interest at a rate of only 6.0%. And very short term treasury bills, discussed above, will pay slightly less.

Because the rate of inflation affects the value of existing bonds (unless you buy one of the specialized U.S. bonds that track inflation (described below)), even buying U.S. government securities is not risk-free. Or put more bluntly, if you need to sell a bond quickly at a time when inflation has gone up substantially, the price you'll receive will be less than what you paid.

> **EXAMPLE 1:** Suppose you buy a bond paying 6.5% interest that, when it matures in ten years, will be worth $1,000. Two years after your purchase, the rate of inflation goes up, and the federal government raises interest rates in an effort to cool off the economy. As part of doing this, the government raises the interest rate it pays on newly issued bonds to 9%. It follows that since investors can now get this higher rate, they won't be willing to buy your bond, paying 6.5% interest, unless you sell it at enough of a price discount that the overall return is 9%.

> **EXAMPLE 2:** Suppose that after you purchase the same bond, a recession looms and the inflation rate drops. The Federal Reserve Bank lowers interest rates to try to spur the economy, with the result that new investors in U.S. government securities are offered only 5% annual interest. Now, if you sell your bond paying interest at a rate of 6.5%, you'll get a premium price, based on the fact that the interest rate your bond pays is higher than what is available on the new bond market.

BONDS THAT HAVE FLUCTUATING INTEREST RATES CAN BE A GOOD IDEA

The U.S. government also issues ten-year bonds in $1,000 denominations which are tied to the Consumer Price Index. If consumer prices increase 2% in a year, both the interest payments and the value of the bond will rise accordingly. Although some investment pros claim that you must pay too big a premium for this inflation protection (and that there are cheaper ways to hedge against interest rate increases) for risk-averse investors who want a good return on their money without worrying about whether interest rates are likely to rise or fall, these bonds can be a decent investment. Like other U.S. obligations, they are sold through regional Federal Reserve Banks and for a small markup through banks and brokers.

Municipal Bonds

As you probably know, states, cities and other governmental agencies, such as public water, harbor or bridge authorities, also issue bonds. The income an investor receives from these municipal bonds is not taxed by the federal government or, for residents of the state where the bond is issued, by the state. This tax-free status is so desirable that municipal bonds routinely pay a significantly lower rate of interest than is paid on corporate—or even U.S. government—bonds. Another way of saying this is that municipal bond investors who don't have to pay federal or state taxes on the income they receive will accept a lower rate of interest than is true for bonds on which interest payments are taxable.

Investing in tax-free municipal bonds can make great sense for people in the higher federal tax brackets, especially those who live in states with relatively high income taxes, including California, Massachusetts, New Jersey, New York, Ohio and Pennsylvania. For example, even though a municipal bond might pay an interest rate of only 5%, a taxpayer in the 39.6% federal income tax bracket who lives in a high income tax state, would have to earn in excess of 8% on a taxable investment to net as much.

To avoid the risk inherent in buying the bonds of just one or a few public entities (remember the insolvency of Orange County, California), the best approach for all but the most sophisticated investors is to purchase shares in municipal bond funds. These funds are similar to stock mutual funds, but instead only invest in bonds. They are available from dozens of investment companies. They buy bonds from a wide variety of governmental agencies that will be paid off at different future dates, thus providing the smart investor with an invaluable risk-spreading service at a low cost. People in high income tax states will almost always want to buy bond funds that invest only in their state, to qualify for both state and federal tax exemptions. If you are interested in this approach, consider the funds sponsored by Franklin Resources Inc. (www.franklintempleton.com), a high-quality investment company whose funds, despite their relatively high fees, score consistently high ratings by *Business Week* magazine and other reputable rating organizations (for information call 800-342-5236). Another good choice is the low-cost funds managed by the Vanguard Group (www.vanguard.com). You can get information about Vanguard bond funds by calling 800-635-1511.

The Easiest Way to Diversify Your Investments

To spread your retirement savings over several different types of investments, a good approach is to purchase a mix of high-quality mutual funds
that specialize in stocks, bonds and short-term government securities. And
don't forget to include at least some index funds (see below, "How to Pick a
Good Mutual Fund"). Another easier, albeit more expensive, approach
(because of the higher fees involved) is to invest in a "balanced" or "asset
allocation" fund. Offered by a number of mutual fund companies, these
funds prepackage a mix of stocks and bonds according to several risk
formulas. For example, Charles Schwab and Co. sells a Growth Fund,
which invests 55% in bonds, 40% in stock and 5% in cash; a Balanced
Growth Fund, which invests 60% in stock, 35% in bonds and 5% in cash;
and a High Growth Fund, which invests 80% in stock, 15% in bonds and
5% in cash. (For more information, call Charles Schwab
(www.schwab.com) at 800-266-5623.)

Corporate Bonds

Many large corporations also issue bonds. Depending on how solvent the issuing
company is thought to be, their bonds receive a high or low rating by the principal
bond rating companies. At the bottom of the scale, unrated "junk bonds" must pay
relatively high rates of interest to find purchasers, who, of course, demand to be
richly compensated in exchange for the added risk they are taking. By contrast, the
highest-rated bonds of top companies pay much lower rates of interest (but still
more than those paid by the U.S. government), because the rating companies
believe it is highly unlikely that the bond holder won't be paid.

As with municipal bonds, you can spread your risk by buying a bond mutual
fund, which invests in the bonds of many companies. Finance magazines such as
Kiplinger's Personal Finance, Money Magazine, Business Week and *Forbes*
regularly rate the performance of these funds.

Stock

As discussed above, a share of stock consists of a small ownership or equity interest in the corporation which issues it. If the company's profits increase, or some other positive event occurs, such as a controlling interest being purchased by another company, its stock will almost always go up—sometimes way up. Of course, the corporation may lose money or suffer other serious problems—for example, be sued by people injured by a defective product. If it does, the price of the stock will drop, sometimes so precipitously that it wipes out a substantial part of your investment.

As noted above, it has become fashionable in some popular personal finance magazines to recommend that consumers invest all their savings in stock, often by purchasing shares in mutual funds. The main argument in favor of this all-eggs-in-the-stock-market approach is that, over the long term, stocks have outperformed other types of investments, including bonds. The argument often is made like this: If 20, 50 or 100 years ago you had invested the same amount of money in the stock of the 30 biggest corporations or in U.S. government or corporate bonds, your stocks would have produced a much larger return. Sounds like an almost irrefutable reason for the long-term investor to prefer the stock market, doesn't it? Slow down. Real people don't invest over 100, 50 or, in many instances, even 20 years. Given the realities of modern life (you may need money for a kid's education or to buy a house or for a family emergency), investing at least some of your nest egg with a ten, five or sometimes even shorter time horizon may be more like it. And as history has proven time and again, in these shorter periods, there is absolutely no guarantee that stocks will do well (or that they will outperform bonds).

Even if you can afford to invest at least some of your money for the long term, I still wouldn't put it all—or even most of it—in the stock market unless you are very sure you will not be tempted to sell when, sooner or later, stock prices take a big fall. My reason for what may seem like overly conservative advice is simple: When the stock market suffers its next major crash, very few investors—even many highly experienced ones—will be able to stand by and watch their hard-earned savings evaporate without the urge to sell and have nothing more to do with risky investments. This exact scenario has occurred so many times in U.S. history that it has become almost a cliché that individual investors buy when the market is too high, and panic and sell when it drops. Far better to have some of your investment portfolio in bonds, which often go up in value when stocks drop, and in cash equivalent investments (money market funds, for example), which will retain their value.

That said, I believe that a significant portion of almost everyone's retirement money, whether in a tax-advantaged plan such as a 401(k) or other retirement savings, should be held in the form of stock. That's because I believe that chances are very decent that over the next 20 years, the U.S and world economy will continue to expand and well-run businesses will do well. For most investors, mutual funds—especially index funds—which are discussed just below, offer the best means to participate in this anticipated growth.

How much of your investment portfolio should be in the stock market? There is no right answer. One good rule is that the longer your investment horizon, the more of your nest egg you should invest in stocks. And, of course, as already stated several times, you should assess your own appetite for risk. People who are highly risk averse should probably put no more than one-third to one-half of their total investments in the stock market no matter how long they plan to leave it there. Less cautious people—especially those who really are confident they won't need their money for many years—might, sensibly decide to put 70% or even 80% of their savings in stocks, keeping just enough in a money market fund to be easily available in case of financial emergency.

BE MORE CAUTIOUS IF YOU ALREADY HAVE ENOUGH RETIREMENT INCOME

People who have already saved or inherited enough money to fund a comfortable retirement will be sensible to keep a substantial portion of their money in conservative investments such as U.S. government or municipal bonds. After all, if you already have enough retirement savings, there is little to be gained and much to be lost by making investments—such as in Internet stocks—with a significant downside risk! And please don't take this advice lightly—I know a good number of people who had all the money they would ever need to live comfortably for the rest of their lives but nevertheless managed to blow most or all of it chasing "get rich quick" investments.

Stock Mutual Funds

Mutual funds were invented for two big reasons:

- to turn the job of picking stocks over to experts, and
- to avoid the risk of an investor with a limited amount of capital putting too much of it in one or a few stocks.

As you probably know, mutual funds accomplish these goals by pooling your investment with those of many others and then buying stock in a number of publicly traded companies. The result is that you own a tiny portion of lots of companies instead of a larger portion of one or a few.

Online Investment Information

Readers who want to learn more about investing online should check out these sites:

- Investing Online Resource Center (www.investingonline.org)—A great source of non-commercial information on online investing.
- InvestorGuide—Your Guide to Investing on the Web (www.investorguide.com)—Includes sections on personal finance and learning about money as well as investing.
- Kiplinger's Magazine Online (www.Kiplinger.com)—All of the personal financial magazines have websites. This is one of the most friendly.

In exchange for this valuable service, you pay the mutual fund company one or more of several types of fees. The first is a sales commission, called a "load" in mutual fund jargon. Many mutual funds, especially those sold by insurance salespeople or stockbrokers, charge these sales commissions. But other "no-load" funds, are sold directly by the investment companies involved and charge no sales commission. In addition, many funds (including some, but not all, "no-load" funds) charge marketing fees, called 12b-1 fees. Finally, all funds charge management fees. Once you fully understand how fees are charged (and that typically the level of fees has little to do with a fund's performance), you'll want to invest only in low-fee funds.

Mutual Fund Basics

Here are a few things to keep in mind if you're considering investing in mutual funds:

- Mutual funds are not created equal. Over time, some mutual funds prove to be excellent investments, and others do reasonably well. But it's also true that many are poor investments; the so-called experts who do the stock-picking for these under-performing funds turn out to be dunderheads.

- Ratings of mutual funds' performance are published by all major financial and personal finance magazines several times a year and are typically archived on their websites (for example, take a look at www.business week.com). Funds that do well over an extended period—at least five years—and have not recently changed managers are often a good bet, especially if they invest in less-risky securities. Be more wary of funds that have recently jumped to the top of the heap after many years of average or sub-par performance or which follow a "high risk" investment strategy. It may have been largely luck that these funds caught a favorable market trend—for example, maybe they bought Internet stocks just before that market segment boomed.

- Because mutual fund performances vary greatly, most investors are wise to diversify their investments among several. And because index funds charge lower fees and subject investors to lower taxes, they tend over time to out-perform most managed funds. (See below, "How to Pick a Good Mutual Fund.")

- Mutual funds come with all sorts of investment strategies. If you believe that over the next decade high tech, healthcare or Internet stocks will do well, you'll have no trouble finding funds that concentrate in these areas.

- As mentioned, there is little or no evidence that funds that charge high fees perform better than those that don't. To the contrary, low-cost funds—especially index funds—are almost always a superior choice, because you end up investing a larger percentage of your investment dollar with them.

- Many investment pros disparage funds that make investments based on socially acceptable criteria (for example, screen out gambling and tobacco companies, as well as heavy polluters and arms makers). Perhaps they should think again. In most recent years, the stocks on the Domini Social Equity Fund (www.domini.com)—a fund which invests in an index of

companies screened for their ethical policies and social responsibility—
have done better than the average mutual fund.

- Funds that trade stocks frequently force investors to pay lots of capital gains
taxes, which of course reduce their overall return. Accordingly, it makes
sense to avoid funds which saddle investors with big yearly tax bills. Again,
index funds are a good choice since they buy and hold stocks, which
means taxes are either avoided or postponed.

How to Pick a Good Mutual Fund

Let's assume you decide, sensibly, that you will put some of your retirement
savings in mutual funds. Which funds should you invest in? If you already have a
401(k) or 403(b) retirement plan that allows you to pick from a small group of
mutual funds, much of your work is done. Your job will be to pick funds from this
list that reflect your long-term goals (aggressive growth or maximum income or
equity preservation) and have done well over the last five or more years. You can
get records of the funds' performance from your retirement plan administrator or
from magazines such as *Business Week*, *Forbes* and *Money*, which periodically
print historical data on risk-adjusted fund performance.

If you are investing on your own, you have thousands of funds to choose from.
How do you make a choice while keeping things simple, profitable and as safe as

possible (especially safe, since, as a savvy peasant, you've undoubtedly learned that it's far easier to hold onto the dollars you already have than to make more)? Do three crucial things:

- Most important, you want to choose top-quality funds with rock-bottom fees. As mentioned above, this means investing primarily in funds with no up-front sales commissions (loads), no 12b-1 marketing fees and very low management fees. After all, any money gobbled up by these fees won't earn you anything now and won't compound to earn you more in the future. Every mutual fund must publish a prospectus listing all fees. Charles Schwab offers hundreds of no-load funds online at www.schwab.com.

- Second, prefer funds whose investment strategy is moderately conservative, meaning most of their money is invested in already successful companies. Most index funds meet this criterion automatically since their investments are weighted to reflect either the market capitalization or market price of the companies in their index (this means they invest more in fast-growing valuable companies and less in small, stumbling ones). Following this approach, our savvy peasant will likely get rich more slowly than a person who puts money in a mutual fund which—the laws of physics notwithstanding—invests in companies attempting to develop the world's first perpetual motion machine. But it is also true that the savvy peasant is far, far less likely to come up a big loser.

- Third, and again, as emphasized several times above, prefer investments which will result in relatively low taxation. Mutual funds which trade frequently in volatile stocks will stick you with a substantial capital gains tax bill at the end of the year, something that is obviously counterproductive to your investment. As discussed below, index funds which by their very nature trade stocks infrequently result in a lower tax bill. (In addition, Vanguard and several other companies sell "tax managed" index funds with strategies to reduce taxes even further.)

As I'm sure you gather by now, I believe a savvy peasant's best long-term mutual fund investment strategy is to invest a significant portion of his or her retirement stash in index funds. Unlike most mutual funds, where supposedly brilliant (and always highly paid) teams of managers choose individual stocks, index funds are designed to mimic either an entire stock market, or a good-sized slice of it. For example, an index fund established to invest in the 500 largest companies listed on Standard & Poor's index would design a computer program to divide all the fund's money among the stocks of these companies, based on the total market price or capitalization of each. The result, of course, will be that your investment would rise and fall in step with the movement of this particular basket —or index—of 500 stocks. Similarly, if you choose a fund based on an index of the Wilshire 5000, your investment will rise and fall in step with the entire stock market.

Although most index funds track broad markets made up of the stocks of many types of companies, it is also possible to purchase funds that index particular market segments. Thus index funds which track international, high tech and health care sectors of the market are available.

You may be wondering why it makes sense to buy all or many of the stocks trading on a particular stock market instead of trusting experts to pick only the best ones. There are at least three reasons:

- First, consistently picking winning stocks is tough—so tough that, as mentioned earlier, many mutual funds under-perform broad market indexes. One reason why picking market-beating stocks is so difficult is that experts from thousands of mutual funds are trying to do the same thing, thereby reducing the possibility that overlooked stocks can consistently be found. In addition, many mutual funds are so big that the very act of making a significant investment can have the effect of driving up the stock's price, thereby eliminating much or all of the opportunity to make a profit. For example, in the five years ending October 1999, the average index fund gained 24.48% annually, while the average managed fund gained only 17.85%. And 1999 was the sixth year in a row that index funds gained more than a majority of their actively managed counterparts.

- Second, since a computer does the walking, it's extremely cheap to run an index-based mutual fund. And because fees charged customers are normally a small fraction of what they are for other types of mutual funds, more of your investment dollar buys stock and less supports the people who run the mutual fund.

- Third, because index funds are set up to mimic an entire market, little buying and selling need be done. The result is that you will not be obligated to pay much in the way of capital gains tax until you sell the fund, which may be many years in the future. In the meantime, all your money keeps working for you. By contrast, mutual funds trying to pick the stock with the best prospects at any one moment usually engage in a significant amount of yearly buying and selling. And when a stock is sold at a profit, you must pay a tax, which reduces the amount of money you have to invest.

To sum up how these factors play out, based on work done by John C. Bogle, a pioneer advocate of index funds who founded The Vanguard Group, as reported in the May 6, 2000, *Wall Street Journal*. Over the past 15 years, if you consider the drag on profits of trading costs, taxes and expenses, the average mutual fund investing in major U.S. corporations produced an after-tax return of 12.2%. By contrast, an index fund investing in the Standard & Poors index of the 500 largest American corporations would have had an average after-tax return of 16.7%. The result would be that the mutual fund investor would end up with just 55% of the dollar amount accumulated by the index fund investor.

⚠ WHEN THE MARKET DROPS, SO DO INDEX FUNDS

As I write this, the stock market, while below its all-time high, is nevertheless pricy in historical terms. That means the price of most index funds (the exception being funds that index out-of-favor market segments) are also high. Because most index funds track either the whole stock market—or at least major market segments, such as all NASDAQ stocks—it follows that should the broad market drop, index funds will fall right along with it. At least in theory, actively managed mutual funds which concentrate on the stocks of conservatively run companies may do better during market downturns, since their managers are supposed to make investment decisions based on both their downside and upside potential (managed funds may also hold cash reserves—something index funds don't do). But I don't think stock picking will prove to be much of an advantage should we experience a prolonged bear market. Certainly not nearly as much as diversifying your investments to put a substantial portion of your nest egg in bonds. The longer your investment time horizon, the bigger percentage of your savings I would put in stocks (stock returns are pretty sure to beat bond returns in the long run). But the reverse is also true. If there is a possibility you'll need to cash in some of your savings in the next ten years, buy some bonds.

Vanguard Really Is Out Front

My favorite family of index funds is offered by The Vanguard Group (www.vanguard.com) of Valley Forge, Pennsylvania (800-662-7447). Like most other large mutual fund organizations, Vanguard offers a number of index funds, several of which are also tailored to reduce taxes. Because Vanguard's fees are always among the lowest in the business, chances are good that over time its index funds will achieve a superior total rate of return. Another good provider of low cost funds is TIAA-CREF (800-842-2252). And you can find comprehensive information about all index funds online at www.indexfunds.com.

Buying index funds from low-cost providers such as The Vanguard Group is not the only way to spread your risk over lots of stocks. Many well-managed no-load mutual funds, where experts do the stock-picking, are also available. And despite the fact that these funds usually charge higher management fees than do index funds, some have an excellent long-term performance record. If you are interested in doing some of your own research in this area, one good place to start is at www.morningstar.com. Or check out www.schwab.com. Charles Schwab sells literally hundreds of no-load funds for no sales fee or load (the mutual fund company—not you—pays Schwab for their work). Working with a company like Schwab can be particularly desirable for people who want to diversify their investments by purchasing a number of mutual funds but don't want to deal with lots of mutual fund companies. That's because Schwab will, at no cost to you, consolidate all your investments in one account, with one monthly statement. (For more information, call Charles Schwab at 800-266-5623 (www.schwab.com).)

Another simple approach many savvy peasants follow is to invest in the funds run by the Fidelity Company. Despite the fact that it charges sales commissions (loads) and management fees for some of its many mutual funds, Fidelity's funds have for many years turned in a very decent performance. Fidelity has upwards of 70 mutual funds, each with a different investment goal. As with other mutual funds, some Fidelity funds concentrate on high dividends, others on rapid growth or capital preservation (low risk). Others focus on investment sectors, such as high technology or bioengineering. Still others buy stock only in certain geographical areas—Brazil, Mexico, Asia. Like Schwab, Fidelity also sells the funds of a number of other mutual companies' families as part of its no-cost-to-you buying service, with the result that you can invest in many different companies through your Fidelity account, rather than having to deal with each company individually. For more information about Fidelity Funds, call 800-544-0109 (www.fidelity.com).

Purchasing Stock in Individual Companies

Purchasing the stock of individual companies is an obvious alternative to investing in the stock market by purchasing mutual funds. Signing up with one of the many low-cost Internet brokers, or establishing an account with a conventional broker is not difficult. But does buying stock one company at a time make sense for a savvy peasant who, according to our original definition, doesn't have lots of time to study the stock market? Logically, no. True, people who invest a portion of their total investment portfolio in the right five to ten companies can do extremely well, sometimes greatly outperforming mutual funds which, by definition, spread their risk over the stocks of many companies. But the real world is rarely so kind to novice investors who, over time, are highly likely to make investments that under-perform market averages. And even if they do score the occasional big winner, investors who buy individual stocks may nevertheless not do as well in the long run as if they had simply bought a lower-performing index fund and held onto it. That's because in today's rapidly changing worldwide marketplace, it is usually unwise to hold a particular stock—no matter how good—indefinitely. Or put another way, occasionally you'll want to cash in your winners, either to avoid the risk of a big price drop or to pursue a better investment. Unfortunately, doing this means you'll be obligated to pay capital gains tax on your profits, thereby reducing the amount of money you have to invest next time. And, of course, if you pick a dog the second or third time around, you can lose your winnings and more in a heartbeat. By contrast, if you instead invest long-term savings in an index fund—which by definition infrequently trades its portfolio—and you hold onto the fund for many years, your ongoing capital gains tax obligation will be extremely low—with the result that all your profits will keep working for you, not Uncle Sam.

But when it comes to saying no to gambling, common sense never completely squares with human nature. Or put another way, if you are like me, you often wish you had bought a particular Internet stock at $10 and sold it at $210. So if your urge to gamble becomes so strong you can't ignore it, go ahead and use a small portion of your nest egg to buy the shares of several individual companies. As long as you don't speculate with more than 10% of your savings, you can't get badly hurt. And hey, if you do well, you'll have something to brag about to your in-laws. But before you do this, ask yourself one more time: What makes you think you know enough to do better than the experts who run America's mutual funds? If your answer is you really can identify one or, preferably, several companies you expect will do extremely well in the future, go ahead and invest. For example, if you are a graphic artist, it's possible you might spot a company in your field with superior new computer graphics technology before Wall Street does and the stock price takes a big jump. Similarly, if you work as a mechanic, you may become enthusiastic about a brand-new line of patented adhesives that are clearly better than anything you have used before.

You may also run across information in your day-to-day life that helps you spot companies that are likely to be successful. For example, if you notice that a couple of your trend-setting friends have begun bragging about the products or services of a particular company, you may have spotted the beginning of a trend that will soon be reflected in the positive performance of the second company's stock. It's no secret that people who took advantage of just this sort of insight to purchase stock in companies such as Amazon, eBay or Yahoo!, did very well indeed.

While I don't have the space here for even a decent beginner's course in buying stocks, if you are determined to give it a try, here are a few rules that should serve you well:

1. As emphasized at the beginning of this guide, don't invest based on the advice of stockbrokers or other advisors who have a financial interest in selling you investments. If you're going to pay someone for stock tips, far better and cheaper to invest through a good no-load, low-fee, mutual fund.

2. Since you don't want advice, don't pay for it by purchasing stock through a full-service broker. Instead, work with a low-cost broker (often called "discount" or "deep discount" brokers) who will execute your buy-and-sell orders without comment. Charles Schwab and Co. is considered by some

to offer a good balance of price and service. But, there are many lower-cost alternatives, including the online services offered by ETrade, Ameritrade or TD Waterhouse.

3. Never put more than 3% of your retirement savings in the stock of one company.

4. If you are positive an entire industry is poised to do well (Internet commerce, cancer drugs, natural gas, wireless communications), consider buying stock in several leading companies to be sure you get the real winner. Or probably more sensible, invest in a mutual fund (either an index or managed fund) that concentrates on that area.

5. Companies that regularly use surplus money to repurchase their own stock or pay off debts can often be a good investment bet. By doing this, the company is usually signaling that it is determined to increase the value of its shares.

6. If you have the time and inclination to read financial magazines, do it to gain more information about companies and industries you are already familiar with—not for tips about companies you know little or nothing about. If you are tempted to speculate by buying stock in companies with which you are unfamiliar, you will almost always be better off purchasing a good mutual fund specializing in that area.

7. Pick stocks you plan to hold for an extended period. If you buy and sell frequently, taxes and trading costs will almost surely result in you doing less well than if you simply purchased an index mutual fund.

8. Just say no to "day trading" strategies which emphasize buying and selling stocks the same day, hoping to make lots of small profits. Once the costs for expensive courses and software are figured in, you have a better chance of making a big score in Vegas.

9. Remember, the stock market is the last place you want to look for a free lunch. Just because you read articles about Internet or high-tech millionaires doesn't mean you'll get rich buying these stocks. In fact, despite the hype surrounding the big winners, the stocks of many Internet companies currently trade below their offering price.

Variable Annuities

Variable annuities are aggressively sold by many investment and insurance companies. They work like this: You hand an investment company some money (either in the form of one big payment or periodic smaller ones). After charging you several chunky fees, the investment company invests your money for a number of years in a mutual fund or investment you choose. Eventually it pays your money back, plus the amount it has earned. Depending on the particular type of annuity you purchase, your payout can be in the form of one lump sum or lots of smaller payments—for example, a monthly payment for a set period of years or for the rest of your life. In addition, annuities usually have an insurance feature—often guaranteeing that if you die before the date at which your withdrawals begin, your inheritors will receive at least as much as you have contributed, even if the value of your investments has declined.

The widely touted advantage of variable annuities is that the money you invest grows free of income and capital gains tax, just as it does in a retirement account. But unlike retirement accounts, where you pay no income tax on money you invest until you withdraw it many years later, earnings you invest in an annuity are subject to federal income tax in the year earned.

Which brings me to the big question: Are variable annuities a good investment choice for a savvy peasant? For people in lower tax brackets, there is little benefit since, after all, variable annuities' main advantage is sheltering your investments from income taxes while they are invested. Does this mean they are a better investment if you're in the highest income tax brackets? Yes, but unfortunately, not much better. The high fees normally charged by the companies that sell annuities (the salesman usually gets 5%–8% of the amount you invest) will more than offset the advantage of having your taxes on earnings deferred. In addition, because annuities lock up your money until age $59^{1}/_{2}$ (there is a 10% penalty on early distribution), money invested in this way is expensive to get at in case of emergency. Finally, annuity earnings are taxed as ordinary income (up to 39.6%), not as capital gains (no more than 20%), as would be true for gains from many other types of investments.

Finally, annuities are a lousy way to pass money to your inheritors. That's because at your death your heirs face income tax on any money that remains in your annuity. By contrast, mutual fund gains outside of an annuity or retirement plan can be left to heirs free of income tax. A better investment approach is usually to first invest the maximum allowable in tax-deferred retirement plans such as a 401(k), SEP-IRA, Keogh or, if you are eligible, a Roth IRA, and then invest the rest in a mix of low-cost mutual funds, such as stock index funds and a tax-free municipal bond fund.

Immediate or Fixed Annuities

In exchange for an up-front payment (for example, $50,000), this type of annuity guarantees you a monthly or annual payment (say, $150 per month) for the rest of your life. Unlike most variable annuities discussed above, your payout will not be dependent on how well your annuity investments do in the meantime. In effect, you're placing a bet with an insurance company: If you live well beyond your life expectancy, you'll collect way more than you paid for the annuity; if you live only a few years, you will collect much less.

Does investing in fixed annuities make good sense? Using a conventional financial analysis, the answer is no; the fairly hefty fees charged by the insurer mean that even people who live several years beyond their life expectancy would come out ahead by investing the same amount of money in a decent mutual fund or even in a bank certificate of deposit. But if you are pretty sure you will live way beyond your life expectancy—say to 108—and want the security of receiving a payment every month, no question—an immediate or fixed annuity will be a great deal.

Real Estate

Another common investment choice is real property—everything from residential rental units to commercial buildings to vacant land. By and large, I consider investing retirement funds in individual parcels of real estate to be a mistake unless you have an intimate knowledge of the local real estate market. And even then, I would not invest more than a third of my savings in this way.
Among my many reasons for caution are the following:

- **The diversification factor.** If you are like most people, you already own a house, condo or co-op apartment. In short, you already have a big portion of your assets tied up in real estate and so should think twice about putting more of your eggs in this investment basket. Far safer to diversify your investments by purchasing stock and bond mutual funds.

- **The lack-of-knowledge factor.** Most people who don't work in real estate or don't spend a great deal of time on self-education never gain a good feel for how much real estate is worth. Unlike mutual funds or individual shares of stock or bonds, there is no daily market to help you determine a reasonable price. As a result, casual investors too often rely on the advice of local real estate people anxious to get a commission, with the result that they pay too much for property. Sure, occasionally the market takes such a big jump that they nevertheless end up with a substantial profit—but often they buy a poor long-term investment.

- **The dirty-hands factor.** The people I know who have done well buying residential and commercial rental property aren't afraid to get their hands dirty. This means that if water pours through a tenant's skylight after a rainstorm, the owner is out in the middle of the night (or at the latest by the next morning) with a ladder to do something about it. If this doesn't sound like you, put your money someplace drier.

- **The liability factor.** People who own real estate are perceived to be wealthy and, as a result, may be sued by tenants, visitors or even a trespasser who claims to be injured. For example, if one tenant breaks a light bulb in the hallway just before another breaks her neck after tripping over a discarded rollerblade, you can bet you'll end up in court. The result is that not only will you need pricey insurance, but you'll probably want to form a corporation or limited liability company to protect your personal assets. All this may be fine for someone in the real estate business, but it is far too worky for a savvy peasant who already has a busy life.

- **The taxes factor.** Some people are tempted to buy vacant land with the hope that, in a few years, development pressures will enable them to sell it at a big profit. This is certainly an easier way to invest than buying rental property, but it, too, has a significant downside. While you wait to cash in, the undeveloped land is probably bringing in little or no income, but costing you money in the form of taxes and insurance. Even though taxes on undeveloped land are relatively low, they still must be paid every year with money you could be profitably reinvesting elsewhere.

- **The hiring-people factor.** If you invest in rental property—and possibly even if you buy bare land—you'll have to do regular maintenance and repairs. Unless you plan to do all the work yourself, you'll have to hire others. This may be fine if you or a trusted manager supervise every job and track every cost. However, real trouble is likely if you plan to be less involved, since chances are good you'll end up paying too much for less than first-class work.

- **The partners factor.** Many people with a little extra money to invest form a joint venture with family members, friends or work colleagues. In my experience, this is likely to make the problems inherent in investing in real estate many times worse. Now, instead of one amateur investor, you have two, three or ten. To raise just one common problem, what happens if several of the other investors want out of the deal when the market is down? You'll likely to be forced to either sell at a loss or raise money to buy the others out. No fun either way.

- **The getting-at-your-money factor.** If an emergency occurs, you'll need to temporarily dip into your retirement funds. If all or most of your savings are tied up in real estate, this can be expensive, time-consuming and sometimes even impossible.

For those savvy peasants who nevertheless believe real estate prices may outperform other types of investments, one easy way to participate is through a real estate investment trust (REIT). REITs operate like a kind of real estate mutual fund to pool investors' contributions and invest them in commercial and sometimes residential real estate. For those who don't want to study the prospects of the many individual REITs, the Vanguard Group is one of a number of mutual fund companies that sells an index fund made up of all publicly traded REITs.

Precious Metals and Exotic Investments

In my view, precious metals (gold, silver, platinum) are a rotten investment for retirement funds. The bet here is that a major financial disaster will cause inflation to go completely out of control or that some other disaster to civilization will reduce the value of paper money or render it worthless. Put another way, when governments are in trouble, gold does well.

Sooner or later, some disaster (for example, a major war in the Middle East which disrupts oil supplies and therefore causes petroleum prices to skyrocket) probably will cause the price of gold to go up. But in the meantime, owning gold or other precious metals not only produces no interest or dividends that can be reinvested, but also costs you money, because you must pay storage fees.

An approach to investing in precious metals that at least avoids the storage problem is to buy stock in one of the companies that mine gold, or in one or more of a number of mutual funds specializing in gold-mining stocks. Still, given the world economy's vibrancy and ability to quickly adjust to even the most serious problems, I wouldn't bet the ranch on an investment that will only do really well if the world faces a prolonged financial crisis.

Other investments, including art and collectibles and exotic animals (ostrich farms and bison ranches), are not worth serious consideration for the average investor. Values are almost always highly inflated by insiders whose main purpose is to transfer money from your pockets to theirs.

NOLO'S ONLINE FUTURE VALUE CALCULATOR

If you have Internet access, you can find out how much your inheritance or other investment money will grow by using one of Nolo's online calculators. Go to http://www.nolo.com/calculator/calculatorinv_fval.html and follow these instructions:

- Enter today's date in the box after "Present date."
- Enter the date when you will cash in your investment in the box after "Future date."
- Enter the current value of your investment in the box after "Present value."
- Enter your expected average annual rate of return in the box after "Interest rate."
- Press the "Submit Query" button.

The number you'll see on your screen will be the amount that your investment will be worth on the date you cash it out. ■

Index

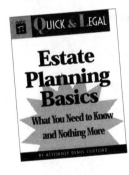
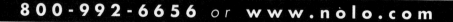

Take 2 minutes & Give us your 2 cents

Your comments make a big difference in the development and revision of Nolo books and software. Please take a few minutes and register your Nolo product—and your comments—with us. Not only will your input make a difference, you'll receive special offers available only to registered owners of Nolo products on our newest books and software. Register now by:

PHONE
1-800-992-6656

FAX
1-800-645-0895

EMAIL
cs@nolo.com

or **MAIL** us
this registration card

REMEMBER:
Little publishers have big ears. We really listen to you.

- - - - - - - - - - - - - - - - - - - fold here - - - - - - - - - - - - - - - - - - -

REGISTRATION CARD

NAME _____ DATE _____

ADDRESS _____

_____

CITY _____ STATE _____ ZIP _____

PHONE _____ E-MAIL _____

WHERE DID YOU HEAR ABOUT THIS PRODUCT? _____

WHERE DID YOU PURCHASE THIS PRODUCT? _____

DID YOU CONSULT A LAWYER? (PLEASE CIRCLE ONE)   YES   NO   NOT APPLICABLE

DID YOU FIND THIS BOOK HELPFUL?   (VERY)   5   4   3   2   1   (NOT AT ALL)

COMMENTS _____

_____

_____

WAS IT EASY TO USE?   (VERY EASY)   5   4   3   2   1   (VERY DIFFICULT)

DO YOU OWN A COMPUTER? IF SO, WHICH FORMAT? (PLEASE CIRCLE ONE)   WINDOWS   DOS   MAC

❑ If you do not wish to receive mailings from these companies, please check this box.

❑ You can quote me in future Nolo.com promotional materials. Daytime phone number _____

LIFE 3.0

N O L O
IN THE
NEWS

"Nolo helps lay people perform legal tasks without the aid—or fees—of lawyers."

—USA TODAY

Nolo books are ..."written in plain language, free of legal mumbo jumbo, and spiced with witty personal observations."

—ASSOCIATED PRESS

"...Nolo publications...guide people simply through the how, when, where and why of law."

—WASHINGTON POST

"Increasingly, people who are not lawyers are performing tasks usually regarded as legal work... And consumers, using books like Nolo's, do routine legal work themselves."

—NEW YORK TIMES

"...All of [Nolo's] books are easy-to-understand, are updated regularly, provide pull-out forms...and are often quite moving in their sense of compassion for the struggles of the lay reader."

—SAN FRANCISCO CHRONICLE

fold here

- -

nolo
**950 Parker Street
Berkeley, CA 94710-9867**

Attn: **LIFE 3.0**